Back Pocket God

Religion and Spirituality in the
Lives of Emerging Adults

MELINDA LUNDQUIST DENTON

and

RICHARD FLORY

OXFORD
UNIVERSITY PRESS

OXFORD
UNIVERSITY PRESS

Oxford University Press is a department of the University of Oxford. It furthers the University's objective of excellence in research, scholarship, and education by publishing worldwide. Oxford is a registered trade mark of Oxford University Press in the UK and certain other countries.

Published in the United States of America by Oxford University Press
198 Madison Avenue, New York, NY 10016, United States of America.

© Oxford University Press 2020

Library of Congress Cataloging-in-Publication Data
Names: Denton, Melinda Lundquist, author. | Flory, Richard, author. |
National Study of Youth & Religion (U.S.), issuing body.
Title: Back pocket God : religion and spirituality in the lives of emerging adults / [Melinda Lundquist] Denton and [Richard] Flory.
Description: New York, NY : Oxford University Press, [2020] |
Includes bibliographical references.
Identifiers: LCCN 2019033307 (print) | LCCN 2019033308 (ebook) |
ISBN 9780190064785 (hardback) | ISBN 9780190064808 (epub) |
ISBN 9780190064792 | ISBN 9780190064815
Subjects: LCSH: Generation Y—Religious life—United States. | Young adults—Religious life—United States.
Classification: LCC BL625.47.D46 2020 (print) | LCC BL625.47 (ebook) |
DDC 200.84/20973—dc23
LC record available at https://lccn.loc.gov/2019033307
LC ebook record available at https://lccn.loc.gov/2019033308

1 3 5 7 9 8 6 4 2
Printed by LSC Communications, United States of America

With deep thanks and appreciation to the many parents and youth who participated in the National Study of Youth and Religion from 2002–2013. We are sincerely grateful for your willingness to share your lives with us.

Contents

List of Figures

Foreword

Christian Smith

YOU HOLD IN your hands the flagship book reporting findings from the fourth and final survey and interviews wave of the National Study of Youth and Religion (NSYR). This wave of NSYR and this book based on it represent the culmination of nearly two decades of sustained collaborative sociological research into the spiritual and religious lives of American teenagers and emerging adults. The idea for such a national, longitudinal study of youth religion germinated around 1999, when leaders at Lilly Endowment Inc. and I began conversations about the need for such a project and the kind of research design that would provide the most valuable data. With extremely generous financial support from Lilly, invaluable methodological advice from a host of sociological colleagues, crucial input from a variety of public advisors on how to make the study most useful to practitioners in various relevant social institutions, and lots of energy and ambition, the NSYR was planned out in 2000 and launched in 2001.

The two authors of this book are perfectly suited to write this final flagship volume. Both have been deeply involved in the project from the beginning. At the time of NSYR's planning and official launch, Melinda Lundquist Denton was a doctoral student of mine at UNC Chapel Hill. She served as the NSYR Project Manager from day 1, and, being highly gifted with particular skills and proclivities that well complemented my own, proved to be an invaluable collaborator on this study. In addition to this book, she coauthored two other NSYR books, *Soul Searching: The Religious and Spiritual Lives of American Youth* (2005, with me) and *A Faith of Their Own: Stability and Change in the Religiosity of America's Adolescents* (2011, with Lisa Pearce). Richard Flory was also involved in NSYR from the first wave of interviews to the last, conducting a multitude of them during the summers of 2003, 2005, 2008, and 2013 in greater Los Angeles, Central

California, the San Francisco Bay Area, and the desert Southwest. Flory, too, has studied and written extensively on youth and religion, including his books *Finding Faith: The Spiritual Quest of the Post-Boomer Generation* (2008, with Donald Miller), *GenX Religion* (2000, with Donald Miller), and *Growing Up in America: The Power of Race in the Lives of Teens* (2010, with Korie Edwards and Brad Christerson). I can think of no better analysts and authors to teach us how a decade of developmental change in the lives of thousands of American youth has shaped their religious lives, and I am grateful for their contribution to our growing knowledge in this book.

Before the NSYR, most of what we "knew" about youth and religion was anecdotal. Even the scholarly body of research findings on the topic was an incomplete patchwork of narrowly focused, somewhat dated, and sometimes methodologically uncertain studies. Most scholars who studied adolescents simply ignored the religious dimensions of their lives, as presumably unimportant. And most social scientists who studied religion ignored teenagers, preferring to study adults and religious institutions and movements. The NSYR thus filled in a gaping hole in our knowledge and understanding of the important subject. It also helped to launch a cottage industry studying religion and teenagers and emerging adults in the sociology of religion. Furthermore, since its treatment of youth turns out to be a fantastic lens through which to view and understand the values and priorities of any larger culture and society, the NSYR has also shed valuable light on the character of American religion more broadly and of the many other institutions and cultural models that shape the lives of young people.

The NSYR built into its research program two major strengths that have paid dividends across the life of the project. The first is its longitudinal design. The NSYR followed the same large and nationally representative sample of American teenagers for 10 years, across the critical period of transitions from age 13 (our youngest subsample of respondents in the first wave) to age 28 (our oldest subsample of respondents in the last wave). That panel design enabled us to overcome the severe limitations of "snapshot" cross-sectional studies when it comes to observable changes over time and temporally antecedent conditions that might shape them. We did not have to rely on retrospective memories. We had recorded respondents' reports back when it mattered. The second major strength of the NSYR was its combining and directly linking of quantitative survey data and qualitative in-person interview data. For each of the four waves of data collected over 10 years, we not only conducted surveys but also interviewed in person, in their hometowns in nearly every state across the country, a subset of the youth survey respondents. That provided us directly linkable survey and interview data for hundreds of carefully selected teenagers and emerging adults across the country. Combining those two strengths in one massive dataset gave NSYR an immense richness and explanatory power that has come out in the many books published on its data, including this book that you hold in your hand.

We who have been involved in the NSYR are proud of the scholarly work we have accomplished, the unique data we have contributed to the public domain, the many findings we have published, and the innumerable conversations and new studies our work has prompted. I personally am proud of this book authored by Denton and Flory. It is the worthy capstone of a massive undertaking well completed. I hope it is widely read and discussed.

Having said that, let us also recognize that times change, cultures change, generations change. Millennials are growing older and raising their own children. Technological developments hit us at a mind-boggling pace. Economic structures are morphing, and inequalities of wealth are growing. Traditional American religious institutions of nearly every tradition are gradually and sometimes rapidly weakening. More generally, we appear to be undergoing a deterioration of social solidarity in the United States. Those who care about youth or religion ought to learn all we can from the NSYR—including, perhaps especially, from this book, *Back Pocket God*. But in time, we will need new and better research on these and related subjects to continue to know what is happening in the world around us and how it is shaping real people's lives. We in the NSYR hope and trust that in due time a new wave of younger, energetic scholars will rise to the occasion. In the meantime, sit back and enjoy this book.

Acknowledgments

THIS IS THE capstone book of the National Study of Youth and Religion (NSYR). We are deeply appreciative of Christian Smith for including us in this groundbreaking project and for inviting us to write this final volume. His trust and support have been a great gift as we worked on the book. The book represents equal partnership and collaboration between us, from the initial analysis of the data to the final writing. Jonathan Hill partnered with us on Chapter 5, and we are grateful for his skilled analysis and contribution to the book.

The larger project of the NSYR and the specific work of this book reflect the efforts of a great number of people who helped make NSYR a successful project from beginning to end. This fourth and final installment of the NSYR project builds on the success of the first three, and we owe our gratitude and thanks to all those who participated in Wave 1, Wave 2, and Wave 3 of the NSYR.

We thank Chris Coble and the Lilly Endowment Inc. and the John Templeton Foundation for their very generous funding support of NSYR Wave 4. Keith Meador, Steve Vaisey, and Margarita Mooney also provided funding for the addition of questions to the Wave 4 survey instrument.

Sara Skiles, the project manager for NSYR Wave 4, has been absolutely invaluable to the success of the project. We owe a great debt of gratitude to all of those involved in the collection of the NSYR Wave 4 survey and semistructured interviews. The in-person, semistructured interviews were conducted by an outstanding team of interviewers: Ria Van Ryn, Lisa Pearce, Trish Herzog, Carlos Tavares, Brandon Vaidyanathan, Hilary Davidson, Kari Christofersen-Hojara, Katherine Sorrell, Karen Hooge-Michalka, Daniel Escher, Shanna Corner, and Jade Avelis. A small army of people also contributed to the project through their efforts tracking our youth respondents across time, managing the fielding of the survey and interviews, and administrating the data collection and preparation process. For their role in these efforts, we thank Daniel Acorn, Amber Barnes, Rachel Beck,

Catherine Braunlich, Gina Bridges, Adrianne Cline, Samantha Coughlin, Alex Cummings, Christine Cummings, Meghan Davis, Carrie Davis, Terry Ely, Melanie Fritz, Lauren Ganshirt, Chelsie Gibson, Karen G. Gilmore, Anne Haas, Jackie Haile, Jessica Haring, Theresa Yoon Haring, Sarah Hart, Paul Hemminger, Carissa Henke, Michael Holtzman, Roseanne Hughes, Amanda Humbert, Angela Hwang, Hayley Jones, Margaret Kendall, Jarrett Knight, Maria Kosse, Abby Kostielney, Caitlin Lackner, Kathy Lanswer, Heidi Lawton, Lex Lorenzo, Katharine Mack, Katie Mattie, Kristiana McClanahan, Lisa Menendez, Rachel M. Molenda, Michelle Mowry, Peter Mundey, Sade Murphy, Lucy Negash, Precious Okonokhua, Megan O. Olson, Alberto Ortiz, Megan P. Pelino, Jennie Potter, Robyn Przybylski, Megan R. Raden, Annie Rhodes, Tracy Richardson, Laura Rosas, Meg Ryan, Peter Ryan, Dan Samide, Annie S. Schoenwetter, Andrew S. Schreder, Christina Senger, Erin Smith, Ashley Snell, Alexa Solazzo, Anastacia Spano, Monica Spitzer, Maddie Swan, Katherine Sylva, Ryann Sypniewski, Hollyn Trudell, Hannah Turgeon, Justin Van Ness, Amanda Varela, Tamara West, Brittany Williams, Andrew Y. Yoon, Rachel Zajdel, and Ilse Zenteno.

We would like to thank all those who contributed time and effort in data analysis and research tasks, including Starla Blake, Julian Culver, Colton Daniels, Reed DeAngelis, Tara Fletcher, George Hayward, Peter Mundey, and Nicole Van Brenna. Thanks also to Claire Chipman Gilliand who constructed the index, and Nick Street, who deftly edited the final manuscript.

This book benefited from the feedback and support of many colleagues, including Lisa Pearce, Jeremy Uecker, Kyle Longest, Aida Ramos, Crystal Columbini, Brad Christerson, Brie Loskota, Diane Winston, and Don Miller. We are also grateful for the receptive audiences who provided important feedback as we presented findings from this project while we were writing the book. We offer our thanks to the anonymous reviewers, whose comments helped shape the direction of the final manuscript. Thank you also to our home departments and colleagues for their support: The University of Texas at San Antonio and the UTSA College of Liberal and Fine Arts, as well as the USC Center for Religion and Civic Culture. Theo Calderara, our editor at Oxford University Press, has guided us through the publication process, and we are grateful for his support.

Finally, and again, to the young people who participated in the NSYR project. We are deeply appreciative of your commitment to the project over the years, for your willingness to tell us the details of your lives, and for the privilege of observing your growth and development over the years.

Introduction

I HAD ARRANGED to meet Michael for our interview at the same Starbucks where I had interviewed him five years before.[1] As was the case with many of the young people I was interviewing, I had spoken to Michael in each of the three preceding waves of data collection for the National Study of Youth and Religion (NSYR).

I had always been impressed with how polite and respectful Michael was and with the thoughtfulness of his responses. I was looking forward to hearing how his life had progressed since we had last talked.

Michael was 14 years old when we first met, and his mother and her then-boyfriend (now her husband and Michael's stepfather) had begun going to church "a lot more" than they had been. Michael was "hoping to become more active over the next few years" in the church they had started attending. In our interview two years later, he reported that he had become more involved in the church and that the family joke was that he was becoming the "preacher's pet." When I interviewed him for the third time, when Michael was 19, he said that his beliefs had "really been shaken lately." He had been researching the relationship between religion and politics and had concluded that religion had "been created to control the masses." As a result, he was becoming disillusioned with religion, was not sure what was true and what was made up by those in power, and in general was questioning his beliefs and moving away from his faith and church community. Now 24 years old and having recently graduated from college, Michael identified as "not religious." I wanted to learn what had happened.

When I asked Michael about his current religious beliefs and practices, he told me that he definitely doesn't acknowledge himself as being religious. He has remained respectful of religion, saying that religion is a good source of moral teachings, but he seemed a bit frustrated that he still makes some decisions based on his past religious ideas: "I still feel like, every now and then, I still hold those values. So, even though I don't want to be religious, I don't feel like I believe in God, but I still feel like every now and then. . . ."

Although he does not consider himself religious, Michael does say that he is "a little spiritual. Not very spiritual." For Michael, being spiritual is "like that good feeling. I know back when I used to be religious, you go to church, you practice or whatever, and at the end of a service you have, like, this good feeling. You feel empowered, your steps feel lighter. That's kind of like what spiritual is."

Michael is not representative of all American young people. But his story does illustrate the changes and struggles that many young people are experiencing as they enter adulthood and find themselves making decisions about aspects of their lives—like religion—that had previously been made for them.

What *do* the religious and spiritual lives of American young people look like as they reach their mid to late twenties, enter the full-time job market, and start families? Most recent media stories, as well as some social scientific research, show that young Americans are rapidly leaving the religions of their youth and now claim no religious identity.[2] Religious leaders have observed large losses of younger members in their organizations and, in many cases, are worried about how to respond.[3] Other reports suggest that, even though these young people are leaving institutional religion, they are busy seeking out alternative spiritualities and can best be described as "spiritual but not religious."[4] This designation suggests that, like Michael, they maintain a sense of spiritual searching and perhaps some forms of spiritual practice, but they generally are looking outside the confines of a traditional religious institution such as a church, synagogue, mosque, or temple.

A different view is presented in a recent book by Tim Clydesdale and Kathleen Garces-Foley, who argue that young people are *not* leaving religion en masse as other sources claim.[5] Instead, in their analysis, young adults attend services at "high" rates, are otherwise religiously and spiritually involved, and maintain a commitment to spiritual practices. Clydesdale and Garces-Foley intentionally present an "optimistic story" about young people and religion as a corrective to what the authors see as the bad news that has been widely reported about young adults and religion.[6] Indeed, their book does present a very positive view of the religious lives of young adults, in the end describing them as "postmodern pilgrims" who are actively seeking out a robust and fulfilling religious and spiritual life.

What are we to make of these two almost opposing interpretations of contemporary youth religiosity? While it is clear from available data that we are witnessing a significant increase in the number of young people claiming they are not religious, what does this actually mean?[7] Are they leaving behind the religious involvements of their youth? Are they simply feeling more comfortable acknowledging a distance from religion that had existed all along?[8]

Setting the Stage

This is the capstone book from the NSYR. The NSYR began in 2002 with a nationally representative sample of youth ages 13 to 17 and followed these same young people through four waves of surveys, ending when they were between the ages of 23 and 28.[9] Each wave of surveys was accompanied by a set of in-depth interviews with a subset of the survey population. This methodology allows us to confidently describe continuity and change in the lives of these young people over a crucial developmental period in their lives.

Over the 10 years of the study and the four waves of data collection, multiple books have been published, each analyzing the latest data while taking into account how these young people had changed since the previous rounds of data collection. Thus, in the first NSYR book, *Soul Searching*, Christian Smith and Melinda Lundquist Denton analyzed the first wave of data collection and developed several themes, including our respondents' difficulty in articulating exactly what they believed. The authors introduced the concept of "Moralistic Therapeutic Deism" to describe how teens conceptualized and interacted with God as a relatively remote being interested primarily in their happiness.[10] In *A Faith of Their Own*, Lisa D. Pearce and Melinda Lundquist Denton described the changes in the religious and spiritual lives of these young people from Wave 1 to Wave 2, and specifically examined how our subjects were devising different strategies to make their relationship with religion "their own," rather than something they simply inherited from their parents, regardless of whether they were moving away from religion or becoming more involved.[11] *Souls in Transition*, by Christian Smith and Patricia Snell, analyzed changes in these young people when they were ages 18 to 23 and introduced the concept of "emerging adulthood" as a framework to understand how changes in religion among the young people in this study were related to broader changes in American society that had created a new social-psychological developmental phase for young people (more on that later).[12]

In this book, we focus on these same emerging adults, now between the ages of 23 and 28, showing where they are now in their lives as well as how their views of and participation in religion and spirituality have changed. We track changes across the 10 years of data collection, thus allowing both an analysis of our subjects' religious lives currently and how their religiousness has changed and developed.

Emerging Adulthood

When the NSYR project started in 2002, all of the subjects were teenagers, and the first two books were about how adolescents understood and approached their religious and spiritual lives as they moved through their teen years. Beginning with *Souls in Transition*, emerging adulthood became an important concept through which to think about how the religious and spiritual lives of these young people related to other aspects of their lives.

Emerging adulthood represents a relatively new stage of development between adolescence and adulthood. Psychologist Jeffrey Arnett, who coined the term and has written extensively on emerging adults, argues that this new period in the lives of young people is the result of changes in society since the 1970s, particularly the fact that Americans are getting married and having children later than they used to.[13] Arnett argues that the sexual revolution, the broad availability of the birth control pill, and the increasing numbers of young people attending college—including a great increase in the number of women in college—have all contributed to the development of this new phase of life.

As a result, there is now an extended period in the lives of young people—Arnett puts this range from ages 18 to 29—when "emerging adults" are still figuring out their lives. Arnett cites five characteristics of emerging adulthood: (1) identity explorations, in which young people are "trying out various possibilities, especially in love and work"; (2) a period of instability for the individual; (3) a time of intense self-focus; (4) a time of transition, or "feeling in-between" as neither adolescent nor adult; and (5) a time of possibilities, as young people face great opportunity to transform their lives.[14] Emerging adulthood is indeterminate in the sense that emerging adults haven't quite figured out who they are or where they are going in life, but it is also characterized by a sense of optimism in that they sense the opportunity to make their own way in the world.

In this book, we retain the concept of emerging adulthood because it remains a useful framing device to help us understand the larger context of the lives of young adults and how religion fits into their lives. Thus, to the extent that the other areas of their lives are in flux, we should expect that their religious and spiritual lives are as well.

Yet, the concept also raises certain issues to keep in mind as the reader moves through this book. As defined by Arnett, the age range for emerging adults is eighteen to twenty-nine, with the argument being that the experiences noted previously are particularly acute among young people in that age range, and they have yet to enter into "full-fledged" adulthood. Arnett provides a precise rationale for why "emerging adult" is the most accurate description for this developmental stage, as distinct from "late adolescence," "young adult," "transition to adulthood," and "youth." A significant part of his rationale is age-based. In other words, emerging adulthood describes young people between the ages of 18 and 29, and their experiences during that time period are common across all individuals in this age range in particular sociocultural contexts that have undergone shifts, including delayed marriage, delayed childbearing, and the like.

The implication is that as one moves out of the emerging adult age range, one will enter "young adulthood." Yet, it is important to note that there is variation within this age group in terms of when particular *individuals* achieve the different status markers that would designate them as an adult rather than as an emerging adult. Thus, it is important to keep in mind that how particular individuals develop along the life course may vary from what is true for the larger group. That is, some people reach the markers of "full-fledged adulthood" well before they reach the upper limit of the 18- to 29-year age range, while others don't reach those markers even as they move into their thirties.

Further, our data show that many emerging adults *believe* themselves to be "adults," regardless of whether they've reached the traditional markers of marriage and parenthood. Thus, it is important to keep in mind not only the psychological and sociological categories that researchers impose on their subjects, but also how their subjects think and act in constructing their own identities—in this case, whether they believe themselves to be "full-fledged adults" as well as how their actions and choices reflect that self-identification.

We also need to point out that the young people in this book are all between the ages of 23 and 28, the older half of the emerging adult age range. Thus, while we use the term emerging adult throughout the book, the reader must keep in mind that we are not referring to all emerging adults, but only to those who are in the 23- to 28-year-old age range.

Emerging Adults and Generations

It has become popular over the past several years to engage in a type of pop sociology that trades on supposed differences between generations—baby boomers, Gen X, and millennials. Although the young people in this book are considered within the age range of the "millennial" generation, we do not refer to them as "millennials." Despite the popularity of using these kinds of generational groupings, any analysis based on differences between generations presents significant methodological problems that make such an analysis difficult, if not impossible. This is particularly true if the analyst attempts to determine how different perspectives on life can be attributed to being born in a particular generation.[15]

Further, this book is not intended to be a "generational" analysis that would demonstrate how this cohort of emerging adults is different from or similar to their parents' or grandparents' generation. Emerging adulthood is a stage through which successive generations will all pass, not one that is unique to one or another generation. Thus, this book is an analysis of the spiritual and religious lives of *emerging adults*: what they currently think and believe about religion, their religious practices and affiliations, and how these have changed, or not, over the course of their development from adolescence to emerging adulthood. It is important to remember that emerging adults are developing through a life stage, and the kinds of changes we see them experiencing—particularly in their religious beliefs, practices, and involvements—are a part of the "identity work" that they are pursuing during this phase of their lives.

Looking Ahead

Throughout this book, we look beyond the stories that argue that emerging adults are either overwhelmingly leaving religion or earnest spiritual seekers whose religious involvements and commitments remain a significant part of their lives. We show that while the dominant trend across the 10 years of this study is that young people are moving away from religious belief and involvement, there is a parallel trend in which a small, religiously committed group of emerging adults claim faith as an important fixture in their lives. Yet, whether religiously committed or not, emerging adults are increasingly personalizing, customizing, and compartmentalizing religion in ways that suit their individual needs and desires.[16]

The God of emerging adults has become increasingly remote from their everyday concerns and rarely enters their thinking or occupies any real place in their lives.[17] Instead, emerging adults have personalized God to serve their idiosyncratic needs and desires. In the process, they have transformed their conception of God from a powerful being or force that exists "out there" to their own personal *pocket God*—a God that they can carry around with them, but that exerts little power or influence in their daily lives. God functions, in a sense, like a smartphone app—readily accessible, easy to control, and useful but only for limited purposes.

As emerging adults strive to become "full-fledged" adults and take on the kinds of responsibilities that are associated with adulthood, they are also making important choices about their lives, including whether and to what degree religion will continue to be a part of their lives going forward. Whatever choices emerging adults ultimately make will inevitably be linked to both their personal desires and aspirations, and the larger cultural and social context in which they were raised and are now entering as adults. In turn, understanding the changing relationship between emerging adults and religion provides a window into the future of religion and, more broadly, American culture. We hope this book begins a conversation about what that potential future may look like as emerging adults take their place as leaders in their religious institutions, communities, and the wider society.

The Teens from Soul Searching *10 Years Later*

SITTING ACROSS FROM me in the crowded Starbucks was a mature, self-assured young woman.[1] Newly married and heading to graduate school in the fall, Melody was happy with the way her life was going and optimistic about her future. As we talked, I felt something like pride as I recalled our first conversation and thought about how far she had come since then. At 15, Melody was thoughtful and mature for her age. But she was clearly struggling to figure out her own identity, differentiating herself from her straight-laced twin sister, trying to balance her impulse toward a counter-cultural identity with her desire to fit in and belong. In the coming years, through follow-up interviews, I saw her grow and mature, wrestle with significant hardships, and come out on the other side confident in her own identity and place in the world. While we had just a handful of inter-actions spread out over ten years, I was grateful for the opportunity to see glimpses of her life as it unfolded.

Melody's story is but one of many that we were able to follow over a full decade. Unfortunately, we can't provide updates on all of the young people that were profiled as teens because some of them dropped out of our study. But most of them continued to participate. In what follows, we catch up with several of the people whose stories have featured prominently in pre-vious installments.

Joy

Joy's life is characterized by resilience in the face of a lifetime of chal-lenges and hardships. When we first met Joy in the summer of 2003, she was 16 years old. She was depressed, doing drugs and drinking a lot of alcohol, and seeking sex with much older men—behaviors that stemmed, in part, from her difficult relationship with her parents. In many ways, she seemed adrift both from any positive relationships with mature and healthy adults and from the Baptist faith in which she was raised.

The second time Joy was interviewed, in 2005, her life had improved somewhat. She had graduated from high school, moved in with her boyfriend, and become pregnant. However, her boyfriend grew distant during her pregnancy and ended up cheating on her with one of her friends, which led to the end of their relationship. Yet, having her baby had a significant effect on her life. She quit smoking and drinking and started to think more about her future, not just the present.

When Joy was interviewed for the third time in 2008, she was 21 years old, and she seemed like a very different person than the teenager who had been interviewed twice before. She was living with her fiancé, Matt, who genuinely cared for her and her baby girl. Joy also reported that in the time between the first and second interviews, she had been placed in foster care a few times and that her foster mother had been an important and caring figure in her life, providing the kind of positive support that she needed and desired but hadn't received from her own mother. And, as a result of attending a Christian teen rally led by a visiting youth evangelist, she had rededicated her life to God and started attending church regularly with her parents and her fiancé.

When we caught up with Joy for our final interview, she and Matt were married and living together with their three children (Joy's daughter, Matt's son from a previous relationship, and a boy they had together) in a double-wide trailer home in a rural, mountainous area in the South. Joy arrived at the interview late—she had overslept—but we were able to conduct the interview at a local restaurant over breakfast. When she arrived, she was wearing a black T-shirt and jeans and had the names of her three children, along with a few butterflies, in a tattoo "sleeve" up her left arm.

As we started the interview, Joy reported that she was slowly rebuilding her life after having a rough time of it over the previous five years. She had given birth to her third child on the side of the road, had several complications, and as a result became addicted to painkillers. She struggled through postpartum depression and post-traumatic stress disorder and had twice checked herself into a psych ward for suicide watch. After being arrested at Walmart for shoplifting—she said that she had been so strung out on pain medication she didn't really know what she was doing—she decided to go to a detox center. Since then, she had relapsed once, but she reported being clean for the past two to three years. Marriage is a struggle; she reported that she and Matt got married before she was sober, and now she feels like she has no idea who she married. They have some problems to work through. Joy said she considers herself to be an adult, "sadly." When we asked why sadly, she said, "I don't know. It'd be great if I could be a kid again." For Joy, "work and kids, you know, real life" are the main things that make her consider herself to be an adult.

Joy appears to be handling the pressures of her adult life relatively alone. Of all the potential supportive older adults in her life, she feels closest to her mother-in-law, who was a teacher for twenty years and has "tons of experience, she raised two kids herself . . . she is very practical and upfront. She will tell you whether you're doing right or wrong, and it helps." As for her own mom, Joy said, "I love my mom, I do my best to take care of her, but as far as being able to talk to her or discuss anything, no."

Two other adult relationships have significantly shaped her life and the trajectory of her faith. At the time of the third interview, Joy identified her foster mother as her main parental figure and a significant positive influence on her life. Her foster mother lives nearby, and Joy had maintained a close relationship with her over the years. However, when we spoke this last time, the two of them had experienced a major falling out. After a period of sobriety following Joy's addiction, her foster mother tried to gain custody of Joy's children, claiming Joy was not a good mother. At the time, Joy and her foster mother had been going to the same church, but after this incident, Joy stopped going to church and really questioned her faith. She believed that her foster mom (and others in the church) were "hypocrites," and she was unable to reconcile their professed beliefs with the way they had acted toward her.

When we asked whether Joy considered herself a religious person or not, she replied, "I am, but I don't go to church. I mean, I would go to church, but there's too many hypocrites." She said that she would go to another church "far, far away, but I can't afford it." Joy had been involved in church and had been baptized. But after the falling-out with her foster mother, Joy said she "just kind of gave up, after all that happened. I'm like, you know what, forget it. I can read the Bible if I want to here at home. I'm not going out there for them to say, 'Oh there she is, still learning how to take care of her kids.'"

During the course of the interview, Joy also revealed for the first time that her stepfather, who was similarly very involved in his church, had molested her from the time she was 10 years old to age 13. He had passed away just a month before we met, and she cried when talking about him. Joy had been his primary caregiver before his death and felt close to him at the end of his life. "I have forgiven him," she said, "I had to move past it because if I didn't, I'd never, you know, be okay. It was me that was suffering and not him."

Although she had forgiven him personally, the impact on her life remained, causing her to question the whole idea of God, religion, and church. She told us, "That's the thing about my stepdad, too. I was always iffy about churches because he went to church and he was like one of the best members of the church, yet nobody knew what had happened behind the scenes." She continued, "It really let me down, like I said and, you know at that time, I didn't know what hypocrite meant [*laughs*], and . . . you know, it did upset me a lot, though, knowing what was going on. . . . I still went to church, I still believed in God, but I did feel like, you know, during my teenage years like where the hell were you at? You know? With God, it really made me question my faith."

Joy described her religious life this way: "I mean, I'm not a real big Christian fanatic, I believe in what's right and wrong." Joy believes in God and that Jesus was "God's son, he was born, resurrected and died for our sins, so on and so forth. . . . He's the only one that would ever be perfect."

She also believes "in heaven and hell. I believe in angels, demons, the devil . . . pretty much everything I was raised on, I guess." What she was raised on came from the local Baptist church. Joy does not have any particular affinity for the Baptist denomination and is open to attending different churches, but she still identifies as Baptist and has never considered changing her affiliation.

We also asked Joy about her private religious practices. "I do pray," she said. "When I was younger I used to only pray when good things happened and thank God, and I felt bad if I prayed for stuff, I know that sounds weird, it felt bad to pray for help." This reluctance to bring her needs into her prayer life has shifted now that she is older. Joy said she prays "when I need to, basically. I have some things going on that desperately, I do need help. And then we do pray at supper time, because we're all there at supper and we do have our family time at supper and we all pray. That's probably the only time I really pray." When asked whether she reads the Bible, she laughed and said, "every once in a blue moon."

Joy said that she feels close to God "at times," and this is "relieving and calming" for her. But she also struggles with doubts. When asked whether she has more or less doubts about God now than in the past, Joy paused for a long time, let out a sigh, and then said, "More, I guess? . . . I don't know, it's a mixture because, you know at first, when I quit going to church . . . I had a lot more doubts about it because of everything that happened there." Asked how hard or easy has it been to maintain her faith in recent years, Joy responded:

> I questioned it, so it's been kind of hard. Not necessarily questioning faith, I didn't mean it that way; I mean, it's just the whole "why do you let people in your church that are gonna act like this." It's not fair, it's criticizing, but . . . you know, I just don't think it's fair, and sometimes I don't understand why God lets it go on. [Do you see it getting easier in the future?] Yeah. I hope so. I pray [laughs].

Joy told us that she believes only one religion is true and that she knows what is true or untrue religiously because of what the Bible says. However, when it comes to her own life and how she knows or decides what is right or wrong, she said, "I . . . subconscious and experience. Like if I have a bad feeling about it . . . a gut feeling, subconscious, yeah, I will usually make a decision from there whether I think it's good or bad, and I'm not gonna do it if it's bad. . . . And experience, you know, like, [I've] already been through it or something similar, so I can use that as an example and go from there."

When asked how easy or hard it is to decide between right or wrong, Joy said, "Pretty easy. I mean, unless it was like an extremely difficult decision, it's pretty simple for me. I don't have to think long and hard about it. I used to, 'cause like: 'Man, maybe I should; man, maybe I shouldn't.' No, now it's like—that's wrong, and I know what should be right and what should be wrong, you know? So it's not really difficult."

When we asked Joy whether she felt she had a purpose in life, she told us that she thinks she is supposed to help other people and that this is her goal in life: "When I help other people, it gives me a sense of importance, and it makes me feel so much better that I've helped somebody." Right now, Joy feels like she is living out this purpose with her kids, and she said she is happy being a stay-at-home mom. However, she hopes to become a certified nursing assistant and sees her future career as a way to live out her purpose. "I love being at home, but you know, sometimes you have to have a break from three kids." She thinks of work not only as an opportunity to help others but also as a part of being a good parent. Going to work "is kind of your escape, even though it's work, it's a different environment, and you come back home and it's okay."

Looking to the future, Joy said that what she really wants to get out of life is to "be happy and to be—I mean my biggest thing is to be happy and to be financially stable. You know, and not have stress constantly." More than anything, she said she values family. But she also places a high value on being treated fairly. She said, "I don't necessarily value money or anything. I'm really big on—like I said, I want to make sure everyone's treated fairly and equally. And I try to teach my kids that, too." Reflecting back on the events of her life, we asked whether she would do anything differently in her life if she could. Joy told us that there was nothing she would change:

> Everything that I've done, everything that I've been through, everything—the way I see it, if I hadn't been through it, I wouldn't be the person I am today. You have to live, and a lot of times, you have to learn the hard way, and I really am happy with the attitude and temperament and all that I do have today. And . . . life lessons. I mean, you either learn, or they make you or break you, is the way I feel about it. So, yeah . . . basically, if it weren't for bad luck, we would have no luck at all, usually.

Joy has had a lot of ups and downs in her 27 years of life. Yet, despite her difficulties, she has a remarkably positive attitude about her current and future prospects. Most of the adults in her life have let her down or hurt her, but she seems to have been able to learn from those difficulties and is figuring out how to be a positive force in her kids' lives, even as she continues to work on her own life.

Kristen

Like Joy, Kristen encountered difficulties early in her life. Her parents separated when she was very young. When she was six years old, Kristen, along with her mother and siblings, found her father shortly after he had taken his own life. Yet Kristen's life has taken a much different path than Joy's. When raising Kristen and her siblings, her mother relied heavily on her evangelical Christian faith. They were deeply involved in their church, and eventually Kristen's mother married a widower who shared a commitment to her faith. In each of the four interviews with Kristen, she has remained consistent in her outlook on life: a happy teen, and now a happy and seemingly well-adjusted emerging adult who is committed to and knowledgeable about her faith. Kristen is a well-rounded, socially involved, outgoing young woman.

When we interviewed Kristen for the final time in 2013, she told us that she had graduated from her Christian college in December 2009 and then went on a four-month-long mission trip to the Middle East. When she returned to the States, she enrolled in a master's degree program in "worship studies" at an East Coast seminary. She expected the program to be oriented toward music performance, one of her passions. However, she instead found herself spending most of her time in libraries and writing papers, which she said allowed her to "stretch" into an area where she was less comfortable. After getting her master's degree in 2012, she joined a group from the church she was then attending to plant a new church in a large city in the desert Southwest. At the time of our interview, she was renting a room in the home that the pastor of the church lived in with his wife and kids. She said that she appreciated being able to have a close relationship with the wife and to watch how her hosts interact as a married couple. Kristen had recently become engaged to a young man who was also a member of the church-planting staff. He, too, had been a student at her seminary, although she said she had not known him well there.

Kristen is 26 years old, is very outgoing and gregarious, and laughed a lot throughout our interview. Looking back at her three previous interviews, her life is incredibly consistent, in both the kinds of relationships she values and maintains with her parents and other adults in her life and how she understands the world as a committed young Christian woman. She said that she is very close to her parents, but since she graduated from college, their relationship has changed somewhat: "In college, when I'm walking to class, there's a lot of dead time, I called my mom a lot. So, I would say that I probably talked to her, in a healthy way, like probably every day if she was available. And now I don't talk to her every day, but she still knows what's going on in my life, or if I have questions, I call them and ask them."

She said that her fiancé is her best friend and she spends most of her time with him. Given the time commitment her church activities require, her primary friend group right now is made up of others who are also involved with her church. However, she still remains in touch with her friends from home, college, and seminary. Religion is a frequent topic of conversation with all of her friends. And, even when she meets new people, issues of faith "just really easily come up in the conversation."

Kristen's faith is a central part her daily life and interactions in a way that is not typical of most of the emerging adults we spoke with.

Kristen thinks that the biggest challenge facing young people is one of identity and said, "A lot of people my age have come from, 'I grew up this way and now I don't really know who I am and . . . I'm still trying to figure out my identity and like what suits me.'" Kristen, however, is confident in her identity. She said:

> I know that I believe that God created me, and so he made who I am. So, finding out who I am is really based on who *he* is, and so a lot of my identity comes from that. Like, I'm a child of God, I'm a daughter . . . in Christ I'm forgiven, like I'm free in that. And, so, there's identity there that speaks into the rest of my life, and so that's where I have found my identity.

Kristen said her faith is "part of who I am, so it affects how I think and what I do, and so in that way, it's part of everyday life." She continued, "What I believe and know to be true affects the way I live. It affects my actions, it affects my thoughts, it affects my attitudes, it affects the way that I deal with situations. It affects the way that I go to events."

Her perspective on morals—knowing right from wrong and doing the right thing—also stems from her religious identity. According to Kristen, striving for moral uprightness is just a part of who she is:

> It's not like when every decision comes, "Well, is this good or bad, right or wrong?" It's a lot a part of, like, who I am, and . . . what I've learned from church and the Bible and from God, and so it's not necessarily like, "Oh, okay, so I have a decision, which one is right?" It usually is evident just because of who I am, but who I am is not because of me.

This ingrained moral compass is a result of the influence of her parents, other adults, her church, her friends, and, ultimately, her relationship with God. She believes that there is definitely right and wrong in the world and, for her, that boils down to "the general principle that it's wrong to be selfish." We asked her to explain what she meant, and she replied, "I think Christianity's the opposite of that, where it's very *selfless*. I think that's the portrayal of Christ: very selfless, and so the opposite of that—selfish. I mean, murder is very selfish . . . speaking poorly about someone else

is very selfish . . . greedy, being greedy. Greed is very selfish. I think that
abortion is very selfish."

Kristen believes that not being selfish is a core principle from which
one can reason out and think about all moral decisions. "I mean if what
people desire is love, like, love isn't selfish, and so I would say that's
what . . . if people are striving for . . . no matter who you talk to, everyone
wants to be loved. They want to feel connected with someone whether they
believe in God or not. So, if we're striving towards love, then selfishness is
a standard of wrong."

As should be clear from Kristen's responses to our questions, her faith
is an integral part of her life, shaping who she is. But it is also—owing at
least in part to her role in her church— the focus of much of her activities.
Kristen spends most of her time with the other church staff, doing community work and holding worship services on Sundays. They also meet
together for an hour and a half each morning for prayer and Bible reading.
She said that for her, prayer is "talking to God":

[Prayer] comes out of whatever we read in scripture, and like whatever I've read. So, thanking him for whatever that is and praising
him for who he is, for what he's done in general and then also in
my life. And then also asking him, like, "God, you know me, and
you see these things in my life, and I'm terrified of this and please
give me clarity on this." So, a lot of asking for myself, and asking
for other people. Like, "God, my sister, she is hurting, like, please
show her love today, or send people in her life to just blow her away
at your love." So, those things.

We asked Kristen to describe her religious beliefs, and she had a ready
answer:

I believe that the Bible is true, that it's the word of God and it can be
proven throughout history to be accurate. I believe that God is the
creator. That he made man, that he made the Earth, and I believe
that God lives in heaven, where it's the perfect place. I believe that
God loves us. . . . I believe that there is sin, and . . . I believe that
there's a payment for that sin that none of us could pay because no
one's perfect, although we try. So, I believe that God sent his son
Jesus, who left his perfect home in heaven to come live here on
Earth and to pay the result of our sin because he was perfect. So,

I believe that Jesus paid for our penalty by dying on the cross. That he was dead and he rose again three days later. And that when we confess our sins, and that we choose to also believe in God, that he forgives us of our sins, and so we have a new identity that once we were dead spiritually but now we're alive spiritually. That's it.

Kristen said that she's "very happy" with how her life is going. When we asked why, she replied, "I'm happy because I know that I am where I'm supposed to be. I think that my purpose is to love God and love other people and to tell them about God." She said that the most important thing in life for her, aside from God, is people. "I think people are what matter. Things, they're all good, they can burn out, but people."

As we were winding up the interview, we asked Kristen what would count for her as having lived a good life. She said, "Being obedient to what I know is true and . . . becoming more selfless and loving. If I go to my grave being selfish, I would be very disappointed." Overall, success and happiness in her life will mean that she is "a part of people's lives. I want to make a difference in people's lives . . . with how the Lord has made a difference in mine, and love people and be generous. I want to be obedient to what the Lord has given me in my life and teach other people how to do the same."

John

When we caught up with John in the summer of 2013, he had recently moved back to the East Coast and was living in his mother's basement for the summer. Five years earlier, in 2008, we had interviewed John in Las Vegas, where he was working as a substitute high school teacher and a semiprofessional gambler. He was barely making enough money to get by, although he still managed to afford trips to California to ski, or to Mexico to party with his friends. His pursuit of a teaching career was mainly to please his parents, and by the time we spoke with him again in 2013, he had given up on teaching altogether. He had, however, continued gambling, primarily on sports, and had expanded into selling tickets for college sports. The summer is his off-time. Once things start up in the fall, he travels to various cities and sometimes stays in motels for a month at a time selling tickets to different events.

During the summer, he was mainly just hanging out and smoking a lot of pot. In fact, many of his answers to our questions seemed pretty disjointed, and he ultimately admitted to having taken a "huge bong hit" just before the interview, saying that he had been smoking so much pot that his tolerance level was "out of control."

In fact, John's whole life sounds as though it is disjointed. He's 28 years old and living in his mom's basement with nothing to do but smoke pot while trying to hide it from her. His dating and sex life are on hold since, as he told us, "I have no money and I'm in my mom's basement." He said that he only has one or two casual girlfriends a year, and these relationships last only a few days. When we asked about his friends, he told us, "I have friends," and that "everybody's around" and he sees them "once or twice a year." But as he thought about it, he concluded that he lacked "a friend's devoted life." At one point in the interview he told us that all of the questions we were asking him made him realize, "I'm not really—I don't really have the . . . human interactions. All these normal parts of life, they're not part of mine."

Yet, John said that things are going "really good" for him even though it's been an "up and down couple of years." He admitted, though, that he's "small time" and that he really needs to turn a corner and make more than "$20, 30, 40 thousand a year doing this stuff." He doesn't have any other career plans, though, telling us, "This is what feeds me for now, and this needs to sort of come to fruition and then. . . . I've thought about, you know, my next business venture. To be honest, it probably won't work, so, when the time is right, I'll dip my toe in the water." For now, though, he said that he gets satisfaction from his work because he travels wherever he wants and does not experience much stress. According to John, his marijuana habit is part of how he copes with living with his mother, but it does not interfere with this work:

> I don't smoke weed when I'm doing my regular life. I might for like a week. I'll buy like a bag for a week when things slow down and all that. But, no, in my regular life I don't—I don't need that stuff. Because the thing is, I'm not some kid anymore. It's just not like in college. If I was in college, I needed to smoke weed no matter where I was but, no, this is just like I'm home at my mom's and like if I didn't step outside every half an hour, [laughs] it would make being at home really bad.

As his comment implies, John is not very close to his parents. This is particularly true of his dad, who often loses his temper. John reported being somewhat close to his mom, but noted that she "doesn't really support my work," which adds to the tension to their relationship. He feels pressure from his parents to pursue a more reputable way to make a living, and to that end he has taken a few graduate courses here and there over the last few years, but "it didn't go anywhere." Regardless, he said that living with his mom—albeit in the basement—is "okay," and that it doesn't take "too much concentration not to get caught smoking weed." When we asked if he thought his parents were happy with how he's turned out, he replied, "Probably not."

When we asked about how he decides or knows what's good and bad and right and wrong in life, John's answers had not changed much from our last interview with him. John does believe that there are definite rights and wrongs in the world. However, the only one he readily volunteered as being universally wrong was that "you can't go like kill somebody and stuff. You can't do that. Everyone knows that." However, John does not think that questions of morality are particularly relevant to his own life and said, "I don't really have these like moral things. Like, they don't really enter my life. I don't know—maybe if I had a life like chasing around like three kids . . . or, you know, living with a woman and all that sort of stuff, but I don't." He continued, saying that "making decisions with moral consequences" is just not part of his life: "You know, like, I only make decisions on like financial stuff, or like if I want to go somewhere. You know what I mean?" John said that he does not attach any moral meaning to these types of decisions. When pressed further on this issue, John responded:

> I think, you know, we all have a moral compass that guides us. But like I said, I don't feel like my moral compass is used much, you know, because I'm not—I mean, I'm still somebody who's worrying about me. My problems just concern me, and a lot of them are out of my control. Just do the best you can.

John is Catholic, mainly because his mother is Catholic. As he puts it, "My mom and I are kinda Catholics," meaning that his Catholic identity does not hold any particular salience or importance for him; rather, "It's what I've always been." He attends church with his mom a couple of times a year, "maybe a little more," although they don't otherwise talk about religion. We asked John what he believes about God and whether he has any doubts about his belief in God. He responded, saying:

I just choose to believe in God. A lot of people choose not to. I do. There's never been any reason to doubt my religious beliefs. They are what they are. It's normal to me. I think the other people are weird. Like how can you not believe in God? There are just different facts to everything. You know, it just doesn't all add up to me. There's some—something more to everything than protons, atoms, and dumb luck. Like I said, I don't [have doubts] because, you know, I'm a pretty humble guy and I don't feel the need to be—have anything proven to me or not.

While he is generally confident in his religious beliefs, when asked specifically about life after death, John said he doesn't really know. He is similarly inconclusive about the idea of karma, though acknowledges that "things have a way of evening themselves out." In spite of these uncertainties, however, John said that it has not been too difficult to maintain his beliefs over the past few years, and he has not experienced any significant religious change over the last half decade. John's religious faith is quite stable, and he does not anticipate any changes in the future. However, this does not necessarily mean that his faith is a particularly important factor in his life. On the contrary, when asked whether his faith is a central part of this everyday life, John said, "I don't know. It's there. Like I said, I'm not—I'm not extreme or anything."

In fact, he seems proud of his ability to maintain his religion without it being "extreme." He goes on to say:

I like to hope that in some ways, you know, I'm an ambassador for somebody who is religious and firm in being religious, but is happy to be casual about it, because in modern society, you know like, religion doesn't seem to be—it seems to be getting sort of squeezed out.

While John is clear in his identity as "just Catholic," he doesn't think that Catholicism, or Christianity more generally, is the only true religion. When we asked him what he thought about whether one or many religions are true, he said, "I don't know. I think multiple. I don't see much conflict between them, you know. They're all sort of similar." He hasn't considered any religion other than Catholicism for himself, and when we asked how he knows what to believe when it comes to religion he replied, "Um, I think . . . I just do. It's my feelings."

As we were wrapping up the interview, we asked John about the future and what he thought it would take for him to be truly happy when he's 40 years old. "Forty. Um. Yeah, I guess I need to just—financial stability and, yeah, I guess I don't want to be, like single when I'm 40. So, somebody willing to put up with me."

It is clear that our questions about his path to the future also highlight some uncomfortable realities about his present circumstances that he tried to deflect, saying, "I'll—I'll start thinking about that stuff when I feel like I'm a person again. I mean I'm just. . . . But whatever. What I am now, it's, you know—you mix me between like a grad student and like a minor league athlete or someone who sells drugs, or you know? I'm a mix of all that stuff into one."

Given his evident uncertainty about his life direction, we asked whether there were things he might have done differently in life. His response shifts the responsibility for his challenges to other people: "No, I don't think so because. . . . But you know, it's. . . . My problems are more other people who are, you know, swirling around like vultures trying to keep me down."

Whether John manages to make a go of it gambling and selling quasi-black-market tickets to sporting events is very much up in the air. Despite his uncertainty about the future, John maintains a sense of optimism. Although he explained how difficult his life is, he still seems determined to succeed in his current undertakings. But could this ever translate into a sustainable career that would provide long-term stability in his life and relationships? Even John isn't optimistic about that possibility.

Heather

We met Heather the Monday after a Saturday night bachelorette party, and she was still on the mend with a significant hangover. She arrived for the interview on time, looking like she had just rolled out of bed, with her blonde hair pulled back, wearing shorts, a T-shirt, and a canvas jacket. When Heather was last interviewed, it was the summer before her last year of college. She graduated in 2009 from a small Catholic liberal arts school in New England. After graduation, she had planned to be a kindergarten teacher. She wanted to move away from the East Coast, and some friends encouraged her to look into the Peace Corps. The Peace Corps didn't work out; instead, she became an AmeriCorps volunteer in schools on the West Coast, where she ended up living for four years.

When we spoke with her at the final interview, she had recently taken a job in sales back on the East Coast and had moved back in with her parents. She became a certified yoga instructor while she was on the West Coast, and yoga remains an important part of her life. She is also considering moving out of sales and into something more related to helping people, maybe going back to school for physical therapy training.

She gets along well with her parents, and even though she had some doubts about moving back in with them as she transitioned back to the East Coast, she said that they are very supportive of her and are now much more like friends than parents. Her mom is "very Roman Catholic" and is involved as a lay leader in her church. Her dad was raised Jewish but was agnostic until recently, when he went on a work-related retreat and discovered the importance of a having some kind of spirituality in his life.

Heather said that since she stopped attending church back in college, things have been "interesting" with her mother. She said that for her, the Catholic faith "just doesn't add up." Even though she went through confirmation, "It just didn't click for me . . . but I just had to wait until I was confirmed" before she could stop attending church. Her mother attributes this to her church's leadership not doing a good job of explaining things. Heather sees it differently and tells her mother that yoga is like her church.

After living away for several years, Heather said that she is getting back in touch with many of the friends she still has in the area and that her social circle is "pretty strong." Her friends have "pretty much nonexistent" religious lives. For some, this is a result of their not being raised by parents with any religious commitments or expectations about religion, while for others, being religious has "kind of like an 'uncool' stigma about it." When we asked her to explain what that was like, she responded that if a person is known to be religious, they are "put in a little box," and people are surprised if they find out that a "cool" person goes to church regularly.

Heather believes that one of the biggest challenges for young people is work, specifically, "finding work that they love." She said that she "wants a job that doesn't feel like work." Rather than just make a living, she wants to find work in which she has "a vested and personal interest." She also feels that relationships are a challenge and that technology such as texting makes it easier to hook up, but not to develop a relationship. For her, there is a loss of the personal touch. She also noted that, in her experience, a hookup happens as a prelude to a possible relationship, but does not often lead to a more serious relationship.

Heather is currently single and has recently broken up with a long-time boyfriend, but she wants to get married someday. In addition to offering support and companionship, Heather also sees marriage as an important part of having children, a way to know that her partner is "really kind of tied down to my side" to get through "the bumps in the road of parenting." When she does have children, rather than raise them Catholic as she was raised, she would want to expose them to multiple options, saying, "And then, you know, they could pick, I guess. . . . [But] I think that too many choices isn't always a good thing."

Heather was a pretty hard partier in college, sometimes binge-drinking and getting "blackout" drunk at parties. However, despite her current hangover, she has curtailed heavy drinking, saying that her body can't take it like it did in college. She does admit that she still smokes pot regularly, for relaxation. She particularly likes to smoke and paint and sometimes will smoke while she is practicing yoga. She said that this lets her "get in my own groove for a while and block myself in." Since she's been home, Heather has turned her parents' attic into a yoga studio. Although her parents are not aware that she smokes, she has been "burning" and doing yoga in the attic. She thinks she'll continue to drink and smoke pot at about the same levels in the future, although once she has kids, she may curtail her use—"You know, for their safety."

Heather believes that life is "all about being happy, I guess doing what makes you happy and finding people that make you happy." For her, that means being with her family on the East Coast—something she admitted she would not have expected to say until relatively recently—as well as having a life companion and finding meaningful work. So far, she hasn't found a career that she's passionate about. She believes that she has a purpose in life to "serve others in some way." She would like to do work that serves her larger purpose, but she doesn't know what that might be right now. She admitted that at the moment she feels a little lost in life. But while she hasn't yet reached her goals of meaningful work and a life companion, she's "on her way" to achieving those things.

Heather said that even though she isn't a practicing Catholic—she doesn't even claim a "cultural" Catholic identity—she does see the value of her upbringing in the Church and believes that "a lot of my values came from the Catholic Church." She doesn't think it is good when people break rules to gain some personal benefit, but she added that this perspective is "another thing that's sort of becoming normal." She continued, saying, "You know, just because we can get away with it doesn't mean that we should." She said that she thinks that this kind of generalized moral sensibility is becoming much more common, particularly among young people. When we asked why, she said:

> I think it's a sense of entitlement, and I'm not really sure where it's coming from. I think that I've heard a lot that my generation has been parented in a—in a different way of kind of like, "How do you feel?" Like, a little bit more fluffy, I guess . . . which I don't think that that's a bad way. But I don't know—I don't know really where it was lost on other people, and I don't know if it's because I did have that religious upbringing . . . there was that—that discipline there. I don't know. I think the moral compass on some young people is a little bit skewed.

For Heather, differentiating between right and wrong comes down to "how is it affecting the other person that you're making this decision with? The other person or community or business or, you know, like whatever it is." Ultimately, she believes that understanding right from wrong is something "internal, like you know that you don't steal. And that's, you know, that is something that I was taught from a very early age."

Heather considers herself "spiritual . . . I don't identify with a religion," and her yoga practice is a large part of that spirituality. And while she appreciates her Catholic upbringing, her appreciation has its limits. She said that there is "some value to their practices," although "they've been tweaked" as she has applied them in her life. Overall, though, she sees the Catholic Church as "more of a—I guess it is a dictatorship" and suggests that the Catholic Church should change with the times. Then she seemed to catch herself, and said, "Not that they—that religion should be changing with the times, because I guess the point is that it's so old." But if she does go to Mass, she said that she feels "like I come out of there not really agreeing with what they're saying or . . . preaching, or that they're a little bit abrasive in terms of their 'you must, you must, you must.' "

Although Heather no longer considers herself a Catholic and doesn't identify with any religious tradition, neither does she consider herself an agnostic or an atheist, as she maintains her own set of spiritual beliefs. She believes "that there's a purpose—I believe that everybody has a purpose. I guess my school of thought would be that, you know, you're— you're here for a purpose and to find your purpose, and then to do it." She believes in "angels and spiritual guides," although when she talks about spiritual guides, they tend to be other humans who help to direct a person onto a better path rather than something supernatural. For example, she mentioned her yoga teacher, who "reconnected me more to like a spiritual path." She also thinks that meditation is "really important" and tries to maintain a regular meditation practice, but said that maintaining a "daily self-discipline" of practicing meditation is difficult.

Heather also believes that people "who passed are watching over," but her beliefs about the afterlife are somewhat colored by her Catholic upbringing. She said that she "has a belief in heaven," but that "I don't think I really do hell. I don't think anybody is burning in hell. And I don't know that there's a Judgment Day where there's, you know, pearly gates are opening."

She does, though, believe "that you go someplace else" after death. But, she said, "I'm not sure of what I think about the whole rebirth thing." We ask if she believes in karma. "I do believe in karma," she said. "I mean, what goes around comes around. And I think that that guides my moral compass. You know, like, if you screw this person over, you know, like you're probably going to get screwed over. But if you kind of keep on the— you know, like if you do good, then it's going to—it's going to come back to you."

Overall, Heather said that she values her family most in life. She said that she values "the way I was brought up, that we were pretty comfortable financially. I think I was unique in terms of . . . my parents having different spiritual backgrounds, and then just being really accepting of whatever, and being open to things." Heather said that this openness is "you know, just like a kind of different . . . world view, I think."

Raymond

When we contacted Raymond, he was eager to sit down with us again. But when we gave him a reminder call about a week before the interview, he had forgotten all about it. Still, he assured us he would be there. On the day of the interview, he forgot the time we had agreed to meet and went to a friend's house instead. He doesn't have a cell phone, but we were able to contact his girlfriend, who got the message to him. Raymond eventually showed up for the interview and gave us an update on his life. This chain of events was not unlike the last time Raymond was interviewed. At that time, he had also forgotten all about it, and we were not certain that he would show up. After speaking with Raymond for this final interview, it was apparent that, like his planning skills, the rest of his life has not really moved forward in any significant way since 2008.

Raymond, now 28 years old, is still living with his grandfather in a small rural town in the Pacific Northwest. He helps around the house, doing yardwork, handyman tasks, working on cars, and generally taking care of "grandpa." Raymond's grandfather, who is 78 years old, owns the property and pays for most everything, although Raymond said that he "chips in" to pay bills when his grandfather asks him to. Raymond said he plans to stay with his grandfather and care for him as long as he can. He acknowledges that he would have to "try a little harder" if he were to live on his own, but also notes that his grandfather "couldn't live without me." It seems to be a mutually beneficial living arrangement.

Raymond has two children from two different mothers; his daughter is now eight years old and his son is two. Though neither of them lives with him, he said he feels close to his children. His current girlfriend lives with him at his grandfather's house, helping out with his grandpa when Raymond is not around, taking him places and doing work inside the house. Living with his girlfriend, he told us, just "kind of sort of happened." He said that his grandfather likes her a lot, so it seems to work out. When we asked whether he is thinking of marriage, he told us that his grandfather has been married six or seven times and that his mother has been married twice. Based on their experiences, he concluded, "You know, I just don't know. Marriage doesn't seem like all it's cracked up to be. It's just paperwork anyway." He quickly follows that comment with, "Not trying to sound like a hippie or anything, but . . ." suggesting that this isn't any sort of countercultural decision, just a reaction to his observations of the marriages in his family, which have shaped his thinking in terms of his own relationship.

As in 2008, Raymond is still working at odd jobs doing "handyman stuff here and there" a few days a week, earning "50 dollars a day or so." He has recently started a two-year business management program at the local community college and is open to going for a four-year degree, "Depending on how things are at the end of the two years, I guess." We ask whether he considers himself an adult at this point in his life, and he said, "Yeah, by now, yeah." He said that for him, being an adult means that you are "able to support yourself. Take care of yourself, and those of yours. You know, your kin, as it were." When we ask about his friends, he talked about having different friends all over the area. However, when we ask how well he knows them, he doesn't sound particularly close to any of them. He said that "in general" his parents are pleased with how he has turned out. And his grandfather tells him that "he's really happy with how things have been going. He's been telling me that for the last two years now."

When we interviewed Raymond in 2008, he reported regular drug use and heavy drinking. At one point, he had even ended up in the hospital with significant health problems as a result. This is one area of his life that has changed in the intervening time since that 2008 interview. He reported in this interview that he hasn't "used that meth stuff since I was 18 or 19." More recently, he has stopped using marijuana and reduced his drinking. Raymond told us it had been about 15 months since he "*drank drank*, you know, in the way to drink and have fun and do whatever we would do." The break from alcohol seems to have been precipitated by an incident that he did not want to talk about, saying simply that "I did some pretty bad things when I was drunk. Part of the reason I haven't [been drinking] for so long." Thinking ahead five to 10 years, Raymond said that he thinks that he still won't be drinking to excess as he has in the past. Then he added, "Weed though. . . . I love marijuana. I do. And I, when I'm, you know, when I'm done with school and stuff, and I'm, you know, in a position that I got money saved away and can do pretty much anything, then, you know, on weekends and stuff, I'll smoke with my friends and hang out and do whatever."

Beyond his responses to specific questions about things like living arrangements, work, and school, Raymond's answers to many of our questions were somewhat vague. He was often unsure what question he was answering or would lose track of the question as he answered. Sometimes he rambled on in his responses, connecting thoughts and experiences that did not seem to be related—several times, in the middle of his response, he would ask, "Now, what was the question?"

This was especially true when it came to religion. When we asked how he described himself religiously, he said, "Um, the Lord is good." When we pressed him as to whether he identified with a specific religion, he replied, "Methodist slash Catholic, I guess." A few minutes later he told us that he was "raised Catholic and RLDS," a branch of the Latter-day Saints movement, although most of his responses seemed more generically Christian and not specifically related to any of those traditions. For Raymond, any differences between Methodists or Catholics and other denominations were all connected to requirements about tithing and how that was linked to getting into heaven. "Methodists, you give what you can.

Whereas Mormons say, you have to give at least 10 percent. You *have* to, or you will go to hell."

Raymond sees Catholics somewhere between the Methodists and Mormons: "The Catholics do say 10 percent I think, too, but not, I don't think you're going to go to hell for it. If you can't give that, at least give what you can." When asked to describe his own religious beliefs, Raymond said:

I believe in God. I believe that we should follow his law. I believe, not maybe not every *single* little tiny thing that teachers of religious law tell you. But I do believe in, in large part, it is all. Oh, I believe in the Our Father, and I believe . . . at least in the Lord. I believe that he put us here, he does in fact have a purpose for us. I do believe that we do all have a purpose and that it is his purpose, whether we know it or not.

When asked what he believes about Jesus, Raymond continued:

Well . . . I believe that he came here to die for our sins. Or at least that he spoke the truth, and it was just the religious leaders did not believe the same as him and he suffered for it. Whether or not you believe, he came here specifically to die for our sins. But, he may not have. He may have just been one of, you know, one of God's messengers to tell us what he wanted us to know. Either way, he was here because God made him, made him to be here. Sent him, however you want to say it. In my opinion, of course, again.

In the end, the most important religious beliefs for him are "well, laws for sure. His law, like not to kill, not to steal, and not, you know, to do all that stuff he says not to do. But to do for [help] others."

Turning to issues of life after death and the existence of heaven and hell, Raymond expressed some uncertainty. Like many of the young people we spoke with, he would like to believe that life doesn't just end after death and that heaven really exists as a perfect place where the soul can be with God after this life is over. But he admitted that he is still undecided and does not know for sure what he believes about these issues.

On the question of reincarnation, he is also uncertain and referenced his Native American heritage in his response. "I don't know. Okay, I'm part Cherokee, so, I don't know. I know plenty of Indians that say that it is [true]. Wolves, eagles, snakes, you know, whatever creatures, but it depends on what you did in life as for what you'll become. I could come back a wise owl, you know, or something like that. *If* that's what happens."

Following up, we asked whether Native American spirituality is important to him, and he related a story of an ongoing experience with an owl and how he is trying to determine whether it is a message from God or perhaps from his grandmother:

> There is this owl. And, as silly as it may sound, for like the last two years, usually when it happens it's at night. I'll hear an owl screech and I'll look up and see him immediately, instead of having to search for him and it's dark. And he's a white one, or gray at least, enough that I can see him in the dark up in the sky at night. And he follows me sometimes and like he hangs around the house, too, in the big tree within a block's radius, he lives in there somewhere. Could be a sign, or I don't know. It—you know, maybe it could be my grandmother, you know, trying to tell me something. So, I guess I do believe that it is possible. . . . I want to believe in it, but I don't know.

After discussing his religious beliefs, we ask Raymond if he has any spiritual practices like attending church, praying, or reading the Bible. He told us that he doesn't attend church, "not like I should. I guess grandpa and I have been being lazy." Instead of going to church, they stay home and watch a TV preacher a couple of times a week, and he reads the Bible along with the service as they watch. He also said he prays three times a day. He does volunteer work at a local Nazarene church, but doesn't attend any services there.

Knowing right from wrong is not very hard at all, according to Raymond. His sense of right and wrong comes from "a feeling, you know. You just, you know. We know what is right and wrong." When asked where this feeling comes from, he said, "I don't know. Being the way I was raised, I guess." He acknowledges that his religious beliefs do often play a role in his deciding what is right and wrong, though "it depends on the circumstance. I could say at least 80 percent." He does not believe that morals are relative, saying, "That's, I mean, just an excuse for people to go and do whatever they want. You know? Or to do wrong things or to be, you know, I don't know. It's an excuse for wrong, sounds like."

Looking ahead in his life, Raymond expressed very pragmatic goals, saying that what will make him happiest when he's 40 years old will be "to have an education and a good job, health insurance, benefits, you know, stuff like that." He's not quite sure what he really wants out of life and is primarily focused on finishing the post-secondary education that he is just now starting. We ask what would count for him as failure, and he replied, "Not having finished the schooling that I'm talking about." Raymond told us that the things in life that he most values are family and the loyalty of friends and that he believes he is living his life in a way that lets him live his values through his volunteer work and helping other people. Raymond told us that he doesn't think he has any regrets about his life so far, and there is not much he would do differently in his life, if given the chance.

Raymond is an engaging, likable young man who has made small but significant changes in his life over the five years between interviews. If he finishes school, that may provide a level of confidence he needs to embark on the life he envisions for himself—a good job with health insurance and benefits, caring for others, and spending the weekends smoking pot and hanging out with his friends.

Conclusion

Although these five stories of emerging adults are not intended to be representative of all American emerging adults, they do echo the themes that we have found, more broadly, in our research. That said, as was noted in the discussion of these same young people after they were last interviewed in 2008, there is more continuity in their lives than there is change.[2]

Of the five emerging adults whom we profile here, Joy is the one who has experienced the most dramatic changes. She seems to have achieved a level of stability in her life. She has been off drugs and alcohol for a couple of years, is in a marriage that is working despite the couple's problems, and is a good and responsible mother. And, almost unbelievably, she has reached a point where she has forgiven the adults who have let her down—even her abusive stepfather. The move toward more stability was prompted in large part by the intervention of a responsible adult and a religious awakening and reinforced by good decisions on Joy's part, particularly quitting drugs and alcohol. It is noteworthy, however, that she has managed to maintain a level of stability even in the face of what she views as a betrayal by her foster mother and her subsequent exit from any church participation.

Each of the others we profiled has experienced much more continuity in their lives. And while the particulars of each of their lives vary widely, the stories of these young people reinforce a theme we have seen across the years of this study: the importance of parents and other adults in the lives of young people. John and Raymond, for example, seem the most marginally stable. But what stability they have is owed in part to the adults in their lives. As with Joy, Raymond seems to have benefited from a positive adult relationship, in his case with his grandfather and the sense of responsibility Raymond clearly has for him. It is hard to know how Raymond might manage if he did not live with his grandfather.

John is clearly just getting by. And even though he isn't thrilled about it, being able to live in his mother's basement seems to provide an important source of stability for him. If living with his mother were not an option, it isn't clear what he would do during the times of the year that he has no source of income.

Kristen and Heather demonstrate more stability and continuity in their lives, despite the differences in their life experiences. It is no coincidence that the two women whose lives are the most settled and stable are also the two who are closest to and have the most support from their families. The influence and support of parents and other invested adults play a significant role in shaping whatever stability and continuity are found among these emerging adults.

Across the stories of all five emerging adults, we see some significant similarities that will emerge later in the book. One of the most interesting characteristics shared by all five—which echoes the characteristics of emerging adulthood briefly discussed in the introduction—is that all of them, regardless of their particular circumstances, are optimistic about their lives and the possibilities that may lie ahead for them. This is true even when the objective evidence suggests little reason to be optimistic. Think of John and his dreams of being a much bigger player in the ticket-selling game, or Raymond and his goal of finishing school and getting a good job with benefits and insurance. They may very well achieve these goals, but it is hard to reconcile that prospect with the evidence of their lives, at least at this point. Yet, these young men continue to expect a brighter future for themselves.

Another characteristic common to each of these young people is their tendency to understand themselves as unfettered individuals standing on their own, fully capable of achieving their goals and making necessary changes to reach those goals, despite their life situations. Raymond is a good example of this. His life has not changed appreciably in the five years since he was last interviewed; he's still living with and taking care of his grandfather and making a small amount of money doing odd jobs. Though he is mostly dependent on his grandfather, he maintains the belief that his future is completely in his hands. He is banking on completing the community college program he just started to allow him to get a good job, yet there is little in his life at this point to suggest that this will happen. If continuity is the norm, then Raymond's future may not be as bright as he imagines it could be. While his future has partly to do with his own abilities and decisions, it will also be dependent on what resources he has available to complete his college courses and how he handles the other responsibilities in his life.

Finally, this sense of individual authority and agency permeates most aspects of these five lives, including how these emerging adults think about religion and morals. We will see much more of this throughout the book, but for now, recall how, with the exception of Kristen, each of the emerging adults expressed morality as being something that they felt in their "gut," that it is a feeling they get, and they "just know" right from wrong. Sometimes they could articulate that this belief might come from somewhere, but in general, morals were something that they *individually* felt or knew.

Similarly, they each (again with the exception of Kristen) have a self-styled set of ideas and beliefs about faith and spirituality. Whether or not they believe themselves to be religious or knowledgeable about religion, there is a significant element of picking and choosing what they like about religion. They seem to be synthesizing their own version of religion or spirituality from a variety of sources, not all of which are religious. How this plays out for emerging adults more broadly is discussed at length later in the book. For now, it is important to point out that these young people are very similar to other emerging adults in their belief in themselves as autonomous individuals in all aspects of their lives.

In the next chapter, we turn to the major themes in the lives of emerging adults as they are moving toward adulthood in order to provide a broader context for their lives in terms of work, friends, family, and the like. Throughout, we focus on how well they are taking on the roles of adulthood as they enter the full-time workforce, start their own families, and otherwise make their way in the world.

2

Setting the Context

TRANSITIONS TO ADULT LIFE

WE CANNOT UNDERSTAND the religious lives of emerging adults without first understanding the cultural moment within which they are living their lives. However they embrace and embody religion, they do so in a way that is embedded in a larger social context that is inhabited by family and friends and shaped by work, school, politics, and a variety of other cultural realities. The goal of this chapter is to provide a broad picture of how emerging adults are transitioning to adulthood and of the general cultural setting within which they are making these transitions. Thus, this chapter focuses on important themes and markers of adulthood that are necessary to set the stage for understanding how religion is lived within these contexts. In turn, the themes from this chapter will come up again in different ways in subsequent chapters. Our goal here is to provide a deeper understanding of the social and cultural worlds from which emerging adults approach religion and of how they may be reshaping religion as they transition into adulthood.

Entering Adulthood

The young people in this book are between the ages of 23 and 28, and many are still at the beginning stages of their adult lives. In most cultures, and until recently in the United States, marriage served as the marker between adolescence and adulthood.[1] Yet, marriage, while still important and meaningful in American culture, no longer functions as the definition of attaining full-fledged adult status. Jeffrey Arnett has argued that the primary marker for emerging adults to be considered adults is that they become *self-sufficient*, which includes taking responsibility for oneself, making independent decisions, and becoming financially independent.[2]

Although there is variation in how they are reaching these markers of adulthood, the young people in this study are moving into adulthood and taking on the traits of self-sufficiency articulated by Arnett. For example, even though most of them have yet to marry and start their families, they are setting out on their own in important ways. More than 70 percent said that they have their own place to live, while 21 percent reported that they still live with their parents. The remainder of the cohort maintain some other sort of living arrangements, such as dorms or other group-style living. This contrasts with many news media stories that suggest that most emerging adults live with their parents well into their 30s.[3] While for some emerging adults this appears to be true, the majority of those in our study are leaving home and establishing their own places to live, which in turn suggests that they are ready to take on more adult responsibilities.

In our interviews with emerging adults, one of our first questions for them was whether they considered themselves to be an "adult." Their responses indicated that not all of them are convinced that they have reached adult status. In general, this hesitancy revolved around how independent and self-sufficient they considered themselves to be. This then led to a discussion about their age, what they thought it means to be an adult, and how those two variables might be related. Most of the young people we interviewed initially expressed ambivalence about their status as adults, suggesting their location somewhere between late adolescence and adulthood, having yet to achieve full-fledged adulthood. Overall, this idea of attaining self-sufficiency informed their responses. They believed that a central part of what it means to be an adult is being able to take on "adult responsibilities," like a decent-paying job, the ability to take care of themselves and the independence that implies, and for those who are parents, the responsibility that goes along with having children.

The more responsibilities they had—whether a full-time job, kids, or simply taking responsibility for themselves—the more certain they were that they had reached adulthood. For example, when we asked whether she considered herself an adult, a 27-year-old woman answered, "Yes, I'm a mother [*laughs*]. I have to be. I wish I was still a kid being able to do my homework and not have to get up every morning and go to work or do the errands and not have to worry about cooking or cleaning, you know? I had to grow up a little bit."

For most, having a job—and the pay that goes with it—seemed to be a key marker for adulthood. Not only did this signal responsibility and the money to pay their own way, but in many cases, it was a source of pride for them, particularly in terms of the adult obligations and concomitant independence that having a job means. This was true even for those young people still living at home, who on average framed their living situation as a chance to save money or pay back loans. They still considered themselves independent, primarily because they were employed, and regardless of their living situation, felt like they were supporting themselves. For example, a 26-year-old woman told us that she considered herself an adult because, "I'm financially stable apart from my parents. I'm independent of my parents." Another answered, "Unfortunately, yes," she did consider herself an adult. She continued, "We've [she and her husband] been having this conversation of like do we consider ourselves adults, and I mean basically like we own a condo, [and] are financially responsible for ourselves." Although she expressed what sounds like disappointment in having reached what she considers adulthood, perhaps betraying a nostalgia for an earlier time in her life, she identified being financially independent of her parents as the marker of adulthood.

Similarly, even those who do not yet consider themselves full-fledged adults primarily pointed to their lack of independence and financial stability as evidence of their not-quite-adult status. Like their peers, they also identified achieving the markers of a stable job, having their own place, and ultimately getting married and having children as indicators of when they would know that they were adults. Michael, who we met in the first pages of this book, said that he still thought of himself as a "young adult," but his age was at the "cutoff" line of becoming a full-fledged adult. When asked what his criteria would be for knowing that he was an adult, he replied, "I say a career. Like a career as being like a, a big piece. Up until this point I've been in school, so I haven't really had a career. I've just been a full-time student. So once I have a career, I see that more as like, what your time is being used for. What you're about. I see that being a part of adulthood."

Family and Friends

In our interviews with emerging adults, the overwhelming majority expressed gratitude for their lives, including for their family and friends. Family came up repeatedly in our interviews as they answered our questions, including mentions of both parents and siblings, as well as their marriages, or desire to be married, and the families they were forming, or hoped to form. Most of the emerging adults we spoke with indicated that their relationship with their parents remained close. Even for those with difficult or distant relationships with their parents, these challenges did not seem to be a major source of anger or frustration for most.

In *Souls in Transition*, Smith and Snell observe a subtle shift in the way emerging adults interact with family and friends.[4] They note that young people seem to have narrowed their social circles, with family and a few close friends becoming more central in their lives while wider networks hold less sway for them. This trend seems to have continued into the final wave of the interviews, with the social worlds for most emerging adults shrinking even beyond what Smith and Snell observed. This development can also have implications for their religious lives. Religion is transmitted and reinforced through networks of family and friends. Thus, as these worlds become more insular for emerging adults, understanding those connections will add nuance to our understanding of their religious lives.

Marriage and Parenthood

A significant marker of adulthood for many emerging adults is the transition from one's family of origin into new family formation through marriage or parenthood. Becoming a parent—and to a lesser extent, getting married—marks a clear transition to adulthood for many emerging adults. And as we will see in Chapter 6, these family transitions are also interwoven with religious engagement in significant ways. While almost 60 percent of the emerging adults in our study have yet to marry, around one-fourth are currently married, and another 10 percent are engaged to be married. Four percent have been previously married but are now divorced or separated. Thirty-one percent of the emerging adults in the study have at least one child. Thus, at least one-third of the emerging adults are busy forming families—getting married and/or having children. While the majority have yet to embark on that journey, this is definitely a priority for most emerging adults in terms of their life goals and desires.

Regardless of whether they are married at this point in their lives, the idea of marriage was a major theme shaping their lives and giving them meaning. For those who have transitioned into marriage or parenthood, these relationships were highlighted as a major source of responsibility and meaning in their lives. But we also heard them acknowledge the significant impact these obligations have on their life choices and opportunities. For example, among those who had children at a young age, parenthood was clearly a factor that influenced their educational outcomes and the kinds of jobs they had taken to provide support for their families.

For most, however, the limitations that having children may have placed on them were outweighed by the positive aspects of family life. This included the realization that they could no longer focus only on themselves. A 26-year-old woman told us that having children "helped me not be so selfish, and [realize] it's not all about me." Similarly, a 28-year-old man told us that his daughter causes him to "take her into consideration before making decisions." One 27-year-old man acknowledged that having children "brought on a whole lot of responsibilities and made me feel [like] more of an adult." Still others said that their children had given them direction and purpose. Another 27-year-old man told us that having a daughter had "changed my life dramatically. It's turned me into the person that I was meant to be . . . [and] I don't think my parents would be as proud of me if it wasn't for my daughter." And, a 27-year-old woman said that her kids provided a "deeper sense of purpose in life, to be more responsible. . . . Having children has changed me 110 percent for the better. It has made me more responsible and given me more drive and more desire."

Relationships with Parents

Over the 10 years of the National Study of Youth and Religion (NSYR) project, a consistent theme has been the importance of parents in the lives of their adolescent and emerging adult children, particularly in shaping the religious trajectories of respondents. Throughout our interviews, we continued to hear about the importance of parents, with many telling us that their parents—either as a couple or individually—were among the people that they most looked up to and respected, and whom they considered as having a significant influence in their lives.

In the survey data, we see that emerging adults reported closer relationships with their mothers than with their fathers, with 66 percent saying that they are very or extremely close with their mother and with 52 percent of those who identified a father figure in their life saying that they are very or extremely close with him. In the in-person interviews, there was a generally positive response to our questions about parents, both mothers and fathers. However, this was often followed by an explanation of the different ways that they were close to their mothers and fathers. Mothers tended to be social and emotional confidants, while fathers were usually framed as a source of practical advice and someone who could get things done for them. A good example is this 26-year-old woman who said that she feels close to her parents in different ways:

> My mom and I do the whole let's talk about like my relationships and you know, that kind of stuff, and my dad and I will have like—I think we have like more . . . serious conversations. Like we'll talk about the news. . . . I feel like whenever I need something, like how to read my lease, or how do I do something or just like random advice on life type thing. I go to him for that.

This difference in how young people related to their parents can help explain the differences between the reported closeness with mothers and fathers, with mothers filling an emotional role more often associated with the idea of relationship closeness.

It is important to note that not all of the emerging adults we spoke with reported being particularly close to their parents. For these young people, their more distant parental connections seem to be a continuation of the kind of relationship they have had with their parents throughout their lives. This was mostly expressed as a neutral or perhaps benign relationship that was neither close nor a priority, yet with the possibility that it could develop into something more significant in the future. A 24-year-old woman gave a response that was typical for these young people:

INTERVIEWER: How close do you feel to your parents these days?
RESPONDENT: I'm closer than I was, I suppose. Our relationship's always just been kind of . . . I can't even really think of a word to describe it. Very, uh, bland, I guess. You know, it's not like we have a really close relationship. We don't have any problems with each other. You know they're not, they're not the type of people that I call up with everything I have to say. I don't share my most *intimate*, you know, things with them, but you know we'll, we'll talk. We get along pretty well.
I: What do you think it's meant to you being closer to them over time?
R: I mean just kind of a coming to terms with the fact that I was a very surly adolescent and feeling that I have to make up for that, you know? Kind of, also, realizing, like, they're my parents. They raised me and I definitely owe it to them to share my life with them.

As seen in this quotation, even when the relationship with parents is not ideal, there is a common recognition of the important role that parents play in their lives.

Friends

When we interviewed these young people as teens, they seemed to have long lists of friends, and in response to our questions about their friends, they would tell us in great detail all about each one of them. As noted previously, as emerging adults, their social worlds seem to be shrinking to family (whether families they are forming or with their parents and siblings) and a few close friends. These friendships tended to be formed around common activities and events related to family milestones or opportunities, with children being a factor for some. One 26-year-old told us that his friends, whom he had known since high school, were all having kids, so their socializing tends to be "go[ing] to our kids' parties and stuff like that," or just to get together and "hang out."

For those with no children, friendships tend to form around their activities with a small group of friends—whether long-term or more recent friends from school or work—who shared interests in the same kind of entertainment, such as music, concerts, movies, video games, sports, and the like. Some weren't even sure what brought them together as friends. This 24-year-old is a typical example. He said, "Most of my friends are different from me. I don't know what brings us together. We usually bond over video games, food, and music. . . . We rarely talk about politics. Never talk about religion . . . a few of my friends are very religious, but it's never been something that we've bonded over as friends. It's usually been just food, video games, music, and playing video games, things like that."

Both friend and family relationships seem to have deepened in many ways, with young people identifying those who are most important to them in response to a question about friendships, rather than enumerating the laundry list of friends that they had described to us when they were teens. So, asking about the ways that they interact with family and friends is important to understanding their participation in and view of the world. In our survey, we asked them to think of up to five of their closest friends, and then asked a series of questions aimed at helping us understand the kinds of people that they surround themselves with: their beliefs, what they talk about, how diverse their friends are, whether they are married or went to college, and other similar things. While an in-depth analysis of emerging adult friendship networks is beyond the scope of this book, what follows are some basic characteristics of the friends of typical emerging adults.

Although most emerging adults in our study have never been married, more than one-half said that they have at least one friend who is married and a similar number of friends who have at least one child. Almost all of them have at least one friend who went to college, and one-third said that they have at least one friend who does not have a job. Although many popular accounts of emerging adults tout their multicultural sens-ibilities, fully two-thirds of our respondents said that they have no friends of another race.

The close friends of emerging adults are an important component of the larger social context within which they are working out their transi-tion to adulthood, and in particular the contours of their religious lives. When it comes to a simple count, most emerging adults do have religious friends. Three-fourths of them said that they have at least one friend who is religious, and 90 percent said that at least one of their friends has be-liefs that are similar to their own. Young people also said that they talk about religion with their friends, with three-fourths of our survey respond-ents saying that religion is a topic they talk about.

While it may be a possible topic of conversation, our in-depth inter-views revealed that emerging adults are not often actually engaging in discussions about religion. One 26-year-old woman told us that she and her friends talk about religion "once in a while, but not very regularly." To the extent that conversations about religion do take place, they tend to be episodic and based on something that our respondents have re-cently experienced. These exchanges do not seem to be particularly deep and engaging conversations about faith. A typical response came from another 26-year-old woman who said that she has "certain friends" that she can discuss religion with, but "not really unless something comes up." This suggests that while religion and spirituality may not be a com-pletely taboo topic for emerging adults, it does not appear to be a par-ticularly important part of their relationships with their friends. Thus, although religion remains a part of the social lives of emerging adults, it figures into their social identities only in a limited manner. They have friends who are religious, but religion does not appear to play a cen-tral role in these friendships, either as a shared activity or as a specific discussion topic.

Work, Career, and Finances

As noted at the beginning of this chapter, self-sufficiency is a major marker of having reached adulthood, usually linked to having work or a career and the financial stability that goes along with that. The majority of emerging adults in this study are working at or near full-time hours, with more than one-half working more than 40 hours a week. Including those who are working between 30 and 40 hours each week, almost 70 percent of emerging adults are working at or near full-time hours. In terms of earnings, the two largest groups of young people in our study are those who are earning between $10,000 and $30,000 annually (37 percent), and those who are earning between $30,000 and $60,000 annually (30 percent). Just eight percent earn more than $60,000 annually. Three percent of our respondents declined to report their earnings, and the remaining 22 percent are earning less than $10,000 annually, with seven percent earning no money at all in the past year.

In our interviews, emerging adults said that work and a career, for them, was not only a marker of having reached adulthood but also an important part of their identity. Many described work as a marker of responsibility, autonomy, and respect. For example, for one 28-year-old man, work entailed the responsibility to "do your job correctly," which for him resulted in gaining "respect from people because you know what you're doing and you know what's expected of you and your job." The desire for responsibility and autonomy was expressed by several emerging adults who spoke about wanting to have their own business someday. Usually, however, they were not quite able to articulate what, exactly, that business venture would be. For example, a 25-year-old woman who was successful in her current job told us that owning her own business was her "dream job." Yet, she couldn't envision what that business would be:

ı: What kind of business would you like to own?
ʀ: See, that's the part I don't know yet. I mean, I manage this whole business [where she currently works], I run that company, and I enjoy it, I just don't know what industry I would choose if I was doing it myself.

Thus, while the themes of responsibility and self-sufficiency often took on different forms, even if only as an abstract expression of ambition, it was clear that these are primary goals in the lives of emerging adults.

Another common theme was the desire for work to be meaningful and to contribute to our informants' larger life purpose and overall happiness.

In Chapter 1, we heard Heather express the hope of one day finding work that makes her happy and allows her to pursue a greater purpose in life. We heard many of her peers express a similar sentiment about their desire to make a difference, either within the company they work for, or by making the world a better place through their work. A 24-year-old woman said, "It's never about the money, 'cause you can get money from anywhere. As long as you're comfortable in what you're doing, then you'll be fine." A 28-year-old man expressed a similar belief, saying that for him, the most important thing in a job or career was "being happy, and if you're not helping better the world, then at least you're not hurting it." Many emerging adults believe work should be more than just a source of financial stability but also offer a sense of identity and purpose. This was expressed as an ideal more often than a lived reality; that is, emerging adults are hopeful that they will one day have work that is meaningful and a source of personal contentment. However, many acknowledge that their current work is simply paying the bills, but is not yet filling their lives with meaning.

Across our interviews, regardless of how religiously committed young adults were, the idea of work contributing to their personal sense of meaning and purpose was frequently expressed. For the most religious informants, this was often, though not always, an obvious outgrowth of their faith or spiritual practice. For the less religious or nonreligious, work may be functioning as an alternative source of meaning in the absence of religiosity. For most emerging adults, regardless of their relationship with religion, work—or the desire for work—was a key part of their identity. Work not only signals that they are responsible and committed people but also serves as a potential, even if not realized, source of meaning and fulfillment in their lives.

Although most young people are working at or near full-time, many are still struggling to make ends meet. We asked emerging adults a series of questions about their relative ability to pay their bills and the amount of their overall debt. One-third said that there was a time over the past year when they were unable to pay a bill, and almost one-fourth said that they had received some form of public assistance at some point in the past two years. When we asked about total current debt, one-third of our respondents reported having no debt or owing less than $5,000 (15 and 18 percent, respectively). Yet, there is a large percentage of emerging adults who have significant debt: 26 percent owe between $5,000 and $25,000, and 12 percent owe between $25,000 and $50,000. Almost one-fourth of the young people we surveyed have debt totaling more than $50,000. Many of them, therefore, are heading into adulthood with a substantial financial burden already on their shoulders.

Given the landscape of financial challenges facing these emerging adults, it is not surprising that significant numbers of young people rely on their parents for various forms of assistance. When asked in our survey about different forms of assistance they may have received from their parents over the past year, about one-third of emerging adults said they had received help from their parents for a place to live, whether providing the place or providing money to pay for rent. Thirty-one percent said that their parents have helped them with groceries, one-fourth had received help with transportation, and close to one-fourth had received help with babysitting and child care. Fewer numbers of these young people had received help with such things as educational expenses (12 percent), money to pay their bills (14 percent), and general spending money (16 percent).

Even though emerging adults receive a wide range of support from parents, when we asked the monetary value of the help they had received, 41 percent said that the total monetary value of assistance provided by parents was zero. Another 27 percent reported receiving assistance of less than $1,000. While young people may not be receiving cash from their parents, they are most certainly receiving assistance with things that would otherwise cost them money that they may not have. Thus, even though the perception of most emerging adults is that this support has little or no monetary value, parents do seem to be supporting their emerging adult children in significant ways.

Despite their current financial struggles and the assistance they receive from their parents, most of the young people we surveyed have a fairly optimistic outlook for their future. Slightly more than half said that they expect to reach a higher standard of living than their parents, while one-third said that they expect to reach the same standard of living. Only 14 percent said that they expect a lower standard of living than their parents. Yet, this optimism, at least among some emerging adults, may be misplaced. Recall Raymond from Chapter 1 and his plans to finish a community college program and move on to a successful life. Despite his desire to succeed in school and become self-sufficient, it seems doubtful that he will fully reach his goals, given the limitations within which he is living and his own difficulties with alcohol and drugs. And, as we will see later, Raymond is not alone in this. Many emerging adults seem to have grand plans with no realistic avenue by which to reach those goals.

Caring for Others

Emerging adults overwhelmingly said that they care about important social issues. Almost 60 percent said that they care very much about racial
equality and the needs of the elderly, while 51 percent said they are very
concerned about the needs of the poor. Another one-fourth to one-third
reported caring somewhat about these issues. But, are young people put-
ting this desire to help others into action? Charitable giving is one way to
act on values with a relatively low level of commitment. Almost 60 percent reported they had given money to an organization at least once in the
past year. However, when they were asked how much of their own money
they had donated, one-half of all givers reported donating less than $200,
with one-half of those having donated less than $100. Although these
numbers are not particularly surprising given the relatively low incomes
and financial struggles reported by emerging adults, neither do they
indicate a strong commitment to financially supporting the causes they
reportedly care about.

So, is it possible that the financial constraints of emerging adults lead
them to give of their time instead? This does not appear to be the case.
When it comes to volunteering or community service, the level of participation was even lower, with only 42 percent saying that they had volunteered at least once in the past year. When we asked young people how
much they had personally helped the homeless or people in need over the
past year, just 18 percent said that that they had helped a lot, despite the
fact that more than one-half of them reported that they care about the poor
very much. Just over one-third reported helping some, and another one-
third said they helped others in need a little.

Thus, there are some disconnects between what most emerging adults
think or believe about caring for others and what they are actually doing.
Most said they are concerned and presumably want to help care for others,
but this level of concern seldom results in actual volunteer activities. In
our face-to-face interviews, some said that they had volunteered in the past
or that they sometimes volunteered, but they had difficulty coming up
with specific examples of volunteering and giving. In general, the young
people we spoke with were not actively participating in volunteer opportunities in any regular or sustained way. A 24-year-old man provides an
example of the desire to volunteer combined with the failure to follow
through on that desire. When we asked whether he had volunteered in the
past five years, he replied, "I don't know. I [sighs] . . . I actually don't know

if there have been any real organized clubs or anything that I've been a part of. I mean, I always normally do stuff, you know, like I collaborate with different people, but it's . . . I don't think there's really been an official organization that I sign on to, pay membership dues, all of that."

To the extent that the emerging adults in our study do engage in some-what regular volunteer activity, this is more likely to be seen among those who are in some way involved in a church or other religious institution, or a community group that provides the organizational structure through which to volunteer. For example, a 25-year-old woman told us that she participates in Junior League and that she does "a bunch of volunteer stuff through them." Similarly, a 28-year-old man said, "One of the leaders in our [Sunday school] class is the chaplain for the [local] rescue mission, so a few times a year we'll usually go and help out with a meal there or running a service."

The pattern we see among emerging adults doesn't seem to be much different than the majority of Americans, who say that they are concerned or care about certain social issues yet report only modest levels of charitable giving and volunteering. In fact, the numbers reported by our emerging adults are somewhat higher than what other data show.[5] A look at national data from the US Bureau of Labor Statistics reveals that only about 25 percent of Americans 16 years or older engage in any volunteer activity.[6] Thus, it is important to note that, despite many popular reports claiming that young people are more interested and involved in volunteer activities than other generations, they are not all that different from the larger population in this regard.[7]

Politics

Politically, the emerging adults in our study are fairly evenly distributed along the spectrum of liberal to conservative and among Democratic, Independent, and Republican political affiliations. Thirty-two percent classified themselves as slightly liberal, liberal, or extremely liberal, while 28 percent located themselves between slightly conservative and extremely conservative. Twenty-two percent said that they were moderate, and 18 percent said they did not know whether they were liberal or conservative. When asked how they identified in terms of political party, they divided similarly, with 26 percent saying they were Democratic and 20 percent saying they were Republican. The largest grouping is the 38 percent of young people in the survey who said that they are politically independent.

The remaining numbers of emerging adults said that they identified with another party or that they did not know whether they would identify as either a Republican or Democrat.

Regardless of how they choose to identify politically, however, the overriding theme among the emerging adults in our study is that they are not particularly interested in or connected to politics. In the survey, more than one-half of emerging adults said that they are either slightly or not at all interested in politics, and only 17 percent said that they are very interested. When we asked whether the subject of politics comes up in conversations with friends, only 14 percent said that it came up a lot, and 37 percent said that it hardly ever or never came up. The frequency of conversations about politics with family shows a similar pattern, although these conversations happen slightly more often with family members. Twenty-three percent of emerging adults said that politics came up a lot in conversations with family members, and 29 percent said that it hardly ever or never came up.

Our in-person interviews confirmed this sense of ambivalence and disconnection that young people feel regarding politics, whether they thought of themselves as conservative or liberal. A 26-year-old woman said that she's "not a very political person" but that she would identify as a conservative. For her, that means that "if I'm voting for someone, if I choose conservative, they're probably gonna be more like-minded with me than someone who is liberal, but that doesn't mean I necessarily agree with them on everything." A 24-year-old woman said that she wasn't particularly interested in politics but that she felt "guilty" about her lack of interest. She expressed an even more varied perspective than the 26-year-old quoted previously, telling us that she was "socially very liberal. Very liberal. And I'm fiscally pretty conservative. I'm all about smaller government where it can be downsized. Like, I'm really into efficiency, and bureaucratic systems that are nightmarishly slow and use a lot of time and money make me horribly angry." And a 28-year-old man told us that while he tried "to be knowledgeable politically," he really didn't like politics. He continued, "I feel like a lot of stuff is just party-line voting, and I . . . have a very jaded view of career politicians. Like, I don't know how beneficial you can be in there."

This was a common refrain from emerging adults—politics is distasteful, and politicians are simply careerists with no real desire or ability to create change, make the world better, or serve the greater good.[8] This was true wherever they placed themselves on the political spectrum. The

24-year-old young woman quoted previously likened American politics to the television show "House of Cards," saying:

> ["House of Cards"] brought to life everything that I think is going on in Washington. I'm like, yes. There's definitely shady things going on, like weird deals, [that] aren't for the people, but are for the people in power. . . . I don't have a very high feeling for politicians. Not because I think they're bad people, but I—I feel like they're working within a system, you know, like, that makes it hard to do good. And so it's frustrating.

A 26-year-old man told us that, in his view, "Politics is just draining and annoying, 'cause they're all just—they all say lies, you know? They're just trying to get your vote. So what they say doesn't necessarily mean they're telling me the truth." This frustration with politics was common across our interviewees. Although we heard emerging adults talk about pursuing a meaningful life and making the world a better place through their work and relationships, it is clear that they generally do not view the political arena as a viable location for realizing these values.

Morals

When discussing moral issues with the emerging adults in our study, we heard a pretty consistent theme. Regardless of whether they identified as liberal or conservative, religious or not, the most common view on social, cultural, and political matters was "live and let live." In general, they wanted little interference from others—whether family, friends, religious authorities, or government—in determining what is good or bad, right or wrong. The majority of young people come down on what most would consider the liberal side on different social issues, yet their responses should be understood through their basic perspective that personal freedoms—whether their own or others—are of primary importance.

Thus, when we see that 62 percent of emerging adults said that gay marriage should be legal, and 52 percent said that abortion should be legal for any reason, these results reflect the fact that emerging adults are reluctant to judge or legislate against what others choose to do in and with their lives. A typical example comes from a 25-year-old woman. When we asked whether she believed there were any rights and wrongs that should apply to everyone, she told us that she had "never really thought about that." She continued, saying that morals were simply a matter of "how you choose live your life, you know?" A 24-year-old man told us that he did not believe there were any rights or wrongs that should apply to everyone, "because I feel that is just like a limit, it's limiting yourself, you know?"

From our informants we repeatedly heard variations on the idea that, regardless of whether they agreed with others on any particular issue or belief, it was not their place to judge those other beliefs, relationships, or actions. Furthermore, they would prefer that various authorities—whether religious or political—also not judge or legislate against beliefs, relationships, or ways of life. Consistent with this position, almost 60 percent of our respondents said that they believe that religion is a private matter best left out of public or political affairs. For example, when we asked whether religion should have a role in public debates, a 27-year-old man said, "I think we should be able to express our opinions and beliefs, but I don't think those should be mandated to people that don't believe them." A 24-year-old woman took a stronger stance on religious beliefs in the public sphere, saying, "No, I think it's personal. Whatever you believe depends on you."

We heard from emerging adults that religion can serve as a source of moral good in society. Specifically, it can provide moral teachings for children and encourage believers to do good things in the world, such as feeding the poor. As a 24-year-old woman told us, "From a practical standpoint, I feel like there are truths within each religion. And I feel like the whole moral part of religion is really useful. The whole idea of getting direction and everything derived from those texts is important."

But this perspective has its limits. From the viewpoint of most emerging adults, religion should not be used to justify the imposition of one's morals or values on others. And in general, emerging adults have a negative view of individuals or groups that they perceive as seeking to limit the freedoms of those who don't share the same commitments or religious values. The distaste for being "too religious" that we heard when our research subjects were younger continues to be voiced as they enter adulthood, with a particular concern about how extreme religious ideology might infringe on people who do not share those views.[9]

This theme of "live and let live" and freedom from moralistic judgment or legislation helps to contextualize our subjects' responses to other survey questions about morality. When asked whether it is sometimes okay to break rules if it benefits them personally, only 8 percent agreed with this, while 86 percent disagreed. This suggests that they hold themselves to a particular moral standard of not breaking the rules. But when it comes to more universally applied moral guidelines, there was less agreement. Thirty-seven percent of young people agreed with the statement that "morals are relative, there are no definite rights and wrongs for everybody," while 56 percent disagreed with this. The remaining seven percent answered, "I don't know."

In a similar vein, emerging adults were almost evenly divided on whether moral standards should adapt to social and cultural changes, with 43 percent saying that they should adapt and 47 percent saying that they should stay the same. These numbers suggest that about one-half of the young people we spoke with were not moral relativists but instead believed in concrete moral principles. And our interviews confirm that many do agree that there are at least some things that would qualify as universally moral or immoral. For example, when we asked them whether there was anything that would be wrong for all people, "killing another person" was the most common reply. Likewise, the idea that it is wrong to do anything that would "hurt others" was provided as an example of a universal moral stance. However, when we asked what they meant by "hurting others," they often had difficulty expressing what that would mean in practice, whether that was restricted to physical violence or would include hurting another person emotionally.

After we moved beyond the moral universals of not killing others and doing no harm, we heard from these emerging adults a moral and cultural relativity that made it difficult for them to articulate general moral principles. They were confident in their ability to determine right and wrong for themselves but did not have much language for talking about morality in a larger sense beyond their own concerns. Most could not think of a scenario in which they were unsure of what was good or bad, or right or wrong, nor could they provide concrete examples of actions or perspectives that were morally good and bad. For most, morals were self-evident and didn't take a lot of thought—you "just know," or in many cases "feel," what is right and wrong. For example, one 26-year-old man told us that, for him, "It's just a natural thing. I think you just—maybe it's because of how I was raised or my religion—it's just there. I'm sure before I was like, 'What makes this right?' But now it's just so ingrained. You just know what you feel is the best way to handle things."

This young man's description of feeling his way toward moral decision-making reflects the concept of "moral intuition," that moral judgments are rooted in embodied, emotional reactions that precede rational explanation.[10] There are some things that are so deeply embedded in culture and everyday interactions that they become ingrained in individuals at an intuitive level, even though they may not be able to express or verbalize this "tacit knowledge." This understanding may be embodied or experienced even if not fully articulated, like being able to recognize a familiar face in a crowd even if we can't explain exactly how or why we recognize someone.[11] When emerging adults are unable to articulate any deeper moral reflection, it is easy to conclude that they lack a moral framework or are uninterested in questions of morality. And this may be the case for some emerging adults. It may also be that they have never been presented with the need to articulate specific moral principles because there is a shared assumption that these things are "just known" and understood within their cultural context.

For example, as we heard in Chapter 1, Kristen was among the few young people we spoke with who said that her sense of morality comes from outside of herself, pointing in part to her religious upbringing. Recall that she said, "It's a lot a part of who I am and . . . what I've learned from church and the Bible and from God. . . . It [right and wrong] usually is evident just because of who I am, but who I am is not because of me." Her comments suggest that "who she is" is the result of the way she was raised, her church involvement, her commitment to her religion, and the like. Yet, even as she acknowledges the influences that created her sense of morality, she now relies on a self-evident, ingrained moral sensibility to guide her decision-making. The assumption is that intuition and personal character can be trusted, and as long as one is a good person, the choices one makes are, by default, the "right" thing to do.

Thus, in what can appear to be a rootless moral outlook, what these emerging adults learned and experienced growing up forms the core of their moral compass, which then frames their own sense of morality in everyday situations. Of course, some young people were better at expressing this idea than others. But while they were almost universally reluctant to judge others' lifestyles and moral choices, they themselves "just know" what is right and wrong because they have absorbed moral guidelines—including the notion that judging others is to be avoided—from parents, schools, peers, teachers, pastors, media, and other sources. For emerging adults, it seems easy to figure out what is right and wrong in any given situation. What is difficult for them is that they are not comfortable making grand moral claims for all people in all places. This may be related, in turn, to their ambivalence about moral and religious authorities who do make such universalistic claims. Yet, even their general disdain for politics and politicians shows that emerging adults do have baseline moral stances that guide their lives, and these have generally to do with honesty, integrity, and treating others well. How these concepts are defined for them, however, is highly dependent on their own individual experiences growing up and on how those experiences have helped to form their moral understandings.

Life Outlook

Overall, emerging adults have a positive, optimistic, and forward-looking outlook on their lives. Almost 90 percent said that they think about and plan for their future very or fairly often, and almost 70 percent said that they are more optimistic now than they were five years ago. Only 13 percent of emerging adults said that they are less optimistic now than they were five years previously.

In our survey, we asked emerging adults to respond to several statements related to how they generally viewed their lives, asking how they perceived their goals or direction in life, whether they lacked direction and purpose, and whether they believed that they had the personal agency required to make important changes in their lives. Approximately two-thirds of the young people in our study agreed or strongly agreed that in most ways their life is close to ideal (62 percent) and that the conditions of their life are excellent (63 percent). Similarly, 73 percent said that they were satisfied with their life.

Similar numbers of emerging adults said that they have direction and goals in their lives. Almost three-fourths of the young people (73 percent) disagreed or strongly disagreed with the statement: "Your life often seems to lack any clear goals or sense of direction," and 74 percent answered the same to the statement, "You don't have a good sense of what it is you're trying to accomplish in life." Seventy-seven percent agreed or strongly agreed with the statement: "Some people wander aimlessly through life, but you are not one of them." When we asked about meaning in life, 69 percent said that life rarely or never feels meaningless. Similarly, almost 50 percent said that they thought about the meaning of life very or fairly often. Another 34 percent said that they thought about the meaning of life sometimes, and only 6 percent said that they rarely or never thought about the meaning of life.

When it comes to focusing on the needs of others versus their own needs, one-half (51 percent) said that they were at least somewhat more focused on the needs of others than they were five years ago. Twenty-six percent said that they were about the same as five years ago, and 23 percent said that compared with five years ago, they are currently more focused on their own needs than on the needs of others.

The way that these young people expressed how they view their lives can be understood as the different ways that they are settling into their roles as emerging adults. This includes not only the increased responsibilities that they are taking on but also how they believe that their lives will progress. Much of their perspective is based on their hopes for the future, yet many of them expressed dreams and goals that seemed unattainable, given their current situations.

In our interviews with emerging adults, we heard them talk of big dreams for their lives and their aspirations to do work that they are really engaged with and that is personally meaningful for them. Yet, often what they described as their life dreams and goals seemed disconnected from any realistic path to get there. That is, their dreams and goals for their lives seemed out of reach in light of their current education, work experience, and relationships. They had no real plans to achieve those goals, which seemed more an expression of their personal interests than the drivers for long-term planning and preparation. A typical response comes from one 25-year-old man. When we interviewed him, he was a bartender and played in a band but told us that he "wanted to finish school and get into the medical field, just to make some money." He added, "But then I would also like to, on the side, start to build my own line of guitar and bass-effects pedals, and maybe build different types of electronic instruments. Eventually I'd like to teach, maybe. I don't know, I want to do a lot of different things."

Another example is found in the statements of a 27-year-old man who worked for a video production company during college. He shared with us that his long-term goals include "running my own business. My dream job would be doing video stuff, writing movies, making movies—stuff like that. Or being in a rock band." While his work experience is more directly related to his stated life goals, he has yet to narrow down his options or map out a path that might get him there.

It is not uncommon for young people to have a variety of dreams and goals that are not yet narrowed down, and in some ways, we should expect them to have this outlook at this stage of their lives. Thus, rather than taking a view that insists they have their life goals mapped out with a logical and reasonable path to achieve them, many are still dreaming big, and sometimes contradictory, dreams. What was notable, however, was how little they seemed to be prepared to actively pursue these goals or to adjudicate between the often-conflicting life paths they imagined for themselves.

Thus, these life goals and dreams seem to be about the kinds of things they *could* do, things that interest them, that in the abstract are still possibilities to consider. The practicality of reaching one or another of these goals seems less important than the notion that they can think about their life potential in these big ways. They seem to understand themselves as still being young and thus having plenty of time to change their mind as their life develops.

Regrets

Throughout the interviews with emerging adults, as they talked about the ups and downs, successes and setbacks across many areas of their lives, we heard some expressions of regret or disappointment with specific things such as educational pursuits cut short or career plans unrealized. Toward the end of the interview, we asked them to look back over their life as a whole and consider whether they had any regrets or whether there were things they wish they had done differently in their lives. Despite some of the specific regrets we heard discussed in earlier sections of the interviews, when asked to provide a global assessment, again and again our informants insist that they have no regrets.

These responses do not necessarily deny the impact of life challenges or poor decisions; rather, emerging adults frame all of their past decisions or experiences as instrumental in making them into the people they are today. To acknowledge regret would seem to them to be equivalent to rejecting their own identity. For example, one 27-year-old told us that he didn't think of events in his life in terms of regret. Instead, he said, "I think that . . . whatever happens, happens for a reason, but it's just kinda . . . you gotta take everything by how it's given to you. I mean, you can regret what you did, but I really do think that if you were to change certain things from your past, that would change who you are. It might not change you in a huge way, but it has the potential to . . . I don't think you would be the same person." A 24-year-old expressed a similar viewpoint about his past experiences making him uniquely who he is now:

R: So far, I've learned not to regret anything, because it's helped me be who I am today. Without those experiences, I wouldn't be who I am today. There's some things that I would change that I can't, really. But at the same time, I can't really say that I would, because I know I would be different if those things were changed. You know, I would like to say that I wouldn't have to go through all those experiences when I was a teenager, with all the drugs and stuff, but without it I don't know where I'd be, I don't know who I'd be.

I: Is there anything wrong with identifying those as regrettable? Is there a problem saying those are regrets?

R: Not really. . . . I mean, some are probably regrets. But they're not regrets. I mean, they're. . . . I've come to this point where I've accepted those things, I've realized what those things were, those experiences were. And I'm happy with them, because I like who I am and I'm happy with who I am, and I know that I'm only who I am today because of all the experiences.

Thus, for emerging adults, regardless of how difficult it may have been, the past is interpreted as being instrumental in the formation of their present lives, making them who they are. Many ascribed to the perspective that everything in life happens for a reason and should therefore be accepted and appreciated as a necessary part of their life. They may acknowledge that they made some bad decisions in the past—whether related to drugs, relationships, or other things—but those relationships, actions, and experiences are valued as a key part of who they are, and they serve as a baseline from which to measure who they want to be in the future. This perspective fits well with their general optimism about the future. It is easier to be optimistic in the face of setbacks when one frames all life events, whether positive or negative, as necessary building blocks for the future.

What Is Important in Life

In our survey, we asked emerging adults to rank different aspects of life in order of their importance for achieving the kind of life that they want to live. The results show that young people overwhelmingly favor close relationships with family and friends over most other aspects of life. The top three ranked items that emerging adults identified as very or extremely important in their lives are to have a good family life (92 percent), a close set of friends (89 percent), and a fulfilling romantic relationship (80 percent). Considering the focus on religion in this book, it is particularly interesting to note that just less than one-half of emerging adults (49 percent) said that having a close relationship with God is very or extremely important for them to have the kind of life they desire. Indeed, when we asked them to select the one item that was the most important for them to have the kind of life they wanted to live, 40 percent said that having a good family life was most important, while only 23 percent said that having a close relationship with God was most important. This percentage of emerging adults is almost matched by the 17 percent who said that having a close relationship with God was the least important thing necessary for them to live the kind of life they desired.

In our face-to-face interviews with emerging adults, we again asked about what they value as most important in life. Their responses were remarkably consistent with the survey responses noted earlier. While some mentioned a job or earning money as an important necessity in life, most discussed relationships, whether with family or close friends, as being the most important thing in life. They recognize that these close relationships are reciprocal, that they get fulfillment out of contributing to the lives of their friends and family members, just as their own lives are enriched through their relationships. For example, a 28-year-old man said, "I think it's probably just your direct relationships with other people. So, probably primarily family, but also just how that extends into friends and church and . . . I think part of that global responsibility. Like, you know, having good relationships." A 24-year-old woman told us, "I feel like the important things are just, like, happiness. So like, how would we define that? I define happiness by having, like, close relationships with the people around me, and . . . laughing a lot, and . . . enjoying things and . . . having the—the freedom to do—and, like, the flexibility to . . . do what I want."

Conclusion

Overall, emerging adults are steadily reaching key markers of adulthood, such as living on their own, working full-time, and, for many, marriage and children. Emerging adults generally consider themselves to be adults, although there is some reluctance and ambivalence about describing themselves as "full-fledged" adults, a status marked by independence and self-sufficiency. Yet, their perceived self-sufficiency is not without potential problems. Although most work at or near full-time hours, they are clustered in the lower income brackets, and significant percentages of them are carrying large amounts of debt. Despite these challenges, most

believe that they will ultimately achieve a higher standard of living than
their parents.

As the social worlds of emerging adults have narrowed since they were
teens, their focus has shifted to family and much smaller circles of friends.
Their friends tend to be more like them than different, and they reported
that marriage and children are an important—or hoped for—part of their
lives. Their primary focus on family, friends, and themselves seems to be
the counterbalance to their view of and participation in larger scale social
institutions. In general, emerging adults are fairly distant from politics
and political institutions and rarely volunteer with local organizations.

Overall, however, emerging adults are taking ownership of their lives
and the situations in which they find themselves. Most have a generally positive view of their lives, although this might seem an overly optimistic perspective for many of them. Their optimism is coupled with a
lack of regret for bad decisions and challenging life experiences; instead
of lamenting setbacks, they tend to frame everything in their lives as "happening for a reason." Their confidence in some form of larger purpose in
their lives suggests some residue of religious or spiritual outlook, even
though, as we will see in the next chapter, they are moving away from any
significant religious or spiritual commitments and involvements. What
do their religious lives look like in more detail? We pursue this question
in Chapter 3.

3

Where Are They Now?

RELIGIOUS AFFILIATION, BELIEFS, AND PRACTICES

THE STORY ABOUT emerging adults and religion that everyone expects—the one that is by now unsurprising—is that emerging adults are becoming less religious. This story is, of course, true, and evidence for it has been outlined in several different reports.[1] And among the emerging adults we have been studying, we see rather significant declines in religious identity, commitment, and practice across the board. In some cases the Wave 4 results continue a long, steady decline in religious affiliation from when this study began in 2002, while in other areas there is a more precipitous drop. In either case, the overarching story is one of decline; emerging adults are leaving religious institutions and commitments behind as they move into adulthood.

In this chapter, we focus on the survey data from Wave 4, with comparisons to the Wave 1 and Wave 3 surveys to tell the story of decline as it is exemplified by these emerging adults. But we also dig deeper for a closer look at what is going on under the surface of the decline. What other stories do we miss by focusing primarily on the aggregate loss in religious service attendance or religious affiliation? We won't ignore the story of decline, but we hope to bring more nuance to narratives of how young people are encountering religion in their lives.

The story of general religious decline among emerging adults has multiple facets. The first is a story of religious affiliation, which can also be understood as a measure of religious market share. In other words, which groups are gaining and which groups are losing numbers in the overall distribution of how young people are affiliated or not affiliated with religion? We look at changes in religious affiliation among emerging adults and examine the patterns of religious conversion, religious switching, and disaffiliation among our respondents.

Moving beyond the focus on religious affiliation, we then turn to an examination of a variety of individual measures of religious beliefs, practices, and levels of religious salience. Looking back over the 10 years of the National Study of Youth and Religion (NSYR), we see how young people have changed religiously, including how much they pray, attend religious services, and feel close to God, as well as other indicators of religious engagement. In the general assessment, we consider the broad story of religious decline in the lives of emerging adults: lower levels of religious attendance, fewer young people who believe in God, less importance placed on the role of faith in daily life. But after examining all emerging adults as one group, we also find that there are different patterns of involvement with religion within different religious groups.

In the next section of the chapter, we take a closer look at how religious change is playing out among those who are *not leaving their faith*, and we see a parallel story emerge. While general religious decline is taking place at multiple levels, there are those who have remained committed to their religious tradition. And, in some cases, this religious commitment is growing *stronger*, rather than weaker. In the final section of this chapter, we turn the tables, and rather than examining the religious lives of emerging adults, we ask what they think of organized religion. How do young people perceive the value of religious institutions, including whether those institutions have any potential relevance for the lives of emerging adults, and in what ways have their perspectives changed since we last spoke with them?

Religious Tradition Gains and Losses

We start by showing the identification with different major religious traditions for emerging adults at ages 23 to 28, with comparisons to when they were between the ages of 13 and 17.[2] This categorization follows the general model established by Steensland and colleagues and includes Conservative Protestant, Mainline Protestant, Black Protestant, Roman Catholic, Jewish, Latter-day Saints (Mormon), and Not Religious.[3] Respondents affiliated with a minority religious group that is not large enough for meaningful analysis are categorized together as Other Religion. The final category is called Indeterminate and includes respondents from whom we did not receive enough information to determine their religious tradition. This measure of religious affiliation prioritizes the tradition of the congregation where they attend services, in the few cases where this is different from the general religious affiliation that was reported.

The overall story is one of loss for all religious traditions and increase in the number of those claiming no identification with a religious tradition or whose religious identity is indeterminate. Table 3.1 shows the percentage of emerging adults in our study who identify with a particular religious tradition at three different points in time: Wave 1 when they are ages 13 to 17, Wave 3 when they are ages 18 to 23, and Wave 4 when they are ages 23 to 28. The final column shows the percentage increase or decrease for that particular tradition over the 10 years covered by this study. This is a type of "market share" measure that shows us the distribution of religious affiliation among emerging adults at three different points in time, with the most current being the numbers at ages 23 to 28.

Emerging adults identifying as Not Religious show the largest change, having increased by 24 percentage points, from 11 percent when they were teens to 35 percent in the final survey. This group of Not Religious emerging adults is what has been popularly described as the "religious nones" in many research and news reports.[4] This grouping includes a diverse set of people who say that they are not religious and thus do not affiliate with any religious tradition or identity. This includes atheists and agnostics as well as those who simply say that they are not religious, without further identifying themselves religiously. We discuss irreligious emerging adults

Table 3.1 Religious Traditions

	Wave 1 Ages 13–17 (%)	Wave 3 Ages 18–23 (%)	Wave 4 Ages 23–28 (%)	Net Change Waves 1–4 (%)
Conservative Protestant	30.6	27.6	19.1	−11.5
Mainline Protestant	11.3	10.8	5.7	−5.6
Black Protestant	10.3	7.2	5.3	−5
Catholic	26.6	19.5	15.3	−11.3
Jewish	1.7	1.1	1.2	−0.5
Latter-day Saints	3.9	3	3	−0.9
Not Religious	11	24.1	35	24
Other	2.4	2.6	3	0.6
Indeterminate	2.3	4.1	12.5	10.2

Source: National Study of Youth and Religion surveys 2002, 2008, 2013.

in detail in Chapter 4, but for now, it is important to remember that this is the group of young people that has grown most significantly over the course of this project, and that while they all claim no religious identification or affiliation, within this group there is variation in how that actually plays out in their lives.

The other category that gained numbers of emerging adults is the Indeterminate category, which increased from 2.3 percent when they were teens to 12.4 percent as emerging adults. Indeterminate means that we did not have enough information from the respondents to determine their specific religious tradition. Almost all of these respondents provided an answer like "just Christian." Thus, while we can't locate them within a specific sect or denomination, they nonetheless identify as Christian. We suspect that many of them are in fact Mainline or Conservative Protestants who are either not familiar with, or decline to identify, the particular denominational affiliation of their place of worship. If this is the case, it means that the losses among Protestants are not as large as they appear.[5] However, it is also telling that these young people do not select any particular identity beyond "just Christian." While they identify as Christian, they are either not aware of or not invested in a particular denominational identity or tradition. It seems that "Christian" is the extent of what they can offer by way of describing their own faith and the place where they attend religious services.

All of the other categories show varying degrees of loss among emerging adults who identify with them. Conservative Protestant and Catholic were the two largest religious traditions when our respondents were between the ages of 13 and 17: 30 and 27 percent of the sample, respectively. It is these two large groups that have declined the most over the course of the study. By the time our respondents reached the ages of 23 to 28, 19 percent of them are identified as Conservative Protestant and 15 percent identified as Catholic, a total decline of just more than 11 percentage points for each group. The remaining groups had smaller market share to begin with and show correspondingly smaller declines in their percentages at Wave 4. Mainline Protestants decreased from 11.3 percent among teens to 5.7 percent at ages 23 to 28. Similarly, Black Protestants were 10.3 percent of the sample in the first survey and are just 5.3 percent of the final sample.[6] The Latter-day Saints and Jewish traditions are small minority groups and remained relatively stable across the study, each with slight drops in their representation. The Other Religion category changed very little, from 2.4 percent of teens identifying with a religion categorized as Other to three percent when they were ages 23 to 28.

No matter how these gains or losses are counted—whether as a percentage of the total sample of emerging adults or as a proportion of those who identify with the tradition at ages 23 to 28, compared with when they were ages 13 to 17—the numbers show that significant change has taken place in terms of how these young people identify religiously. Another way to think about gains and losses in religious affiliation is to consider the pathways of religious movement, or what social researchers call religious switching. That is, based on what we know about how these emerging adults identified religiously as teenagers, what identity had they moved to when we asked them at ages 23 to 28? Table 3.2 shows a cross-tabulation of religious identity when the respondents were teens and then at ages 23 to 28. Each column includes all those who were identified with a particular tradition as teens and shows what percentage are now affiliated either with the same tradition or with other traditions.

For example, looking at the first column for Conservative Protestant, we see that, of those teens identified as Conservative Protestants as

Table 3.2 Transition between Religious Traditions, Waves 1 to 4

Religious Tradition Wave 4 (Ages 23–28)	Religious Tradition Wave 1, Ages 13–17 (%)								
	CP	MP	BP	RC	J	LDS	NR	OR	IND
Conservative Protestant (CP)	**46**	10	12	6	~	5	4	7	6
Mainline Protestant (MP)	5	**23**	3	2	~	5	1	~	9
Black Protestant (BP)	2	1	**41**	2	~	~	4	1	4
Catholic (RC)	2	4	1	**53**	4	~	5	6	2
Jewish (J)	~	1	1	~	**42**	2	~	3	~
Latter-day Saints (LDS)	~	~	~	~	2	**61**	1	~	~
Not Religious (NR)	24	41	16	30	52	25	**74**	39	70
Other Religion (OR)	1	1	3	2	~	~	4	**42**	~
Indeterminate (IND)	19	17	23	6	~	2	7	2	**10**
Total	100	100	100	100	100	100	100	100	100

Note: Bold numbers indicate the percentage of emerging adults remaining in each tradition based on their Wave 1 religious identification.

Source: National Study of Youth and Religion surveys 2002, 2013.

teenagers, 46 percent can still be categorized as affiliated with the Conservative Protestant tradition. Continuing down the column we see the current religious tradition for those who are no longer identified as Conservative Protestant: five percent are now Mainline Protestants, two percent Black Protestants, and two percent Catholic. Similarly, we see that 53 percent of teens who identified as Catholic have maintained their Catholic identity, which means that almost one-half have switched to some other religious—or not religious—identity. Thus, we see that six percent of Catholics are now identified as Conservative Protestant, two percent as Mainline Protestant, and about two percent as part of Black Protestant denominations.

Among most religious groups, retaining the same religious identity is the most common response. Just less than half of all respondents (47 percent) retained the religious identity from their teenage years, with the Catholic and Latter-day Saints traditions having the highest retention rates. However, there are still significant numbers of emerging adults who have switched their religious identity from what it was when they were teens to something else. About one-fourth of the respondents switched from one religious tradition to another religious tradition. But across the religious traditions, the most common path of religious switching was to go from affiliating with a religious tradition to being not religious. More than one-fourth of all emerging adults moved from a religious identity to the Not Religious category. The only religious group for whom Not Religious is not the largest receiving category is Black Protestant. One-fourth of Conservative Protestants and 30 percent of Catholics have moved into the Not Religious category over the course of the study. Mainline Protestant is the one group for whom becoming not religious outpaces religious stability; 23 percent of Wave 1 respondents remain Mainline Protestants, while 41 percent now identify as Not Religious. Among those who were classified as Other Religion, the numbers are fairly even, with 40 percent now reporting that they are not religious, compared with the 42 percent who have remained in the Other Religion category.

The pathway from a given religious tradition to Indeterminate was the second most common category of switching. However, it is interesting to note that this switch was common among the Protestant groups and not the other religious traditions, with Conservative, Mainline, and Black Protestants most likely to shift into the Indeterminate category. The majority of individuals in this category are identified as such because their survey responses suggest that they still view themselves as religiously affiliated. However, that affiliation is generally not more specific than "just Christian" and is not connected to a particular denomination or group. Most of these indeterminate "Christians" are likely affiliated with some form of Protestant church, whether Conservative or Mainline. We do not see a similar trend among Catholics, perhaps because Catholicism is in itself a specific Christian identity. When Catholics drift away from a religious congregation, many continue to identify themselves as Catholic. However, when Protestants do the same, their identification is more likely to shift away from a specific religious tradition to a "just Christian" identity.

Examining the movement of the previously Indeterminate teenagers is also instructive. About 15 percent of those who were Indeterminate as teenagers moved into Conservative or Mainline Protestant categories at the final survey. Perhaps, as these young people got older, they were better able to identify and locate themselves within a particular tradition. On the other hand, 70 percent of those who were Indeterminate at Wave 1 are classified as Not Religious in Wave 4. We have suggested previously that classification as Indeterminate can be interpreted as signifying some degree of disconnection from religion. These are young people who still profess some level of religious identification; however, they are not engaged enough to be able to identify their particular religious tradition beyond the generic response of "Christian." This disconnection from religious particularism appears to have been a step in the process toward more complete disengagement. At least for this subgroup, while they were "just Christian" in Wave 1, they now identify themselves as Not Religious—that is, having no religious affiliation.

This suggests that those emerging adults who we currently classify as Indeterminate in their religious identity may be in the process of moving further away from religious involvement and commitment. That is, the pathways of the majority of those who were categorized as Indeterminate when they were teens—from their indeterminate religious identity to now being not religious—suggests that many of those who are now Indeterminate will eventually move into the Not Religious category as well.

There are multiple ways to analyze the patterns of religious affiliation. Again, regardless of which method we use, the general story appears to be one of aggregate religious decline. When we look at those young people whose religious affiliation has changed over the 10-year period of the NSYR, we see that while some have changed to a different religious affiliation, many more have moved further out of mainstream religious traditions, with more and more young people identifying themselves as not religious. Yet, there is another way to look at the data, one that has not been emphasized in all the talk about the increase in religious "nones." Taking into account all of the movement we see in Table 3.2, 26 percent of all the emerging adults in our study moved from a religious identity (including Indeterminate) to Not Religious.[7] However, there is a larger contingent of young people who have maintained their religious affiliation. Fifty-nine percent of respondents continued to describe themselves as religious, whether in their original tradition or another tradition, and three percent moved from not religious to identifying with some religion. Thus, while the number of emerging adults who moved from being religious to being not religious is significant, the 59 percent who remained religious—and the three percent who became religious—have a story that also deserves attention.

Orientation to Tables and Religion Measures

Religious affiliation and identity is but one facet of religiosity, one way of understanding the religious lives of the young people we followed over the course of the project. We also have measures that tap into a wide range of religious dimensions, such as beliefs, practices, salience, and attitudes toward religious organizations. Readers who have been following the NSYR since the publication of *Soul Searching* will be familiar with these measures.[8] And we know that many have been waiting with keen interest to see how our sample of young people would respond to these questions 10 years after they were first asked to consider them when they were teenagers.

There are many possible ways to present these data, with different comparisons that can be drawn and multiple stories that can be told. Each reader will come to the data with their own questions of interest and their own perspective that informs how they interpret and understand the numbers presented here. We offer a full table for each religion measure, closely mirroring the measures used in the previous three books (*Soul Searching, A Faith of Their Own,* and *Souls in Transition*).[9] Rather than discuss each religious measure table in detail, however, we will instead focus on a few of the story lines that emerge when we consider them as a whole package. Readers with a specific interest in prayer, for example, can study that table at their leisure. For our purposes, we are less interested in each particular measure and more interested in the larger stories that these individual measures help us weave together about the patterns of religious engagement among emerging adults. Further consideration of the measures will follow in Chapter 4.

In the tables for this chapter, we look at a wide range of survey questions measuring different facets of religiosity and examine how the responses to these questions vary by religious tradition.[10] The longitudinal nature of our survey data allows us to map these responses over time in various ways. In each table we present four columns of percentages. The responses are sorted according to the main religious traditions in the United States: Conservative Protestant, Mainline Protestant, Black Protestant, Catholic, Jewish, Latter-day Saints, and Not Religious. The first three columns report the responses to each question at Wave 1, Wave 3, and Wave 4, grouped by the religious tradition that the respondents were affiliated with as teenagers at the time of the first survey (ages 13 to 17).[11] Examining the responses based on the Wave 1 religious identity tells us something about changes in the religious lives of individuals who were raised in a particular religious tradition, regardless of their current religious identity.[12] For example, if we consider all of the respondents who at Wave 1 were identified as Conservative Protestant, how many of them believed in God then, and how many of those same young people still believe in God at Wave 4? This tells us something about how this group of individuals has changed over time, regardless of current religious identity. A significant portion of those respondents continue to be identified as Conservative Protestants. However, as noted earlier in this chapter, a substantial number of them are no longer a part of the Conservative Protestant tradition. Their responses are also included in the third column of these tables.

The final column in each table limits the responses to only those individuals who are identified with a particular religious tradition at the time of the Wave 4 survey, and excludes those who affiliated in the past but are no longer identified with the religious tradition. This final column provides a sense of the current composition of the different religious traditions and the level of particular religious measures within that religious tradition.

For example, what is the level of religious salience among those emerging adults who currently identify as Catholic, Protestant, or Jewish? This allows us to compare, for example, the current religiosity of all the individuals who are Mainline Protestant today (column 4) with the religiosity of all the individuals who were Mainline Protestant as teenagers (column 3). Column 4 also includes those who have moved into the tradition since they were teenagers. It does not include responses from individuals who started in the religious tradition as teenagers but have since moved out of the tradition. A comparison of columns 4 and 1 will highlight any changes in the composition of each religious tradition at the time of the respective surveys.

The first row in each table provides the total percentages for the entire sample. Since there is no division by religious tradition for the total sample, Wave 4 percentages are only displayed in the first Wave 4 column (column 3). This first row of percentages provides us with several important pieces of information. First, the Wave 4 columns give us a sense of where emerging adults are today as a group in relation to each of these religious measures. Comparing the Wave 4 and Wave 3 percentages tells us how much change has taken place since the last survey five years previously, when respondents were between the ages of 18 and 23. Finally, we have included the responses from the original Wave 1 survey to allow for a general sense of the total change across each religion measure over the 10 years between the first and last surveys of this group of young people.

Overall Change in Emerging Adult Religion

As was noted in the introduction to this chapter, when we look at the responses for the full sample across a wide range of religious measures, the story that emerges is one of general religious decline. On almost every measure, our sample of young people reported lower levels of religious engagement as emerging adults than they did as teenagers. In most cases this change is modest, while for a few variables it is quite dramatic. Notably, it appears that the overall decline in traditional religiosity was underway between the first and third waves of the survey, while the change that has taken place in the most recent five years, during the later years of emerging adult life, reflects a modest continuation of this trend.

The most dramatic change among the emerging adults in our study was in attendance at religious services (Table 3.3). Over the course of the study, attending religious services weekly or more often has dropped from 40 percent to 19 percent of respondents. Reports of never attending religious services has increased 33 percentage points over 10 years, from 18 percent of the sample in 2003 to 51 percent of the sample in 2013.[13] While there has been a significant drop in attendance at religious services, the other measures of religion have seen more modest aggregate declines. Over the life of the project, the percentage of those who believe in God has dropped 10 points, from 84 percent to 74 percent (Table 3.4). In addition

Table 3.3 Religious Service Attendance

	1	2	3	4
	Religious Tradition, Ages 13–17			Religious Tradition, Ages 23–28
	Wave 1 (%)	Wave 3 (%)	Wave 4 (%)	Wave 4 (%)
Total				
Once a Week or More	40	20	19	
Never	18	35	51	
Conservative Protestant				
Once a Week or More	55	28	29	45
Never	4	24	39	5
Mainline Protestant				
Once a Week or More	44	12	9	18
Never	9	38	58	17
Black Protestant				
Once a Week or More	41	25	18	29
Never	7	18	29	4
Catholic				
Once a Week or More	40	15	12	16
Never	11	38	53	36
Jewish				
Once a Week or More	8	10	9	13
Never	22	62	82	53
Latter-day Saints				
Once a Week or More	71	60	50	79
Never	4	22	34	10
Not Religious				
Once a Week or More	~	5	4	~
Never	95	73	81	99

Source: National Study of Youth and Religion surveys 2002, 2008, 2013.

to the decline in those who believe in God, there was also a shift among those who do believe in God in how they describe their view of God (Table 3.5). Up through the time the respondents were 18 to 23, almost two-thirds of those who believed in God reported that they believed in a personal God who was involved in the lives of individuals. At the time of the final survey, when respondents are between the ages of 23 and 28, those who believe

Table 3.4 Belief in God

	1	2	3	4
	Religious Tradition, Ages 13–17			Religious Tradition, Ages 23–28
	Wave 1 (%)	Wave 3 (%)	Wave 4 (%)	Wave 4 (%)
Total				
Yes	84	78	74	
No	3	6	12	
Unsure	12	16	14	
Conservative Protestant				
Yes	94	87	84	95
No	1	2	7	1
Unsure	5	11	9	3
Mainline Protestant				
Yes	86	68	66	95
No	2	7	13	1
Unsure	13	25	21	4
Black Protestant				
Yes	97	97	97	98
No	~	0	2	~
Unsure	2	3	1	2
Catholic				
Yes	85	80	76	89
No	1	5	9	2
Unsure	14	14	15	10
Jewish				
Yes	72	50	55	76
No	5	19	22	0
Unsure	23	31	22	24
Latter-day Saints				
Yes	84	83	84	99
No	~	4	6	0
Unsure	13	13	10	1
Not Religious				
Yes	49	47	41	40
No	17	17	33	30
Unsure	34	35	26	30

Source: National Study of Youth and Religion surveys 2002, 2008, 2013.

Table 3.5 Views of God

	1	2	3	4
	Religious Tradition, Ages 13–17			Religious Tradition, Ages 23–28
	Wave 1 (%)	Wave 3 (%)	Wave 4 (%)	Wave 4 (%)
Total				
A personal being involved in the lives of people today	65	63	51	
Created the world, but is not involved in the world today	13	10	4	
Not personal, something like a cosmic life force	14	17	13	
None of these views	5	1	20	
Does not believe in God	3	6	12	
Conservative Protestant				
A personal being	77	74	68	84
Created the world	10	9	3	2
Cosmic force	8	11	8	3
None of these views	4	<1	15	10
Does not believe in God	1	2	7	1
Mainline Protestant				
A personal being	69	57	42	67
Created the world	13	9	2	5
Cosmic force	13	24	20	13
None of these views	3	2	22	15
Does not believe in God	2	7	13	1
Black Protestant				
A personal being	74	78	63	78
Created the world	13	9	11	5
Cosmic force	7	9	4	2
None of these views	5	2	20	14
Does not believe in God	~	<1	2	<1
Catholic				
A personal being	64	62	47	59
Created the world	17	13	6	6
Cosmic force	14	17	14	14
None of these views	4	1	24	20
Does not believe in God	1	5	9	2

(continued)

Table 3.5   Continued

	1	2	3	4
	Religious Tradition, Ages 13–17			Religious Tradition, Ages 23–28
	Wave 1 (%)	Wave 3 (%)	Wave 4 (%)	Wave 4 (%)
Jewish				
A personal being	44	32	16	42
Created the world	12	11	1	5
Cosmic force	33	32	24	22
None of these views	5	2	38	32
Does not believe in God	5	19	22	0
Latter-day Saints				
A personal being	76	78	71	88
Created the world	7	5	0	0
Cosmic force	9	14	12	5
None of these views	8	0	11	7
Does not believe in God	~	4	6	0
Not Religious				
A personal being	30	36	24	17
Created the world	15	9	6	5
Cosmic force	31	34	17	21
None of these views	7	2	20	27
Does not believe in God	17	17	33	30

Source: National Study of Youth and Religion surveys 2002, 2008, 2013.

in a personal God make up just more than one-half of those who said they believe in God.[14]

Measures of private religious salience include reports about the importance of faith in daily life and feelings of closeness to God. Reporting that faith is very or extremely important in daily life declined 5 percentage points since 2008 and 12 percentage points over the course of the 10-year study (Table 3.6). The percentage who said they feel very or extremely close to God increased slightly from the Wave 3 survey and is just five percent lower than it was in the original survey in 2003 (Table 3.7). More than one-third of respondents reported praying daily, a slight increase from the previous survey. At the same time, however, the percentage who reported

Table 3.6 Importance of Faith

	1	2	3	4
	Religious Tradition, Ages 13–17			Religious Tradition, Ages 23–28
	Wave 1 (%)	Wave 3 (%)	Wave 4 (%)	Wave 4 (%)
Total				
Very/extremely important	51	44	39	
Not at all/not very important	18	27	30	
Conservative Protestant				
Very/extremely important	67	57	51	76
Not at all/not very important	7	15	18	2
Mainline Protestant				
Very/extremely important	50	33	30	50
Not at all/not very important	16	37	42	9
Black Protestant				
Very/extremely important	73	72	63	69
Not at all/not very important	5	6	8	~
Catholic				
Very/extremely important	41	34	34	37
Not at all/not very important	18	28	30	17
Jewish				
Very/extremely important	13	16	16	40
Not at all/not very important	37	61	62	21
Latter-day Saints				
Very/extremely important	68	59	58	85
Not at all/not very important	15	23	16	3
Not Religious				
Very/extremely important	14	17	14	5
Not at all/not very important	57	57	62	71

Source: National Study of Youth and Religion surveys 2002, 2008, 2013.

that they never pray increased from 15 percent in 2003 to one-fourth of re-spondents in the current survey (Table 3.8).

In our final inquiry about how the salience of religion has changed in the lives of emerging adults, we turn to a question that asks them to assess this change for themselves. Respondents were asked whether, over the

Table 3.7 Feeling Distant or Close to God

	1	2	3	4
	Religious Tradition, Ages 13–17			Religious Tradition, Ages 23–28
	Wave 1 (%)	Wave 3 (%)	Wave 4 (%)	Wave 4 (%)
Total				
Extremely close/very close	36	29	31	
Very distant/extremely distant	8	12	8	
Conservative Protestant				
Extremely close/very close	48	35	39	52
Very distant/extremely distant	4	8	5	3
Mainline Protestant				
Extremely close/very close	40	22	25	32
Very distant/extremely distant	6	17	13	3
Black Protestant				
Extremely close/very close	49	45	59	65
Very distant/extremely distant	5	6	2	1
Catholic				
Extremely close/very close	31	23	24	27
Very distant/extremely distant	5	10	6	8
Jewish				
Extremely close/very close	10	7	12	34
Very distant/extremely distant	21	17	21	19
Latter-day Saints				
Extremely close/very close	44	55	51	68
Very distant/extremely distant	6	10	5	1
Not Religious				
Extremely close/very close	9	12	15	9
Very distant/extremely distant	24	23	11	13

Source: National Study of Youth and Religion surveys 2002, 2008, 2013.

course of the past five years, they had become more religious, had become less religious, or had stayed about the same. These responses look very similar to the information we received when we asked the same question five years earlier (Table 3.9). Fifty-six percent of emerging adults in our study said that they had remained about the same, while 24 percent said

Table 3.8 Private Prayer

		1	2	3	4
		Religious Tradition, Ages 13–17			Religious Tradition, Ages 23–28
		Wave 1 (%)	Wave 3 (%)	Wave 4 (%)	Wave 4 (%)
Total					
	Once a day or more	38	30	34	
	Never	15	20	25	
Conservative Protestant					
	Once a day or more	49	42	48	64
	Never	5	10	12	1
Mainline Protestant					
	Once a day or more	32	24	24	36
	Never	11	23	32	6
Black Protestant					
	Once a day or more	55	43	55	61
	Never	5	6	9	3
Catholic					
	Once a day or more	33	22	26	29
	Never	13	20	24	8
Jewish					
	Once a day or more	9	8	9	26
	Never	34	45	59	42
Latter-day Saints					
	Once a day or more	57	54	53	71
	Never	12	23	24	6
Not Religious					
	Once a day or more	11	18	14	8
	Never	51	48	56	60

Source: National Study of Youth and Religion surveys 2002, 2008, 2013.

they had become more religious, and 19 percent said that they had become less religious.

Regardless of their responses to individual religious measures, in their overall assessment of their own religiousness, the majority of respondents did not report any religious change. When they did report change, it was

Table 3.9 Self-Reported Religious Change over the Past Five Years

	1	2	3	4
	Religious Tradition, Ages 13–17			Religious Tradition, Ages 23–28
	Wave 1 (%)	Wave 3 (%)	Wave 4 (%)	Wave 4 (%)
Total				
Became more religious		24	25	
Became less religious		17	19	
Stayed about the same		59	56	
Conservative Protestant				
Became more religious		27	29	43
Became less religious		20	19	11
Stayed about the same		53	52	46
Mainline Protestant				
Became more religious		16	19	27
Became less religious		23	24	18
Stayed about the same		60	57	55
Black Protestant				
Became more religious		37	40	42
Became less religious		13	14	14
Stayed about the same		49	45	44
Catholic				
Became more religious		16	24	24
Became less religious		17	24	18
Stayed about the same		66	52	58
Jewish				
Became more religious		15	8	19
Became less religious		19	12	6
Stayed about the same		66	80	76
Latter-day Saints				
Became more religious		51	22	32
Became less religious		13	16	8
Stayed about the same		33	62	60
Not Religious				
Became more religious		20	15	7
Became less religious		7	10	28
Stayed about the same		73	75	65

Source: National Study of Youth and Religion surveys 2002, 2008, 2013.

more likely to be an increase in religiosity than a decrease. This seemingly paradoxical finding in relation to the aggregate declines we see across the majority of the other religion measures was also present in the second and third waves of the study and has been discussed in detail elsewhere.[15] However, it highlights a few points to keep in mind. First, while aggregate numbers reflect overall religious decline, there is movement going on in both directions—both toward and away from religion—as well as a fair amount of stability, reflecting the experience of people whose religious lives have not really changed dramatically over the past five years. These nuances of change can be lost in the aggregate summaries of the data.

A second point to consider is that religiousness is more than just the sum of its parts. The measurement of individual facets of religion—practices, beliefs, experience—does not always paint the same picture as a holistic assessment of an individual's religious life. People are complex, combining and compartmentalizing their lives in unique ways. When we ask people for their self-perceptions of their own religious vitality, we have to keep in mind that each person is drawing on a complex assortment of facts and feelings about their religious lives. Their own perceptions may not always match up with the reported behaviors and beliefs of other survey questions. In the case of the young people in our study, they are each assessing their own religious lives through particular social lenses. The specific nuances of these social lenses merit future research into the dynamics of how they are assessing their own religiousness. At present, however, it is worth noting that more of them than we would expect, based on other religion measures, perceive themselves to have become more religious in recent years.

Tradition-Specific Change

Up to this point we have been painting with a broad brush the general patterns of change among the emerging adults in our study. Moving forward, we look more closely at the individual religious traditions and examine the ways in which the tradition-specific changes align with or diverge from the larger trends.

Continued Decline

The general decline that we see in the aggregate sample is reflected most clearly among Catholic emerging adults. As we saw in the larger sample, the greatest decline in religious engagement was highlighted by the measure of religious service attendance. At the time of the first survey, Catholic teenagers reported weekly attendance of 40 percent, the same as the full sample. By the time of the final survey, weekly attendance had declined even more than among the full sample of emerging adults. Among those who identified as Catholic as teenagers, regardless of their current identity, just 12 percent continued to report attending services weekly. Yet, even if we narrow the focus to only those who currently identify as Catholic, the weekly attendance rate is just 16 percent, lower than the average for the total group of our respondents.

The rest of the religion measures show less dramatic decline among Catholics, but the overall pattern is consistent with movement away from religious engagement. As discussed earlier in the chapter, there are two potential comparisons to draw when examining religious change over time. The first is to examine the group of individuals who were a part of the religious tradition as teenagers and compare their reports from that point in time to their present reports of the various religious measures. The second is to compare the levels of religious engagement among the group of religious adherents from the first survey to the levels of religious engagement among the current adherents at the time of the final survey. By either measure, Catholic young people are reporting lower levels of religious engagement at the time of the Wave 4 survey.

While none of the other measures decline as much as religious service attendance, Catholic emerging adults at Wave 4 are less likely, compared with their responses as teenagers, to report feeling close to God or to say that their faith is important to them. At the time of the first survey, 85 percent of Catholic youth said that they believed in God. When we asked those same young people this question again in Wave 4, only 76 percent still said they believe in God. However, if we limit the responses to only those who have maintained their Catholic identity as emerging adults, belief in God increased to 89 percent. At the time of the first survey, 41 percent of Catholic teenagers reported that their faith was very or extremely important to them. Ten years later, 34 percent of those respondents identified faith as being important to them. Narrowing the responses to those who continue to identify as Catholic, we see that 37 percent said that faith is important in their life.

These findings are consistent with the previous waves of the survey and with the more detailed discussions about Catholic young people found in other books from the NSYR.[16] Although the beliefs and practices of

Catholic youth and emerging adults cause them to appear to be more dis-engaged than Conservative or Mainline Protestants, Catholic religious identity retention is greater. Fifty-three percent of the young people who identified as Catholic as teenagers are still classified as Catholic in our final survey. This is higher than the 46 percent of Conservative Protestants and the 23 percent of Mainline Protestants who retained the same reli-gious identity over the course of the study. This group of emerging adults appears to be maintaining some connection to Catholicism, even as they distance themselves from the beliefs and practices of their faith tradition.

Solidifying Religion

While the main story is one of decline, there is a parallel story about those who are not experiencing religious decline. Among certain groups, we find evidence of increased religious commitment and participation. Comparing the Wave 1 and Wave 4 responses tells a story about what is happening within particular religious traditions. Among the Conservative Protestant, Latter-day Saints, and Jewish traditions, there is a general pat-tern of higher religious engagement among the affiliates of the tradition at Wave 4 compared with Wave 1 (column 4 compared with column 1). At the aggregate level, these religious traditions show increased religious en-gagement among current adherents. In the context of the overall religious decline that we examined earlier, what might explain these increases?

There are two ways to understand what may be going on here. First, attrition or a winnowing process is operating. Within any religious group, there are individuals who, although affiliated, have relatively lower levels of commitment. Over the time period of this study, these individuals might have moved from the fringes of a group to outside of the group entirely. Thus, those individuals who were originally somewhat marginal in their commitment move from religious affiliation to identifying as Not Religious. While this attrition is an important story in and of itself, another way to understand this is through what happens within these religious traditions after this attrition takes place. As less committed individuals move out of the group, the religiosity of the group gets stronger, and we see higher levels of commitment and engagement when measuring those remaining in the religious tradition.

A second explanation is that those who remain committed to their re-ligious tradition over the course of the study may experience a strength-ening of their own religiosity. This sample was originally collected while the respondents were teenagers living with their parents. For many who identified at that time as belonging to a particular religious tradition, that identification was as much about their family upbringing as it was about their own election of faith. In *A Faith of Their Own*, we heard from youth who expressed the desire to make their faith something of their own choosing, and not just something imposed on them by their parents.[17] As these young people get older, they have increasing autonomy about their religious lives.

Now, as emerging adults, those who continue to identify with a religious tradition are more likely to remain in the tradition of their own accord. Being old enough to make these decisions for themselves, they have had to confront their own beliefs and perspectives about religion and choose for themselves the religious identity they will carry into adulthood. As they move into adulthood, those for whom faith "sticks" are committing more wholeheartedly to this faith that they have chosen not to abandon. Therefore, rather than a unilateral decline across the board, it seems that those on the high end of religious engagement may, in some ways, be reaching deeper or firmer levels of commitment.

Among the Conservative Protestant, Latter-day Saints, and Jewish traditions, most of the religious measures strengthened within the group over time. Although there has been attrition and a general decline among those who started out in these traditions as teenagers, reports of religious engagement are generally higher for those who identified with these faith traditions at the final survey than for people in these groups at Wave 1. For example, the percentage of respondents within all three groups who said that faith is very or extremely important is higher at Wave 4 than it was at Wave 1. The most significant change was among Jewish respondents. At Wave 1, only 13 percent of Jewish teenagers thought faith was very or extremely important. Among emerging adults, 32 percent of those who are Jewish reported that faith is very or extremely important. At Wave 1, 68 percent of teenage Mormons said that their faith is very or extremely important, while 79 percent of the Mormon emerging adults at Wave 4 reported this level of religiosity. Though the change in importance of faith is smaller for Conservative Protestants, the pattern is the same, with a shift from 67 to 77 percent.

A similar pattern holds for reports of how close respondents feel to God. When comparing Conservative Protestants at Wave 1 with those who are identified as Conservative Protestant at Wave 4, there is a modest increase in the percentage who said they are very or extremely close to God.

Larger increases are seen among Jewish respondents (from 10 to 28 percent) and Latter-day Saints (from 44 to 61 percent). These increases in the percentage of those within the religious tradition identifying faith as important or saying that they feel close to God suggest that there is a kind of strengthening of the core of these religious adherents, while those who were on the periphery to begin with may have moved out of the religious traditions altogether.

Black Protestants are a special case within this trend. The main pattern for Black Protestants is that most of the religious measures remained stable over the course of the study. For example, the percentage of Black Protestants who said they believe in God at Wave 1 is similar to the percentage who said they believe in God at Wave 4. There are a few measures where we see the same types of increases we saw among the Conservative Protestants. However, these increases are not as common. One reason for this is that, as a group, Black Protestants often have the greatest level of religious engagement across a wide range of religious measures. At each wave of the survey, they reported relatively high levels of religious belief and salience. Given that they are already highly religious, there is a ceiling effect: They have less room for increasing the aggregate levels of religiosity.

Therefore, while we do not see as much religious intensification at Wave 4, this is in part because Black Protestants are already the most religiously engaged group. The religious measure that taps into levels of religious salience provides evidence that, even with the already high levels of engagement, there is a similar process of religious strengthening happening among Black Protestants. Across all four waves of the survey, we asked respondents, "How close do you feel to God?" At the time of the first survey, 49 percent of Black Protestant teenagers told us that they felt very or extremely close to God. In the final survey, 64 percent of emerging adult Black Protestants said that they feel very or extremely close to God. In addition, 41 percent of Black Protestants between the ages of 23 and 28 reported having become more religious over the previous five years. Black Protestants and Conservative Protestants (42 percent) are the two groups with the highest rate of self-reported increase in religiosity.

A solidifying of religious salience was also taking place among the Not Religious, although in the opposite direction. At the time of the first survey, 14 percent of the irreligious teens still said faith was important in their daily life. But as emerging adults, only five percent continued to say that faith is very or extremely important in their life. The percentage of those who said they believe in God also declined, from 49 percent of the Not

Religious teenagers to 40 percent of the emerging adults who identified as Not Religious. As has been argued elsewhere, being religiously unaffiliated does not necessarily mean having no religious sentiments or beliefs, and that is true among our respondents as well.[18] However, we do see that over the course of the study, not only is there a growing number of individuals who are religiously unaffiliated, but also those religious "nones" appear to be more comfortable with their distance from religion and more confident in their nonreligious identity. As a group, the not religious also seem to be embracing their identity and are more willing to say that faith is not at all important in their lives and that they do not believe in God.

The increased number of emerging adults who are embracing their lack of religion mirrors those emerging adults who exhibit an increased commitment to religion. Emerging adults who no longer identify with any religious tradition seem to be exercising their personal autonomy and disaffiliating from whatever religious identification they formerly had.

Thus, there appears to be polarization, with young people moving more definitively toward the two ends of the continuum of religious engagement. This trend may be linked to some of the developments we saw in Chapter 2, where there is an aversion to judgment of others exhibited by young people. That is, the cultural landscape within which emerging adults live provides a context where one can believe—or not believe—whatever they want, without much fear of disapproval. The solidification of a religious or nonreligious identity may also be linked to the greater level of polarization being experienced in society at large, where we are also witnessing a hollowing out of the middle in politics and culture, as people cling more tightly to their left- or right-of-center ideology. It is within this larger context that emerging adults are evaluating their own religious allegiances, and the results seem to mirror the larger cultural movement away from the middle of a variety of societal spectrums.

Attrition or Holding Steady?

The final religious tradition to which we now turn our attention is Mainline Protestants. This group occupies a middle ground between the clear religious decline of the Catholics and the religious solidification of the other traditions. The first story we see among Mainline Protestants is one of marked attrition. Mainline Protestants have the lowest retention rate of any of the major religious traditions. Just 23 percent of the youth who identified as Mainline Protestant in 2003 are still affiliated with that religious tradition at the time of the final survey. Among those youth identified as Mainline Protestants as teenagers, more than 40 percent now identify as Not Religious. This shift in affiliation is reflected in declines across each measure of religious engagement when we compare the Wave 1 and Wave 4 responses of those who were Mainline Protestants as teenagers. While 44 percent of Mainline Protestant teenagers attended services weekly, just 18 percent of this group attend weekly as emerging adults. Belief in God and reporting that faith is very or extremely important also declined by 20 percentage points for Mainline Protestants as they transitioned from teenagers into emerging adults. And young people who were Mainline Protestants in their youth were the most likely to report having become less religious over the past five years, providing further evidence that there is clear movement away from religion as they move into adulthood.

Yet, there is another story to be gleaned by focusing on the group of emerging adults who are currently identified as part of the Mainline Protestant tradition. Less than half of the individuals in this group were Mainline Protestant as teenagers. The other half of the current Mainliners consists of young people who have moved into the Mainline Protestant tradition over time. Most notably, 29 percent of current Mainline Protestants identified as Conservative Protestant during the Wave 1 survey. Given the considerable shift in the membership of this religious tradition, we examine the religiosity of current Mainline Protestants and how this compares with the religious engagement of this group 10 years earlier (column 4 compared with column 1).

In doing so, we see that there is not a clear-cut story of either religious decline or religious strengthening. The percentage of Mainline Protestants who reported that faith is very or extremely important is the same in Wave 4 as it was in Wave 1. As a group, current Mainliners are somewhat more likely to report that they believe in God, yet they are less likely than those in the earlier cohort to report feeling very or extremely close to God. On most other measures, the current group of Mainline Protestants reported engaging in religious beliefs and practices at similar rates or slightly higher rates than the group of Mainline teenagers at Wave 1.

Finally, when asked to report on their own perceptions of religious change in their lives, 27 percent said they have become more religious in the past five years, and 18 percent reported becoming less religious— numbers that closely mirror the larger sample. Taken as a whole, the story for the current Mainline Protestants is one of holding steady. The religious beliefs and the salience of faith for Mainline adherents in Wave 4 has shifted a bit across measures but overall is not significantly different from the level of engagement that we saw among Mainline Protestants in 2003.

Mainline Protestant beliefs and religious salience may be holding steady in part because of the influx of former Conservative Protestants who now make up nearly one-third of this group. There is evidence that some younger Conservative Protestants are shifting into Mainline congregations because they are seeking religious communities that provide a greater connection to Christian history than is available in evangelical churches.[19] Although they compose a group that is not particularly large, these former Conservative Protestants may bring with them the relatively higher rates of religious commitment and practice that are characteristic of Conservative Protestant traditions and, in doing so, may provide new buoyancy to the otherwise sinking ship of Mainline Protestantism.[20] This raises the question of whether Conservative Protestants moving into Mainline Protestant congregations will remain and contribute to the revitalization of these congregations they join, or whether this migration is simply a stop on their way out of religion altogether. Given the larger trends we see, the former possibility seems less likely than the latter.

Attendance

Regardless of what is happening with all the other religion measures, one thing that almost every group shares in common is a decline in the reports of religious service attendance. Understanding attendance patterns requires that we pay attention at both ends of the attendance spectrum. On the one hand, there was very little change in the percentage of respondents who reported regular weekly service attendance between Waves 3 and 4; most of the drop-off in weekly attendance happened before Wave 3. At the time of the Wave 1 survey, 40 percent of teenagers reported weekly service attendance. By the time they were interviewed five years later at Wave 3, just 20 percent were attending regularly. After five more years, at Wave 4, this number had dropped just one percent—to 19 percent attending weekly.

The most dramatic change uncovered in the fourth survey was not in regular attendance but in the percentage of the young people who have stopped attending altogether. Five years earlier, 35 percent of the young people we surveyed said that they never attend religious services. At the final survey, this number had jumped to 51 percent; more than half of all of the emerging adults in our study reported that they never attend religious services. When we look at column 3—those who were in each religious tradition as teenagers—we see that every group has a substantial increase in those who never attend when comparing the Wave 1 and Wave 4 responses. Jumps in the numbers of those who never attend are less dramatic when we limit the analysis to only those who are currently affiliated with each religious tradition (column 4). Yet, even among current adherents, there are increases in nonattendance for all groups except Conservative Protestants and Black Protestants.

The fact that religious service attendance shifted more than any other religion measure is noteworthy and raises questions about the relationship that these emerging adults have with the institution of religion and the congregations that represent this institution. This move away from congregational involvement may signal a deeper distrust of organized religion. We examine this in the next section.

Attitudes about Organized Religion

To this point in the chapter, we have been examining the religious lives of emerging adults, assessing the general decline in the importance of religion in their lives and the shifts and changes in their religious beliefs, experiences, and practices. We now turn the tables and allow these young people an opportunity to assess mainstream or organized religion, such as churches, synagogues, mosques, and temples. What do they think about religious institutions in our society?

Emerging adults' views about organized religion are less positive than they were when our interviewees responded to the same questions five years earlier. The next series of tables shows this decline across several different questions. When asked to respond to the statement, "I have a lot of respect for organized religion in this country," those responding that they agree or strongly agree declined from 79 percent in Wave 3 to 55 percent in Wave 4 (Table 3.10). Conversely, there was an increase in those who said that they disagreed or strongly disagreed that they had a lot of respect for organized religion, from 21 to 33 percent. This increasingly negative view of organized religion was mirrored across emerging adults in every religious tradition as well as among the Not Religious. Young people who began our study as Catholic or Not Religious showed the greatest decline in their respect for organized religion, while Mormon and Black

Table 3.10 Respect for Organized Religion

	1	2	3	4
	Religious Tradition, Ages 13–17			Religious Tradition, Ages 23–28
	Wave 1 (%)	Wave 3 (%)	Wave 4 (%)	Wave 4 (%)
Total				
Strongly agree/agree		79	55	
Strongly disagree/disagree		21	33	
Conservative Protestant				
Strongly agree/agree		84	60	70
Strongly disagree/disagree		16	28	16
Mainline Protestant				
Strongly agree/agree		73	48	73
Strongly disagree/disagree		27	43	21
Black Protestant				
Strongly agree/agree		89	75	79
Strongly disagree/disagree		11	14	12
Catholic				
Strongly agree/agree		81	53	68
Strongly disagree/disagree		19	32	18
Jewish				
Strongly agree/agree		58	36	51
Strongly disagree/disagree		42	58	41
Latter-day Saints				
Strongly agree/agree		91	77	96
Strongly disagree/disagree		9	19	3
Not Religious				
Strongly agree/agree		60	34	25
Strongly disagree/disagree		40	54	63

Note: Survey question wording was, "How strongly do you agree with the following statement: *I have a lot of respect for organized religion in this country?*"

Source: National Study of Youth and Religion surveys 2002, 2008, 2013.

Protestant emerging adults showed the least decline, with only 14 percent fewer saying that they had a lot of respect for organized religion.

The questions about organized religion were not asked in the original survey, so we are not able to make comparisons to the Wave 1 data.

However, when we limit the results to those emerging adults who currently identify with a religious tradition, we see that among those who are still religiously affiliated, regardless of the tradition, support for organized religion is higher than among the larger group of those who were affiliated with each tradition as teenagers. For example, only 53 percent of those who were Catholics and 48 percent of those who were Mainline Protestants as teenagers currently have a lot of respect for organized religion. Yet, of those who still identity as Catholic or Mainline Protestant, 68 and 73 percent, respectively, reported having respect for organized religion. There is even stronger support among those who currently identify as Mormon or Black Protestant. Interestingly, among current Conservative Protestants, only 70 percent said they have a lot of respect for organized religion. This result, however, should be understood in the context that, in general, Conservative Protestants tend to think of "organized religion" in negative terms, viewing it as not sufficiently spiritual. Regardless, this does suggest that there are a number of Conservative Protestant emerging adults who are not particularly pleased with organized religion as they understand and experience it.

Similar changes are evident in other responses to questions about religious institutions. When asked if they view organized religion as "a big turnoff," 38 percent of all Wave 4 respondents said that they agree or strongly agree, up from 29 percent in Wave 3 (Table 3.11). In general, across each of the different religious traditions, the same pattern characterizes the responses: an increase in the number of emerging adults who said that organized religion is a turnoff, and a decrease in the number who disagreed with that statement. Once again, if we look at the responses among those who are currently affiliated with a religious tradition (column 4), the negativity toward religion is, not surprisingly, lower across the board. However, even among those who are affiliated with a religious tradition, we see at least some level of disapproval for religious organizations in general.

Emerging adults responded in somewhat different fashion when asked whether they agree with the statement: "Mainstream religion is irrelevant to the needs and concerns of most people my age" (Table 3.12). For this item, there was actually a decrease in the percentage of those who agreed that mainstream religion is irrelevant, and this pattern was generally repeated across the different religious traditions. However, there were also fewer young people who said that they disagree with the statement. Instead, there was an increase in the percentages who elected "I don't

Table 3.11 Organized Religion is a Turnoff

	1	2	3	4
	Religious Tradition, Ages 13–17			Religious Tradition, Ages 23–28
	Wave 1 (%)	Wave 3 (%)	Wave 4 (%)	Wave 4 (%)
Total				
Strongly agree/agree		29	38	
Strongly disagree/disagree		70	52	
Conservative Protestant				
Strongly agree/agree		23	30	15
Strongly disagree/disagree		76	60	72
Mainline Protestant				
Strongly agree/agree		36	45	25
Strongly disagree/disagree		63	46	72
Black Protestant				
Strongly agree/agree		14	19	12
Strongly disagree/disagree		85	7	80
Catholic				
Strongly agree/agree		26	38	26
Strongly disagree/disagree		72	51	63
Jewish				
Strongly agree/agree		52	65	38
Strongly disagree/disagree		48	29	53
Latter-day Saints				
Strongly agree/agree		21	29	9
Strongly disagree/disagree		79	67	90
Not Religious				
Strongly agree/agree		51	63	71
Strongly disagree/disagree		49	28	20

Note: Survey question wording was, "How strongly do you agree with the following statement: *Organized religion is usually a big turnoff for me?*"

Source: National Study of Youth and Religion surveys 2002, 2008, 2013.

know" as their response, reflecting emerging adults' increasing ambivalence about the importance of organized religion.[21]

The final question regarding how emerging adults view organized religion asked them to respond to the statement, "I have very positive feelings

Table 3.12 Irrelevance of Mainstream Religion

	1	2	3	4
	Religious Tradition, Ages 13–17			Religious Tradition, Ages 23–28
	Wave 1 (%)	Wave 3 (%)	Wave 4 (%)	Wave 4 (%)
Total				
Strongly agree/agree		42	34	
Strongly disagree/disagree		56	47	
Conservative Protestant				
Strongly agree/agree		38	28	21
Strongly disagree/disagree		60	56	63
Mainline Protestant				
Strongly agree/agree		40	36	25
Strongly disagree/disagree		59	45	62
Black Protestant				
Strongly agree/agree		43	30	24
Strongly disagree/disagree		54	56	68
Catholic				
Strongly agree/agree		42	36	29
Strongly disagree/disagree		55	45	52
Jewish				
Strongly agree/agree		55	37	37
Strongly disagree/disagree		42	31	39
Latter-day Saints				
Strongly agree/agree		28	21	7
Strongly disagree/disagree		72	68	87
Not Religious				
Strongly agree/agree		48	45	50
Strongly disagree/disagree		50	30	27

Note: Survey question wording was, "How strongly do you agree with the following statement: *Most mainstream religion is irrelevant to the needs and concerns of most people my age?*"

Source: National Study of Youth and Religion surveys 2002, 2008, 2013.

about the religious tradition in which I was raised." This item was asked only of respondents who were raised in a religious tradition and asked about their specific experience, rather than the more abstract concept of organized religion in general. Over the five years since the previous survey, positive regard for the religious tradition they were raised in has declined. As a whole, agreeing or strongly agreeing with this statement dropped from 80 percent to 62 percent of the sample (Table 3.13). Those

Table 3.13 Positive Feelings about Religious Tradition

	I	2	3	4
	Religious Tradition, Ages 13–17			Religious Tradition, Ages 23–28
	Wave 1 (%)	Wave 3 (%)	Wave 4 (%)	Wave 4 (%)
Total				
Strongly agree/agree		80	62	
Strongly disagree/disagree		19	18	
Conservative Protestant				
Strongly agree/agree		84	72	86
Strongly disagree/disagree		15		8
Mainline Protestant				
Strongly agree/agree		76	61	78
Strongly disagree/disagree		23		13
Black Protestant				
Strongly agree/agree		90	82	87
Strongly disagree/disagree		9		10
Catholic				
Strongly agree/agree		77	57	78
Strongly disagree/disagree		22		9
Jewish				
Strongly agree/agree		76	68	79
Strongly disagree/disagree		19		6
Latter-day Saints				
Strongly agree/agree		84	74	90
Strongly disagree/disagree		16		8
Not Religious				
Strongly agree/agree		~	32	28
Strongly disagree/disagree		~		33

Note: Survey question wording was, "How strongly do you agree with the following statement: *I have very positive feelings about the religious tradition in which I was raised?*"

Source: National Study of Youth and Religion surveys 2002, 2008, 2013.

who were raised Catholic showed the biggest declines in agreement that they have positive feelings about the religion they grew up in, followed by Mainline and Conservative Protestants. Jewish, Black Protestant, and Mormon emerging adults reported a somewhat smaller decline in positive feelings about the religion in which they were raised. Although positive feelings have declined among those who were raised Conservative Protestant, it should be noted that this tradition still has one of the highest rates of respondents who feel positive about the religion of their youth; they rank just behind Latter-day Saints, with 72 percent agreeing with this statement.

When we focus on those young people who remain affiliated with the religious tradition of their upbringing, the affirmative response to this question is even greater. Among those who currently identify as Conservative Protestant, Black Protestant, or Mormon, more than 85 percent reported positive feelings about the religion in which they grew up. And for Jewish, Catholic, and Mainline Protestant respondents, agreement was just under 80 percent. These higher percentages among the currently affiliated provide support for the larger story of a divide among respondents. While there are significant numbers of emerging adults who are disaffiliating and disengaging from organized religion, there are also young people who remain religious and are continuing to strengthen their commitment to and regard for religion and religious institutions.

In sum, emerging adults are fairly divided on how they view organized religion. For those who are still involved, more said that religious organizations are important and can be relevant to young people. For those who have left, or are on their way out, organized religion is less likely to be viewed positively. Yet, even within the group of less religious emerging adults, religious institutions have not been rejected completely because there are still some who maintain a positive view of religious organizations.

Conclusion

In this chapter we have told two different stories of emerging adults and their religious lives. The first story is one of emerging adults' disaffiliation from the religious institutions of their teenage years and an increase in those saying that they are not religious, accompanied by a decline in religious practice and the importance of religion in their lives. The second story describes those who continue to identify with a religious tradition and appear to have solidified their religious commitment. These young people are more likely to consider religion an important part of their lives, to attend religious services, and to pursue other religious and spiritual practices. In general, they are more interested in and committed to their religion and its place in their lives.

In the first story, we see emerging adults who are leaving the religious traditions in which they were raised, continuing a trend we saw in Wave 3.[22] There is a distinct decline in religious affiliation among emerging adults, paralleling declines in religious practice and belief in the relative importance of spirituality in their lives. If there is a "winner" in this story, it is the Not Religious category, which reflects a significant increase in the percentage of emerging adults who no longer identify with any religious tradition. A less obvious part of this trend is that there has been an increase in the number of emerging adults in our Indeterminate category of religious identity. This could be for a number of reasons, and although this uptick in the number of religiously indeterminate young adults is a much smaller increase than in those who now claim that they are not religious, it is likely an indicator of increasing religious ambivalence, decreasing particularism, and the more general state of transition that characterizes the lives of young people. It remains to be seen whether this religiously indeterminate status represents an intermediate location as our respondents make their way out of religion altogether. However, a large percentage of those who were religiously indeterminate as teenagers are now not religious, suggesting that the "exit door" is perhaps the most likely trajectory for these emerging adults.

All of the major religious traditions are losing emerging adults, mostly as these young people begin to identify themselves as not religious. The general decline also shows up in other key areas of the lives of young people. For example, fewer emerging adults said that religious faith is important in their lives or that they are interested in learning more about their religion. Similarly, slightly fewer said that they believe in God, and there is a definite shift from belief in a personal God to some other version of God. Fewer believe in the afterlife or that heaven is a real place. Many still seem to want to believe in God as well as the notion that there might be more to reality than just the physical world, but they are just less certain of who or what that "something else" might be. It follows, then, that with this shift to being less formally religious, regardless of what they said they believe, emerging adults as a whole place less importance on the formal aspects of religious and spiritual practice, such as prayer or attendance at religious services.

Finally, emerging adult views about organized religion are not entirely what we might expect, given the story of religious decline. We might have expected that, owing to the increasing numbers of young adults who are "checking out" of religious institutions, there would be increased animosity toward organized religion. On the contrary, there seems to be a lingering soft spot on their part for organized religion. Certainly, there are those who have no use for religion and see it in negative terms, and support for religious institutions is declining overall. Yet, there are larger numbers of emerging adults who continue to say that they have respect for organized religion and that it is not irrelevant for people their age. Despite the large increase in the number of emerging adults who say that they are not religious, they remain generally supportive of religious organizations, although their involvement with organized religion is decreasing.

In the second story, we saw that those who still identify with particular religious traditions seem in general to be more committed to and interested in their religion. Compared with those who say they are not religious, these emerging adults are much more likely to attend religious services regularly, pursue other religious and spiritual practices, say that religion is important in their everyday lives, assent to more conventional religious beliefs, and have more positive views of organized religion.

There are, however, interesting similarities between those emerging adults who still identify with a religious tradition and those who are not religious. For example, while religiously affiliated emerging adults are more likely to positively view the religion in which they were raised, many nonreligious emerging adults also reported similar feelings. The two groups are also similar in their generally positive views of organized religion and in some of their beliefs about God and the supernatural.

This chapter has focused on the trends shown in the survey results, both overall for the emerging adults in our study and within different religious traditions. What is missing are the voices of the emerging adults themselves. How do they articulate their understanding of their own religious commitments and involvements? Are there other ways that emerging adults are both similar to and different from each other in how they approach religion? We turn to these questions in Chapter 4.

4

Emerging Adult Religious Commitment and Identity

THE MOST SIGNIFICANT shift in religious commitment among emerging adults has been a move away from identifying with a particular religious group or tradition. As we saw in Chapter 3, substantial percentages of young people from across all of the major religious traditions now identify as Not Religious. As a result, scholars and the news media have steadily begun to pay significant attention to what some are calling "the rise of the religious nones," referring to the rapid increase in the number of individuals in the United States who claim no religious affiliation.[1]

In this chapter, however, we want to move beyond simply making the case that emerging adults are increasingly identifying as not religious. We will examine what this phenomenon actually looks like "on the ground" and uncover the complexities in the lives of the current generation of emerging adults, who have often been characterized in recent research and media coverage as a monolithic group of either "religious" or "not religious" individuals.[2] We will consider the different ways that religion is part of the identities of emerging adults, the extent to which they identify with and are involved in the life of congregations, and how they fashion their religious and spiritual lives across the multiple facets of religiosity.[3] We will look more deeply at the story of decline, but also the accompanying story of what appears to be a solidifying of religious commitment, as well as those who seem to be somewhere between commitment and disaffiliation.

Self-identification as either religiously affiliated or not religious is only one way to assess religion in the lives of young people. The rate of attendance at religious services, an important measure that is left out of most reports on the increase in the number of religiously disaffiliated, serves as a baseline measure of connection to organized religion and public religious practice. Using attendance as a measure of an individual's general connection to organized religion and practice is important for many reasons, perhaps especially because it suggests that the more individuals are involved in the life of a religious organization and the larger community of participants, the more that religion is an important part of their personal lives.

As we saw in Chapter 3, attendance at religious services is the religion measure that has shown the greatest decline over the four waves of the study. In 2002, 40 percent of the young people in our study reported attending religious services at least once a week. By 2013, this number has dropped by half, to less than 20 percent. More noteworthy is the fact that 51 percent of the emerging adults in our study now say that they never attend any religious services. This is a dramatic increase even from five years earlier, in Wave 3, when just 35 percent said they never attended services. Although we expected a significant rise in the number of those who never attend, when we first saw these results, we were surprised at the findings: More than half of all the emerging adults in our study are disengaged from public religious practice and largely disconnected from organized religion.

Religious self-identity and attendance at religious services are two distinct measures of religiosity that often overlap but are not perfectly correlated. Given the growing interest among scholars and practitioners in the movement away from organized religion among emerging adults, it is important to consider both of these ways of measuring religiousness in the lives of young people.

In what follows, we take into account religious self-identity and public religious practice to divide emerging adults into four groups: (1) Not Religious: those who are atheists, agnostics, or simply say that they are not religious; (2) Disaffiliated: those who claim a religious identity but no longer attend services and are not associated with any particular religious institution; (3) Marginal: those who attend religious services sporadically (once a month or less) and are thus on the margins of religious institutions, and for whom religion remains on the margins of their lives; and (4) Committed: those emerging adults who regularly attend religious services (at least two to three times a month), suggesting a more religiously committed life.[4] Within each of those groupings, we look at four areas of their religious lives: (1) religious beliefs; (2) centrality of faith, or the importance of religion and spirituality in their daily lives; (3) religious and spiritual practices; and (4) attitudes about organized religion and religious institutions.

In Chapter 3, we examined the differences in survey responses across religious traditions. In this chapter, we look at similar measures of religion. However, instead of comparing across religious traditions, we compare the responses across the four orientations to religion just described. While religious tradition continues to be important, it does not make an appearance in this chapter other than as a descriptor of the respondents whom we quote. Instead, we have divided our sample into these four broad categories that aim to identify the "how" of religious life rather than the "what." In other words, rather than focus on the particularities of individual religious traditions, we look at the commonalities of how religiosity is lived out at varying levels of commitment among the emerging adults in our study. As we noted in Chapter 3, there certainly are religious particularities that are important to understand. But we also recognize that, increasingly, there are normative scripts for how young people incorporate religion into their lives that are not necessarily bounded by religious tradition. So, in this chapter, we look once again at the range of religion measures from our survey using a different lens.

Religious Groups

The emerging adults in our study are divided into four groups that take into account religious service attendance and self-reported religious identity (see Tables 4.1 and 4.2). We classify as Not Religious those respondents who said they never attend religious services and who answered "no" to the follow-up question, "Do you think of yourself as part of a particular religion, denomination, or church?" This group accounts for 35 percent of the full sample of respondents. A portion of those who said they never

Table 4.1 Religious Groups by Percentage

Not Religious	35
Disaffiliated	16
Marginal	23
Committed	27
Total	100

Source: National Study of Youth and Religion survey 2013.

Table 4.2 Religious Service Attendance

	Not Religious (%)	Disaffiliated (%)	Marginal (%)	Committed (%)	All (%)
Never	100	100	~	~	51
Few times a year	~	~	46	~	10
Many times a year	~	~	33	~	7
Once a month	~	~	21	~	5
Two to three times a month	~	~	~	30	8
Once a week or more	~	~	~	70	19
Total	100	100	100	100	100

Source: National Study of Youth and Religion survey 2013.

attend, however, answered "yes" to the follow-up question of religious identity. These respondents who continue to identify with a religious tradition but reported that they never attend religious services are categorized as Disaffiliated and constitute the smallest group, at just 16 percent of our sample.

A third group of respondents we label Marginal. These respondents consider themselves to be religious, or at least reported some level of identity with a religious tradition and reported some level of attendance at religious services.[5] Attendance at religious services for this group ranges from a few times a year to once a month. The Marginal group makes up 22 percent of the sample. The final category encompasses those we are calling Committed. These are the respondents who identify with a religious tradition and reported that they attend religious services two to three times a month, once a week, or more than once a week. This group constitutes the remaining 27 percent of the sample.

Social Characteristics of Religious Groups

When we divide our sample of emerging adults into these four religious categories, some distinct demographic patterns emerge (Table 4.3). First, we see a pattern related to religion and gender. In the sample as a whole, 53 percent of our respondents are female. However, females make up just 45 percent of the Not Religious. The Disaffiliated are 55 percent female, while the Marginal and Committed groups are 59 and 58 percent female, respectively. Next, we examine the relationship between religion and race.

Table 4.3 Social Characteristics of Religious Groups

	Not Religious (%)	Disaffiliated (%)	Marginal (%)	Committed (%)	All (%)
Female	45	54	59	58	53
Age					
23–24	31	27	29	29	29
25–26	40	46	42	42	42
27+	29	26	29	29	28
Race					
White	77	74	63	67	71
Black	6	11	18	18	13
Latinx	9	9	10	11	10
Other	7	6	8	4	7
Family					
Have children	24	28	38	36	32
Married	17	16	23	43	25
Education					
High school or less	19	19	21	20	20
Some college	36	36	34	36	36
BA/BS or more	45	44	45	44	45

Source: National Study of Youth and Religion survey 2013.

The Not Religious have the highest percentage of white emerging adults of the four groups; 77 percent of Not Religious are white. Seventy-four percent of Disaffiliated are white, while 64 percent of the Marginal and 67 percent of the Committed are white. Latinx emerging adults are similarly represented across all four groups. However, black emerging adults are overrepresented among the Marginal and Committed, with each group having about 18 percent black respondents, compared with 13 percent in the full sample. Age and levels of education appear to be distributed similarly within each of the four religious categories.

When we examine current family status, we see clear differences across the four religious categories. Among the Committed, 43 percent are married. This is about twice the proportion of married people in the other groups. The Marginals have the next largest proportion of married individuals, at 23 percent, while the Disaffiliated and Not Religious each include about 18 percent of married individuals. The presence of children in the lives of respondents is more evenly distributed across the groups, though still highest among the more religiously engaged. We discuss the link between religion and family life in more depth in Chapter 6, but for now this helps to create a picture of how these groups differ, beyond just their connection to religion.

Thus, the demographic patterns across all four religious categories are similar, and with the exception of marital status, there are no large differences in the demographic distributions in each category. However, the Committed emerging adults are still somewhat more likely to be female, less likely to be white, and more likely to have families of their own than their less religiously engaged peers. At the other end of the religious continuum, the Not Religious have the highest percentages of emerging adults who are white, male, unmarried, and without children.

In what follows, we describe each of the four religious groups using Wave 4 survey data to show the general trends within each group, while also drawing on our interviews of emerging adults to hear how they talk about issues related to religion and spirituality. Tables 4.5 through 4.13 include survey data for all four religious groups in the areas of beliefs, centrality of faith, religious and spiritual practices, attitudes toward organize religion, and spiritual but not religious identity. For easier reference and to avoid repeating the tables for each group, Tables 4.5 through 4.13 appear at the end of the chapter.

Not Religious

We met Josh on a nice sunny day in the same location where we had first met him 10 years previously, outside of a local library located in a quiet suburban neighborhood. Josh is not religious; in fact, he describes himself as a committed atheist—although not, as he said, the "mean type." Josh was 14 years old when we first interviewed him. When we asked whether he had any religious upbringing, he said, "I was raised, well just nothing, not atheist but not a specific thing, just kinda blank. It's not like [my parents] are against it . . . it just isn't there." His parents, however, did encourage him to seek out religion if he wanted to, and although he said he never really had any desire to be part of a religion, he was always curious about religion and its claims about morality and the cosmos.

Josh, now 24 years old, is about 6'3" tall, thin, with longish, curly hair. In fact, his hair is distinctive enough to elicit a comment from at least one passerby during our interview, who called out to him: "Love your hair!"

In general, he has that sort of young artist look—black jeans, gray shirt, black boots, and of course sunglasses. He graduated with an economics degree from a well-known university on the East Coast two years before our meeting and has been looking for permanent work ever since. He is currently working with his mother in her freelance business and lives with his father and stepmother in a house at the back of their property.

Josh is very much at ease with himself and very thoughtful and articulate in his answers to our questions. When we first met Josh in 2003, he told us that he spent a good amount of time at the library, encouraged by his parents to pursue his appetite for ideas and even checking out books from different religious traditions, such as the Tao Te Ching. He seems to have kept up the reading habits he developed when he was younger, and throughout our conversation he interspersed comments related to philosophers, social theorists, and the so-called new-atheists, along with lots of other subjects of interest to him, as well as his propensity to read books about different religions.

When we asked him about his interest in religion and whether this was part of a spiritual quest on his part, he said:

> I don't think that it's completely separated from some kind of spiritual quest. 'Cause on *some* level it would be really nice to find something that I would believe in, you know? I wish that I could do that a lot of times, because of all the benefits you get from peace of mind and purpose and all this, that would be awesome. But—so that's part of why I've looked into so many different [religions]. Sorta to try them out, does that make sense?

Josh does understand the appeal of religion for people, suggesting that the certainty that religion provides is really a type of nostalgic pull to the things one may have learned in childhood. He noted that as some of his friends have faced the difficulties of adult life, they "have started to go back to childhood things, like faster than I thought that they would, you know like become more religious, or . . . more traditional." He continued, saying:

> I mean it makes sense. The world is complicated and scary a lot of times, so I think that's what they knew when they were younger, and that's the toolbox that they had built into the back of their brain. So, then it makes sense that when stuff gets too hard for them, they

go back and . . . do that stuff. So yeah, I think it's in response to fric-
tion from the outside world, probably.

In the end, even though he tries to remain open to the possibility that one
or another religion may be true, they all fail to satisfy his criteria for truth-
fulness in that they all ultimately require a sort of blind faith that he just
can't accept. He said, "I'm a very strong atheist, I would categorize myself
as, you know . . . not in the emotional sense of, like, 'God is stupid!' Not
like that . . . I basically . . . don't believe in any kind of mysticism that you
can't explain. Just reason and logic, basically."

In some ways, Josh is a unique case, with his persistent pursuit of understanding religion coupled with his insistence on using only reason
and logic to evaluate the truth claims of different religions. In other ways,
however, he offers an illustration of the type of emerging adults who are
identifying themselves as not religious. As we listened to him talk about
his beliefs about religion and his views of the world, we heard echoes of
the themes from our interviews with other Not Religious young people.
Even for Josh, a committed atheist, religion is not entirely absent from
his life. Like many other Not Religious young people, he is not completely
closed off to or antagonistic toward religion. He is open to religion as a
theoretical possibility, one that works for some people. However, there is
a distinction between religion as a theoretical possibility and religion as
personally relevant. For most of the Not Religious young people we spoke
with, like Josh, religion is just not something that holds particular relevance for them personally.

Diversity of Identities

As noted previously, Josh does not believe in God and is a self-proclaimed
atheist. His atheist identity is rare, even among those who say they are
Not Religious. Contrary to what some observers have at least implied, not
all young people who say they are not religious are explicitly secular or
identify as atheists or agnostics.[6] A first step in understanding this group
of Not Religious young people is to recognize the range of ways that they
themselves want to be identified—whether atheist, agnostic, or simply not
religious.

Table 4.4 shows how Not Religious emerging adults identify themselves
in the Wave 4 survey. Atheists make up just 13 percent of all of the Not
Religious respondents as a group and only five percent of the entire sample

Table 4.4 Self-Identity of Not Religious

	Not Religious (%)	Total Sample (%)
Atheist	13	5
Agnostic	21	9
Just not religious	38	16
Something else	28	17

Source: National Study of Youth and Religion survey 2013.

of emerging adults. Identification as agnostic accounts for 21 percent of the Not Religious group and about 9 percent of the full sample. These numbers are greater than in the general population and have increased over the years of the study, but still represent the minority belief among Not Religious emerging adults. Some reports suggest that people who do not believe in God are reluctant to identify as atheists because they fear social disapproval of their atheism.[7] Among the young people in our study who said they do not believe in God, just 30 percent identified as atheist in a separate question, though the emerging adults we interviewed did not necessarily express particular aversion to the atheist label. However, those who did identify themselves as atheists were quick to say that they were not overly aggressive in their atheism—the "mean type," as we heard Josh say. Others made similar qualifications, such as this young man, who told us:

> I used to, you know, identify as atheist . . . and for a long time [I] sort of just started being angry with some things about religion, shit like wars that happened over religion or influence in politics. Like you know what, it's just a waste of life trying, just being angry about something. . . . If people want to be religious, whatever, that's fine, that's going to happen. You know I'm not religious, but I'm not going to be actively against it anymore and go on ahead with my life, because . . . it's just not a part of my life and it never really comes up, so there's no use in even, in even thinking about it, really. I don't need it to live the kind of life I want to live and be responsible and have morals and be good to people. I know I'm on the right path and that I'm good to people.

Although there are some who identify as atheist or agnostic, it is more common for Not Religious emerging adults to report that they are "just not religious" rather than adopting a specific identity as atheist or agnostic. Some expressed the view that they were simply uninterested in those discussions and arguments and that, for them, atheism and agnosticism are just other ways of being religious. These emerging adults were happily not religious, and while they did not believe in God, taking on a specific identity as an atheist would (ironically) require a level of interest in religion that they simply did not have. For these young people, arguments either against or for God's existence were simply irrelevant to their lives. This exchange with a 23-year-old Not Religious young man was typical of this perspective:

INTERVIEWER: So you say you wouldn't describe yourself as a religious person at all?

RESPONDENT: No.

I: Do you consider yourself to be an agnostic or atheist?

R: I consider those religions.

I: You consider those religions?

R: Yeah, I mean they're . . . they're belief, so I just, I don't affiliate myself with anything.

I: Nothing?

R: Nothing.

I: You don't feel passionately about being nonreligious?

R: It's—I just think it's a choice that I've made, I don't believe in God, I don't believe in any religion, and being agnostic and atheist—those things are the religion of not being a religion. I mean, I'm not an atheist, but I'm not—I'm not anything. I guess I don't really consider myself any religion.

Another issue regarding nonreligious identity is that some religious traditions are closely linked to cultural identity. For some of the young people we interviewed, religious and cultural identity overlap, while for others, these cultural markers hold distinct meaning in their lives. In such cases, people may continue to hold on to their cultural identity even though the religious component of their identity is not particularly salient. For example, one young woman identified as Jewish while also identifying as Not Religious. In this case, the identity marker of Jewish is about her cultural heritage and does not necessarily reflect her religious identity. In reporting the demographic information of these respondents, we try to follow their own language and note both their cultural identity and religious category when they appear in the text.

Beliefs

Just as Josh was clear in his identity as an atheist, he was also clear in his rejection of all beliefs in religion or spirituality. For Josh, the bottom line was that whatever he believed had to be explainable through reason and logic. As Josh expressed it: "It's fine to believe that, but you have to be very explicit about saying I don't have a rea—like, I don't have evidence to believe this, but these are my beliefs separated from my understanding of the world."

While there are others like Josh who reject all religion and spirituality, this was not necessarily true of all the Not Religious young people we talked to. In fact, surprising numbers of Not Religious hold religious beliefs of one kind or another. Of those emerging adults who consider themselves not religious, 39 percent believe in God, compared with 31 percent who said they do not believe in God and 30 percent who are unsure. Of those Not Religious respondents who said they believe in God, 40 percent of them identify God as a personal deity who is involved in people's lives, rather than a more general concept of a supernatural force or a higher power. However, looking at the Not Religious group as a whole, just 16 percent expressed belief in a personal God.

Although many respondents acknowledged a belief in God, they seemed to be distinguishing between their belief that there *is* a God and the fact that they don't necessarily believe *in* God or feel any connection to what they believe is God. For example, this 28-year-old woman told us:

> I believe in a God and one ultimate creator, an intelligent designer of the universe. I suppose I most closely relate *him*—if you know, you have to put a term on it—so I would closely relate *him* to the Christian perspective because it's what I'm most familiar with. But I guess I'm somewhat shying away from that as I get older, in the respect that you know Christians believe that there is only one God and that is "The Christian God." I believe that there is one God, and every religion worships the same one, they just do so differently. That's kind of where I stand on God, or intelligent designer, whatever you want to call it.

Turning to beliefs about the afterlife, 32 percent of the Not Religious said they believe in heaven. For example, one young man who identified as an atheist told us what many across the spectrum of religious involvement expressed—that good people go to heaven and only really bad people end up in hell:

R: I believe that when you pass on, I don't believe that's the end of life. I do believe there is an afterlife.
I: So do you believe in a heaven and hell?
R: Yeah, pretty much. I do believe there's both.
I: What are those like to you? How do people get there?
R: To me, you know. . . . Hell is for, I mean, I look at someone who's killed someone and to me, they're going to hell. They took another person's life, you know, that's a big step to take. And then like, heaven, I look at it like my grandmother: She did everything she could in life to better her family, to better herself, you know, and I think she put all her effort in that, you know, to me, she's going to go to heaven. She did what she can to teach her children about everything and teach them—and she even taught them about God, you know, so that's the way I look at it.

Others expressed similar views. We spoke with one 27-year-old woman who describes herself culturally as Muslim, though she no longer identifies as religious, either in her beliefs or practices. She said, "I think everyone goes to heaven. I don't think there even is a hell. I think that that's something people use as a scare tactic. But I think [heaven] is just another plane where others exist. Other souls exist, other consciousness exists. . . . Just conceptually. . . . I still don't understand it, but I just know that there's something, an alternate life beyond what you know here."

Not all of our respondents were as certain about their beliefs in the afterlife as those two young people. We also heard these beliefs framed as either cosmic uncertainties or general hopes about what might happen after death. Even Josh, who said he relies on reason and evidence for his beliefs and view of the world, expressed it as something he just couldn't come to a conclusion about:

I would like to believe that there is some kind of . . . what do you call it, reincarnation? But I don't know. I, you know, I try to come at it, think about what it would be to be nothingness. And I don't know, 'cause it's nothingness. I find it really interesting to think about, but I don't have an opinion on what I think happens when we die.

Still others expressed their disbelief and disinterest in the whole idea of an afterlife as well as heaven and hell. When asked if she believed in life after death, or heaven or hell, the 28-year-old noted previously, who believes in "one ultimate creator," responded:

> Maybe. I don't . . . that really just doesn't interest me. You know, whatever may or may not be after here is not for me to know or decide, and there's absolutely no way that I could ever possibly know, so I just don't bother myself with it. I just try to live a life that I feel like is good for me and for other people too. And if there is someone with a gavel upstairs, then I hope things go in my favor, you know?

The range of perspectives about God and the afterlife among Not Religious emerging adults is mirrored in their take on religion more generally. Identifying themselves as not religious does not mean that they are closed off to the ideas of religion altogether. In fact, many are open to the possibilities of religious teachings, even if they do not personally subscribe to them. Fifty-four percent of the Not Religious reported that they think many religions may be true (compared with 41 percent who said that there is very little truth in any religion). The Not Religious are also the emerging adults most likely (69 percent) to endorse the idea that individuals are not obligated to accept all the beliefs of a particular religion but can pick and choose what to believe from any tradition. This 28-year-old woman provides an example of this type of eclectic gathering of beliefs by saying:

> I kind of take a few things from different religions, I guess. Like . . . I believe in in God, per se, whatever he looks like, or you know or whatever you want to call him. I'll just call him God. And then, like . . . I believe that we've all lived before. I believe in karma. I believe like, just different things that make sense to me [laughs]. There are some things that don't, so that's why I just can't see that being true or believing in that fully.

While there is an openness to the potential that religion may be true, this is tinged with doubt and questions. This 26-year-old woman said that she doesn't practice "one particular religion. I think I'm more of like a live by morals and treat other people with kindness—send out positive energy to people" type of person. When asked whether she had any spiritual or religious beliefs, she said, "I mean, I don't know. I really haven't thought about it lately, you know? I don't know. I don't know. Yeah, no, I just, is there a God? That's a question. I don't know." The Muslim woman whom we heard from previously responded to the same question, saying, "I actually . . . recently, kind of came—not came to conclusion, 'cause you never can really come to conclusion when it comes to God—but, I kind of . . . I'm now viewing God as something that's within us. . . . In our ability to heal, our ability to just be magnificent creatures."

Centrality of Faith

Among Not Religious young people, we see a clear distinction between beliefs *about* religion and the personal importance of religion *in* their lives. Despite having some level of belief in God, very few of those who said that they are not religious told us that spirituality or faith was particularly important in how they lived their lives, or that they expected to be more religious in the future. And less than 10 percent reported feeling close to God. For many Not Religious emerging adults, religion or spirituality is simply not a part of their daily lives or anything they regularly think about. Most are comfortable with this lack of religiosity and did not feel that they were missing anything by not being religious.

There are, however, some Not Religious young people who acknowledge that religion or spirituality still plays a role in their lives. For example, this 27-year-old said that spirituality is a part of every day for her. She said, "Yeah, it makes me more in tune to my surroundings, to the people around me, a better judge of other people. I put myself in better situations and . . . pull myself out of negative situations. I think it's just, it's kind of like what's been my guiding light."

This level of intentional spirituality, however, was rare among the Not Religious. Spiritual practice or reflection was more likely to be something that operates in the background of their lives, in some cases a residual habitus from former religiosity. For example, this 25-year-old former Baptist woman told us:

I wouldn't say I was a practicing Baptist or even practicing really anything. I believe in God, but I don't have, like, daily devotional time or, really, to be honest with you, I don't really think about it that often. But I do think that it's kind of part of my foundation, or my

background, so I guess it's still a part of me, even if it's not like the
first thing that comes out, or anything like that.

When we asked how much that modest amount of religion or spirituality is part of her everyday life, she said, "probably less than two percent,
maybe even less than that." This 28-year-old woman expressed a similar
perspective, saying:

> I'd say the spirituality aspect is definitely pretty much always pre-
> sent. It's always in the back of my mind when it comes to making
> decisions, how I interact with people. It's like love what you got with
> all your heart, love your neighbors—those are the two foundations
> for how I kind of live life.

Beyond this background presence that some spoke about, religion
does not appear to be particularly salient for most nonreligious emerging
adults. Recall, however, that this does not mean that they are closed off
to or opposed to religion. When we asked them whether they would like
to learn more about religion, many of them reported that they would.
Like Josh's continuing study of different religions, they are not opposed
to learning about religion as an intellectual exercise, so long as they are
not being asked to engage personally with religion. However, it is another
question entirely as to whether most Not Religious emerging adults would
ever engage in learning more about religion or spirituality, whether based
on their own past involvements or on curiosity about other religious traditions. Most likely, owing to their other statements about how irrelevant
religion and spirituality are in their lives, their claim to be interested in
learning more about religion is more aspirational than actual. Rather than
ever actually seeking out different forms of religious or spiritual knowledge, their stated interests are likely to remain a theoretical possibility.

Religious and Spiritual Practices

Not Religious emerging adults are by definition disconnected from religious institutions. But another important question is whether they incorporate any personal religious practice or spirituality into their lives. As we
discuss later in this chapter, 17 percent of the respondents in our study
reported that they would describe themselves as "spiritual but not religious," indicating that some elements of spirituality are present in their

lives. We asked respondents across all four religious groups about a wide range of religious practices, including public practices such as attendance at religious services, and private practices such as prayer, meditation, and reading religious or spiritual materials. Respondents were also provided a list of religious traditions and asked whether they incorporated any practices from those traditions into their own spirituality. Among the Not Religious, 37 percent reported that they do not practice any form of spirituality, while 24 percent indicated that they practice spirituality but do not include any elements of the listed religious traditions. The remaining 38 percent of the Not Religious respondents identified at least one tradition from which they incorporate elements into their own spiritual practice.

While a substantial minority of Not Religious young people make a nod to some form of spirituality in their lives, the evidence of this is sparse when we ask about specific types of religious or spiritual practices. The spiritual practice that was reported most frequently was meditation, with 19 percent reporting that they have meditated in the previous year. Yet, our in-person interviews revealed that it is rare that meditation holds any sort of spiritual meaning for the young people we spoke with. Most who meditated did so as a way to "settle their mind" or "get their thoughts together," without claiming it had any religious or spiritual meaning for them. The following 25-year-old woman provides a good example of this. She told us that she does yoga and, although she sits quietly during her yoga routine, for her it isn't spiritual or religious: "No, it's just—I guess quieting my mind, and not being, like, so frazzled. But I don't think it's like a spiritual thing." So, while they may be practicing meditation from time to time, we are hesitant to point to these data as evidence of spirituality in the lives of the Not Religious emerging adults in our study.

Twelve percent of the Not Religious reported having read religious or spiritual material within the past year, and less than 10 percent reported regular prayer. Observing a weekly day of rest or a period of fasting or self-denial was even more rare among the Not Religious, at three and four percent, respectively. Although personal prayer is not frequently reported by this group, 16 percent said they have experienced an answer to prayer within the past five years. Another 14 percent said they have witnessed a miracle during this same time period.

Thus, as we might have expected, Not Religious emerging adults reported very low rates of religious or spiritual practices such as prayer, reading spiritual or religious material, setting aside a day of rest, or giving up something as a form of spiritual discipline. Of course, it is possible that they are engaging in other types of spiritual practices that were not captured by the questions in our survey. However, the responses to our in-person interviews do not indicate that this is the case. Among the young people who identify as Not Religious, the extent of the spiritual practices we heard about were occasional references to casual prayers and maybe some meditation, though as noted, meditation was not framed as spiritual or religious in nature. In general, Not Religious emerging adults are not engaged in regular or intentional spiritual practices. To whatever extent some of them may have moved toward a "spiritual but not religious" iden-tity, it does not seem to include the element of spiritual practice.

Attitudes about Organized Religion

When scholars began to see a significant shift in the larger population to-ward identifying as a religious "None," one important explanation for the trend had to do with individuals' distancing themselves from, and dissat-isfaction with, organized religion.[8] Rather than disavowing religious be-lief and salience, the new "Nones" represented a growing distrust of the institutions of religion. While there appears to be more than that going on today, it is the case that the Not Religious emerging adults in our study are the most distanced from organized religious institutions. In response to a series of questions asking about organized religion, the Not Religious have the lowest level of confidence to report. About one-fourth of the Not Religious respondents said that they have a lot of respect for organized religion and that they have positive feelings for the religion in which they were raised. These comparisons are reversed when we asked whether mainstream religion was irrelevant for most people their age, and if they saw organized religion as a big turnoff. Not Religious individuals were far more likely to answer in the affirmative to both of those questions, with 50 percent agreeing that religion is irrelevant for their age group and 72 percent agreeing that organized religion is a big turnoff.

In comparison to the other three religious groups, the Not Religious are the most distant from and suspicious of religious institutions. In our interviews, Not Religious young people expressed this distance and dis-trust in a variety of ways. One theme we heard was a critique of the finan-cial and bureaucratic trappings that they perceive to be associated with institutions in general, and their disappointment at seeing these traits as part of religious organizations. For example, a 25-year-old told us: "I don't love it that [religious institutions] have become very corporate, like it's more of a business than it is actually a place of worship." Another 25-year-old man is representative of those emerging adults who view the leaders of organized religions as more interested in building their own empires than in serving others. He said, "I don't like organized religion. I feel like it's a scam. Everything's run by money, and they pass that plate around asking for money all the time. I don't know. Organized religion throws me . . . it leaves a bad taste in my mouth." Expressing similar sentiments, a 28-year-old said that, for him, organized religion should have "more transparency, particularly around the way that they have their finances. I think that churches kind of get a free ride to do whatever they want, and they don't pay taxes." And a 27-year-old said that for her, "Institutional religion is the same thing as any kind of institution. There's always a hierarchy, there's always some sort of bureaucracy, and that's not what . . . religion should be. In my eyes, I think religion should be more spiritual."

For others, the suspicion was related to the role of religious organizations in the lives of people. One 24-year-old said that he didn't like "institutionalized religion because I think it takes away from the human capacity to make moral decisions." A 25-year-old man spoke of religious institutions as misleading, saying that religious institutions are a source of comfort, but that was why he viewed them as "awful, because [people] look to that for their comfort, and a lot of people are just like, 'Well, I don't care if my life sucks in this world because the next world is going to be great.' And it's like no, to me, this world is heaven or hell and you make it such. There is nothing else that we know of, this is it."

Still others expressed personal experiences that had turned them off from formal religious organizations, like this 25-year-old woman:

R: You know, it's just never been a pleasant experience to be in a church and be gay, it's just not. If they don't know, they're completely okay with it. The minute that they find out, then it's a little different.
I: Have people treated you differently?
R: Oh yeah.
I: What do they say?
R: It's not as much as they say, it's how they act.

Viewed from an alternative perspective, however, we see that at least one-fourth of the Not Religious gave answers that are generally supportive of organized religion. To understand the nuance and variation within this group, it is important to keep this in mind. In our interviews,

this perspective tended to be expressed as the belief that religious institutions are fine for those who need or want to participate in them, even
though interviewees themselves weren't interested, with a clear caveat
that extreme versions of religion are not okay. One 25-year-old said that
he was "okay with it. I just am not a fan of extremism, and I'm not a fan
of what I think are wrong beliefs, because it's harming people or it's
uneducated, causing like actual institutional change. But I'm okay with
it other than that." And this 25-year-old woman said that, although she
wasn't interested in organized religion, she saw the benefits for some
people:

> It's just something I don't really do. I think that there's, like, extreme
> institutional religion and I do think, like, the extreme extremes kind
> of make me uncomfortable because I feel like some of them almost
> take away the gut feeling of right and wrong and influence people
> too much. But in general, I don't have a problem with them. I mean
> I think it's a good thing for people to have. I think a lot of people ben-
> efit from it. It's a place people can go for guidance or help and you
> know, tranquility. And for some people it gives them purpose. But
> I think the thing that really makes me uncomfortable is the extremes.

Thus, among the Not Religious, there are those who have positive regard
for religion and see its potential benefits, even if they don't personally subscribe to or affiliate with religion. And while most of the emerging adults
we interviewed said that in the future they will not become religious, some
did recognize the possibility that they *could* become involved with religion
again under the right circumstances.

For some Not Religious emerging adults, the possibility of becoming
religious in the future is related to the inevitable tough times in life that
they anticipate may prompt a return to parts of their lives that they had
left behind. Recall what Josh observed about people he knows, who in response to a "complicated and scary" world, have "started to go back to
childhood things . . . [and] become more religious." For others, this was related to particular stages of their lives, whether getting married and having
children or simply a part of the process of development that happens as
they are getting older.

For example, one 26-year-old man linked the possibility of his becoming religious to having children sometime in the future, seeing one

possible future as similar to his father's life: "My dad was actually kind of like me when he was my age, but when he had kids, he became actually religious." We asked whether he thought that might happen to him, and he replied, "That may happen to me, I mean I'm open to the idea. I don't like the prospect of it, but it may happen." And a 26-year-old woman told us, "I don't know. I think I'll still be spiritual. I would like to think that I will have developed a more regular practice by then. And I guess that I would hope that I do a little bit more homework in terms of religion and spirituality before I have offspring that I intend to be teaching those things to."

In the case of some interviewees, a possible return to religion was framed as a function of what their potential marriage partners might want or if their children were interested in religion, rather than something that they would independently choose for themselves. When asked whether she will be more religious in the future, this 25-year-old said, "I don't know. I think a lot of it will depend, like you know, on if I'm married, who I married, what they believe. I mean I could see myself being more religious." Similarly, a 24-year-old linked the possibility of her becoming religious to a shift in how interested in religion her boyfriend or her son might be, saying, "I probably might still be the same way [not religious]. Unless my son kind of drove me into something, or my boyfriend tries to get a little more religious. I would support him, but . . . maybe they might end up changing the way I see it, who knows?" And this 24-year-old man expressed a similar reluctance about the possibility of his future religiosity when he acknowledged, "I want to say less religious, but in reality, I'd imagine it's up and down. So, imagining I'll be religious again for a little bit and I'll lose it again and so on and so on. I see that go like a rocky path."

For others, the possibility of becoming religious in the future was even more unlikely, unless some miraculous event either drove them back to religion or somehow verified for them that religion was true. When we asked, "What do you think you'll be like religiously when you're 40 years old?" these two young people had similar responses:

Not religious at all (chuckles). Unless, like I said, unless something major, you know, happens to show me that there is something to believe in. I don't see it happening, but if it did, you know, I'm open minded. (25-year-old man)

Probably pretty similar, unless I have one of those supernatural experiences. That could shift things a little bit. (27-year-old woman)

The potential for any return to religion for the Not Religious emerging adults seems to represent much more of a murky potential development for them, rather than a real, concrete option, at least as they conceive of the prospect of increased religiosity now. That is, they *could* return to religion given the right circumstances, or if their needs were such that they could envision a religious institution as being able to provide for those needs. But even in this theoretical return, it is interesting to note the lack of personal agency in their responses. A return to religion would only be spurred by something outside of themselves, whether prompted by a spouse, children, a miracle, or the inevitable "rocky path" of life. Becoming more religious is not framed as an intentional decision or choice; rather, it is something that "may happen to me," as if a life of faith is something that would be imposed on them, rather than something that they could cultivate and develop. Overall, they think and talk about religion as something that they are not interested in and that is completely irrelevant to their current lives. And if it were ever to become relevant, it would not be of their own doing because very few expected to be internally driven or motivated to seek out religion in their future.

In sum, Not Religious emerging adults are largely disengaged from religion and spirituality, even though they are not completely irreligious. Religion still operates in the background for some. Some are open to the possibilities of religion, but they are not personally connected to or motivated by those possibilities. For Not Religious emerging adults, religion operates as a kind of theoretical option, but one that could only be realized under particular circumstances. The Not Religious do still maintain some beliefs, although these are more an intellectual assent rather than actual belief or faith in any religious tenets, leaving whatever belief or connection to religious institutions they have largely unrealized. For Not Religious emerging adults, religion, spirituality, and faith, while maintaining a small place in their lives, are largely irrelevant to their daily life. To the extent that religion exists at all on their radar, it is at a residual or potential level and as an unlikely option for their lives in the future.

Disaffiliated

Andrew was born into a Catholic family, and although his parents still attend church every week, he neither attends nor is interested in attending or having anything else to do with the Catholic Church. For Andrew, being Catholic is simply the result of his having been born into a Catholic family—nothing more, nothing less. Andrew's approach to his religious identity is pretty simple. He said, "If somebody asked me, 'Why are you Catholic?' Just 'cause I was raised that way, I guess." For Andrew, religion operates merely as a background part of his identity:

R: I didn't make any like big decisions like oh, I like this religion. It doesn't, in your everyday life, it doesn't come up.
I: What I'm hearing you say is that this doesn't really matter.
R: It doesn't.

Andrew is 26 years old, with closely cut hair and a light beard. He's about 5'10" tall and looks like the former high school football player he is. He is unfailingly polite in his responses to our questions and at times seems amused that we keep asking him about religion, despite the fact that he keeps telling us that none of it matters in his everyday life, that he doesn't believe any Catholic religious teachings, and in general, that he doesn't have anything to do with the Catholic Church.

We interviewed him in an outside courtyard of a shopping center, next to a Starbucks and some other fast-food stores, in an exurban area that has rapidly developed over the past 20 years and has diversified significantly over that time. He is living with his girlfriend but is in no hurry to get married. He thinks he will eventually marry her, but he makes that sound more like it would be okay, rather than something he really wants to do. He has one son with a previous girlfriend and another with his current girlfriend, who is also pregnant with his third child.

Despite the fact that he personally never attends religious services or does anything else with the Church, Andrew is not opposed to religion or Catholicism. His six-year-old son goes to Catholic school because that's what Andrew did when he was growing up, and he thinks that it is a good source of morals for his son. He's not even opposed to his son going to church, although he doesn't take him. Rather, Andrew drops his son off at his parents' house so that they can take him to church with them. Despite his lack of interest in church, he thinks that religion could be important for people his age; it just depends on where one's priorities lie.

Yeah, I mean if you want to . . . if that's in your life, it can be very relevant. If you're a believer, it's relevant to everything that you do.

So, it's . . . I guess it's to each their own. If you're a believer, yeah, it's going to be very relevant to anybody my age. But if you're not, it's just it's equally not relevant.

He continues by suggesting that religion is just another expression of where people decide to put their commitments in life:

People tend to think religions are a lot different than a gym, but they're not. It's the same thing. It's just . . . you value religion more than getting in shape. And for some people, getting in shape is a religion. So, it's kind of that every faith is fighting for everybody to get them in. 'Cause more people is better than no people.

In the end, though, Andrew said that it's just not something that he is particularly interested in: "I don't really pay attention to how they do it, though. I don't follow it."

Beliefs

When it comes to belief in God, 89 percent of Disaffiliated emerging adults in our study reported that they believe in God. More than one-half said that the deity they believe in is a personal God who is involved in people's lives. However, in contrast to the more religiously involved young people, the beliefs articulated by the Disaffiliated sound more like a general acceptance that religious claims are, or may be, true rather than any deep commitment to a religious or spiritual perspective. For example, a 28-year-old Disaffiliated who identifies as simply a "Christian" said:

I believe that you don't have to go to church in order to believe. I believe that you should, like they say, you know, treat other people the way you want to be treated. That's a spiritual thing. And then, I do not believe that you should force your spiritual beliefs on anybody. Everybody has their own choice, their own opinion, and their own option. I do believe that there are right and wrong religions, personally, but I think that everybody who's religious kind of believes that.

This 25-year-old Jewish Disaffiliated describes her ambivalence about believing in God, given the bad things that can happen in the world. She said,

"I kind of believe in God and I kind of don't. Like, I believe that he made us; I believe that he made the world; but then . . . times like 9/11, what happened in Boston—he's not there. Because I believe if he was really there, all these bad things wouldn't happen, so . . . that's why I think he's there but he's not." A similar ambivalence is noted by a former Conservative Protestant, who said that while she believes in God, she's not at all sure what that means: "I believe that there is a God, I don't know if there's a specific one God."

For others, these perspectives are more "hopes" than actual beliefs. For example, when we asked Andrew, the disaffiliated Catholic, what he believes, he replied:

> I think I have more of a hope than a faith. And the big thing about, like, Christian religion is faith. You have to believe without knowing. And I'm just hoping [*laughs*]. Like, it would be awesome. Like, if there is a God, that would be awesome, you know? My biggest thing is fear of when I die, that it just shuts off. That sucks. And that's kind of what I believe. Like your brain's done, that's it.
>
> ɪ: But you're hoping?
> ʀ: So, I hope. . . . That would be awesome. . . . It's hard to be much of a believer when I just don't, you know?

This uncertainty expressed as hope, rather than belief, was a fairly common response to our questions from those who are less involved in religious institutions:

> ʀ: God, my beliefs are so fluid. I can't even pin anything down.
> ɪ: Do you believe in God?
> ʀ: I think so [*laughs*].
> ɪ: Okay, tell me about that.
> ʀ: I would like to think that we have a purpose that's bigger than just being dropped into this earth and then just leaving. I would like to think that. (24-year-old Disaffiliated Jewish woman)

> ɪ: Do you believe in a God?
> ʀ: [*Pause*] Maybe a higher power. Maybe not . . . maybe not a being . . . a person, um . . . maybe just . . . sometimes it sounds so, like . . . contradictory. You know [chuckle]? I'm . . . higher power, yeah. I think . . . yeah. I guess. (26-year-old Disaffiliated Mainline Protestant woman)

This continued belief—or hope—among the Disaffiliated that religion just might be true is apparent in that the majority said they believe that many religions might be true and that it is okay to "pick and choose" religious beliefs, either from within their own tradition or across multiple traditions. A good example of this view is this self-identified "nondenominational Christian," who shows a typical curation of multiple sources from both within and outside of her tradition:

I: How would you describe yourself to me in terms of your religion, faith, and spirituality?

R: I am eclectic. I'm nondenominational Christian. I believe in free interpretation of the Bible based on current, personal, situational relevance. I believe in gut instincts being a direct influence of God on an individual's motives. I think that doing the right thing, trying to be the best person that you can be, making the right decisions when the time comes, really thinking it through are the things that make the difference when all is said and done. And I feel like there are elements in this earth that were put here for our healing. I wear a chakra rock for good karma.

Disaffiliated emerging adults also tend to be less certain of their beliefs about what happens after death. In answering questions about whether heaven is a real rather than imaginary place, Disaffiliated emerging adults tended to frame their responses as a belief that all—or at least most—people end up in heaven after they die, and that hell is primarily reserved for murderers and thieves. This 28-year-old Catholic was certain about heaven, less so about hell. From her perspective, hell is reserved for those who commit the most heinous of sins:

R: I believe in heaven. I don't believe in reincarnation or anything like that.

I: Do you believe in hell?

R: [*Long pause*] Yes.

I: How does someone get to hell?

R: I think murdering certain . . . um, you know like, murdering, raping, like unforgivable sins. I think there are certain things you can do and I think as long as you turn your life around. Depending on what it is. If you murder somebody, I don't really know if you're going to be forgiven for that.

Andrew illustrates how Disaffiliated emerging adults' beliefs about the afterlife—as with their beliefs about God—were mostly framed as uncertainties or hopes about what might happen after death. His uncertainties about religion in general extend to his thoughts about the afterlife:

I: Are you hoping that there's an afterlife of some sort?
R: Yes, that would be ideal. I hope that your . . . your whatever it is that you want to save . . . your soul or whatever, just the process of thinking, just goes on and that's it. That's what I hope, but it just seems so farfetched.
I: So, what do you think about things like reincarnation or . . .
R: That would be awesome, too. I kind of would like to take from all religions. Like oh, that would be awesome if that was true . . . but I really don't think any of them are going to happen.

A 28-year-old Disaffiliated Jewish woman provides a similar example of this uncertainty:

> I suppose I believe in some sort of heaven. I don't think I really believe in hell, but, I think we all go somewhere after this, and there's something more you know, our soul leaves, our bodies stay but our soul leaves, and there's something. I don't know what it is though.

Disaffiliated emerging adults are neither complete unbelievers nor atheists. They are open to the possibilities of religious beliefs. But beyond believing, or hoping, that there is a God, the particulars are a bit fuzzy. They like the idea of religious beliefs but can't quite articulate what those beliefs might be. And even though they hope that there might be something beyond themselves, this possibility doesn't seem to occupy a lot of their time or thinking. Rather, they seem satisfied to remain in this ambivalent space where they are neither believers nor unbelievers, not really knowing what they finally believe about religion, God, and the afterlife.

Centrality of Faith

Disaffiliated emerging adults in our study are similar to the Not Religious in their hope that there may be some truth to religious claims, but they seem to be keeping their options more open regarding the role of religion and faith in their own lives. As we spoke with Disaffiliated emerging adults, it became evident that these sentiments seem related as much to their residual religious identity and upbringing as to their current status as Disaffiliated. Recall Andrew's statement that his Catholic identity is a product of his upbringing, but it doesn't matter for his everyday life. He is not alone in his view; only about one-fourth of the Disaffiliated young people in our study reported that their faith is very or extremely important in their daily lives. Like Andrew, many Disaffiliated emerging adults expressed a disconnect between their religious identity and its importance in their lives. For example, this 24-year-old Disaffiliated woman who identifies as Jewish, framed Jewishness as a key part of her identity, but with no real religious significance:

I: How much would you say that Judaism is part of your everyday life?

R: Um, it's not. I wouldn't say it really is. No.

I: Is it a big part of your identity, do you think?

R: Yeah! I would say like it's not part of my life like when I make decisions, I don't like refer to Judaism. But I would say, like, when I would describe who I am, that's like one of the first things . . . it's like an individualizing factor.

And when we asked this 24-year-old Disaffiliated Conservative Protestant if religion was a part of his daily life, he answered, "I'd like to say yes, but nah, really, I really can't say that, no." Thus, religion is still a part of these Disaffiliated young people's lives in that they continue to identify with a particular religious tradition, but beyond acknowledging the religious identity in which they were raised, it simply is not at all relevant to their lives.

There are other Disaffiliated emerging adults, however, who seem to be caught between feeling that religion and spirituality have little or nothing to do with their daily lives and thinking that they *should* have more of a presence in their lives. A 27-year-old man provides a good example of this response:

I: How would you say that your faith or religion influences your life?

R: Not as much as it should [laughs].

I: Okay [laughs]. What makes you say that?

R: Just, you know, some of the stuff,—you know, nobody, nobody's the, the perfect ideal of a Christian or whatever, I mean it. And it, just, you know, there's a lot of things I could maybe do better on. Do differently, I guess.

Similarly, a 24-year-old Disaffiliated Conservative Protestant said that, for her, religion was a part of her life, "a hundred percent. It's always in the back of my mind," but leaves undefined what that actually means for her. It seems that, although religious beliefs are present, they are not particularly salient for this group of young people. While 89 percent of the Disaffiliated emerging adults believe in God, just 27 percent said that they feel very or extremely close to God. Those who said they are becoming less religious outnumber by two to one those who said they have become more religious in the past five years. The majority, 63 percent, reported staying the same religiously during this time period.

These responses help us understand one of the key distinctions between the Not Religious and the Disaffiliated. They are equally distant from religion in that neither group attends religious services. However, in addition to maintaining a religious identity, many Disaffiliated emerging adults still have some sense that religion should be part of their life, even if it isn't in practice. In leaving the door open to religion, whether through vague religious beliefs or an acknowledgement that religious institutions have some positive benefits, these emerging adults see religion as something that they *could* call on in times of need.[9]

Religious and Spiritual Practices

Disaffiliated emerging adults are less likely than the Marginal or Committed, but more likely than the Not Religious, to engage in spiritual practices such as prayer, reading spiritual or religious books, or regularly setting aside a day of rest or giving up something as a form of spiritual discipline. However, when we asked whether they drew any spiritual practices from other religious traditions, only 14 percent of the Disaffiliated said they did not practice spirituality at all. The remaining 86 percent identified at least some spiritual practices in their lives. For example, 17 percent have read religious books at some point in the last year, while about one-fourth of the Disaffiliated reported that they pray at least daily.

The particular nature of their spiritual practices, however, seems to fit with the larger picture of the Disaffiliated as connected to the possibility of religion, if not the practice and implementation of religion. For instance, this 24-year-old Disaffiliated Jewish young man talked about prayer as a form of self-reassurance rather than as a means of connecting to God or a higher power:

i: Do you ever pray?

r: [*Sighs*] Kind of. Um, not so much traditionally. There were many times in college where I would go through periods of acute stress and self-doubt, usually when we got our finals, when everyone's experiencing that, and prayer for me was never something for it to be answered. It's more results in opportunity to like . . . it's a mixture of reassuring myself through prayer and also [*laughs*] almost like covering my bases. Say like, 'Hey, feelin' lost, 'n like I could use some help.' Like [*laughs*], you know, I could use a hand here.

Similarly, this 26-year-old Disaffiliated Catholic female said: "I pray often. Maybe not every day, but a couple times a week." When we asked what she prayed for, she replied, "To keep everybody safe and healthy, I think that's the main thing I pray about." And this 24-year-old said that she prayed, "probably several times a week" and that her prayers were mainly to ask God "to watch over my family and friends and if I have, like, something going on, to help me get through it or, you know, like I hope you have a plan for me, that kind of stuff, to get better or to have a better job or to help me with this."

Thus, Disaffiliated emerging adults are still holding on to some elements of religion and spirituality in their lives. They are not religiously engaged, but they still acknowledge the possibility of religious meaning and are not ready to give up their own religious identity, however distant it may be from religious organizations.

Attitudes about Organized Religion

Responses from Disaffiliated emerging adults to the questions about organized religion continue to highlight their liminal state. Although they do not attend religious services, the Disaffiliated are more than twice as likely as the Not Religious to say that they have respect for organized religion and are almost three times as likely to say that they have positive feelings for the religion that they grew up in. When asked whether organized religion is irrelevant or a big turnoff, just over one-third agreed. The remaining two-thirds of the Disaffiliated do not have particularly negative views of organized religion. These young people were more likely to answer that religion was—or at least could be—relevant and to disagree that it was a turnoff. As we heard from Andrew at the beginning of this section, "If you're a believer, it's relevant to everything that you do. But if you're not, it's just, it's equally not relevant."

Others told us that they believe that religion serves a good purpose in society, although they tended to frame this in a way that at least implicitly emphasized their distance from organized religion. A 23-year-old Disaffiliated emerging adult said that she appreciated the diversity of religious groups in the United States: "It's nice that we have people in this country that believe in lots of different things and have the freedom to practice and believe in what they want to." A similar sentiment was voiced by a 26-year-old Disaffiliated Catholic, who said, "I think religion in general can be a very helpful thing for society . . . if it's practiced with a bit of care, and following the core of its beliefs. In all reality religion—all it does is promote a more peaceful, loving, caring society, in most cases."

Thus, for the Disaffiliated, it seems that their lack of involvement is not likely driven by negative feelings about religious institutions themselves. While negative feelings toward religious institutions may characterize a small subset of the Disaffiliated, the majority continue to demonstrate the "benign positive regard" for religion that we have seen throughout the years of this study.[10] It also does not seem that they are rebelling against their own religious upbringing, given that 71 percent reported positive feelings for the religion in which they were raised. But having positive feelings, or seeing the good that religion can do in society, does not necessarily translate into a willingness to be engaged and committed to their religion or to religious groups.

In sum, while the Disaffiliated are neither completely unbelievers nor atheists, they maintain only a fuzzy set of beliefs and a liminal connection to religion. Still, they have not severed that connection completely. The Disaffiliated tend to hope there is something bigger than themselves but are not quite sure what that might be or how they can make any rational sense of it. They remain doubtful—not willing to reject the possibility of God or the supernatural completely, yet uncertain what they really believe about religion.

In contrast to Not Religious emerging adults, who don't seem to feel the same sort of regret about their distance from religion, some of the Disaffiliated think religion should be part of their lives, even though it is not currently and seems to be an unlikely addition to their lives in the future. Religion is just not a viable option for their expenditure of time and commitment. It occupies a secondary space where it would be nice if it were true, and they may even participate in some limited forms of spiritual practice. But these practices, such as they are, are idiosyncratic to these individuals and their backgrounds. The Disaffiliated are not opposed to religion and do not exhibit strong negative feelings toward it, but they aren't particularly interested in committing to any religious beliefs or communities, and, in their view, religion doesn't really affect their lives in any practical sense.

Marginal

Maria is a fascinating person to have a two-hour conversation with. When we last interviewed her, she had just graduated from dental assistant school. In the five years between interviews, she had gone on to get other certifications so that she would be qualified to assist with more advanced procedures, such as oral surgery. She is very confident in herself and her abilities and is driven to make more of herself. In her own words, she has set her sights on "moving up the corporate ladder."

Maria is a 27-year-old woman who was very comfortable answering any question we asked her. In fact, she often answered our questions before we finished them! In her telling, she had to take charge of her life from an early age and really enjoys it. She talked about her parents as drug addicts and how she's taken over their house and mortgage. She has big plans for herself—although those plans primarily have to do with making more money and are short on specifics. She's thinking ahead in her life to the next thing she can do to make more money and be more successful. Maria has two daughters (ages six and one). She also gave birth to a still-born child, an experience that changed her outlook and ultimately made her more serious about how she approaches her life and what she wants to accomplish.

When we asked about her perspective on religion, she revealed an interesting amalgam of religious beliefs and views. She and her "significant other"—they have been together for nine years, are not married, and have no plans for marriage—recently started attending services at a local Calvary Chapel about once a month. Maria said that she believes in God and that Jesus was just another human. She prays about four times a week and believes in reincarnation (which is a holdover from her experiences on a local Native American reservation) as well as karma. When we asked about her experience at Calvary Chapel, she said that "they sing too much" and that she would "rather hear the scriptures than hear all the singing." When we asked her about the importance of religion in her life she said, "Oh, I would say, like, five-percent. I don't know."

i: What would that five percent look like?

r: Well, I mean, it doesn't really bother me. I'm not sitting here, like, what would Jesus do in this situation, or am I going to be judged for this? But, as long as I live my life the way I should and I'm not doing harm to others or doing things where karma would bite me, you know what I mean, then I think I'm kind of okay.

For Maria, religion is one involvement among many that vie for her attention, and not necessarily for obvious spiritual reasons. She attends Calvary Chapel as a way to get some spiritual content in her life—she finds it "peaceful" and "people-oriented"—but it also has a nostalgic appeal, because that is where her mother would occasionally take her when she was a child. In the end, she doesn't see religion as particularly relevant or integral to her life:

I think I can get by without having a religion, you know, I think a lot of people could. I know I don't have to sit there and go to church every day, I don't need to pray every day or anything like that, I can still make it, but it's just nice to know that you have something out there other than yourself watching out for you.

For Maria, this view extends to others in her generation: "I think a lot of teenagers, young adults these days don't need [religion]." When we asked whether church could be an option for young people, she replied, "I think it's . . . a slim option."

Maria is an example of a group of emerging adults we are referring to as Marginal. Marginals are those who attend religious services at least occasionally—for our purposes, generally once a month or less. Marginal emerging adults are similar to the Disaffiliated in how they express their beliefs and in the way that they pursue religious and spiritual practices. What sets them apart from the Disaffiliated is their willingness to be somewhat active in a faith community, however marginal their participation may be. In the following sections, we examine the facets of religiosity expressed by this group and illustrated by Maria.

Beliefs

Marginal and Disaffiliated emerging adults are very similar in their religious beliefs. The rates of belief in God and belief in heaven are the same for both groups, though Marginals are more likely to report belief in a personal God. Marginals lean a little bit more in the direction of religious exclusivity, though not by a lot. Sixty-seven percent said that many religions may be true, and one-half reported that it is okay to "pick and choose" among religious beliefs. Overall, they share much more in common with the Disaffiliated than with the Committed.

In our interviews with Marginal emerging adults, most expressed their belief in God, but they sounded somewhat unsure of what, or who, God is. Some had fairly orthodox beliefs, while others had developed their own conception of God. When we asked them to describe how they understood who or what God is for them, we got a mix of answers that, in different ways, demonstrated their limited involvement with religion. Most, like this 27-year-old Catholic woman, framed their understanding of God in uncertain generalities. She told us that she believes "there's something that created us and the world that we live in. I don't necessarily think that he, you know, messes with, like, the day-to-day occurrence of, you know, what we're doing. But I think he's, I think there's something, there." When we asked whether she believes in Jesus, she answered, "I don't know [*laughs*]. Maybe [*laughs*]. I mean, I think there probably was a man named Jesus who, you know, was a miraculous being, but I don't know if he was the Son of God."

Similarly, this 26-year-old Mainline Protestant described her view of God as somewhat remote, but available if she had any problems or needed guidance:

> I always envisioned him up in heaven. Yeah, I mean, I don't think that he has all the answers and I don't think that he's there to give you the answers. Otherwise that would just be too easy. But I do think he's there to be able to give you advice and guidance when you might feel those moments of struggle, just to be able to have someone to talk to I guess [who] might be able to show you a sign, maybe, which direction you should take.

When asked, she described Jesus as "someone that could be inspiration, just for the, you know, the struggle and the sacrifice that he made."

Other Marginal emerging adults, however, gave a more abstract description of how they understood God. For example, a 25-year-old Jewish woman told us that, for her, God was "an explanation for things you can't explain." And a 26-year-old Catholic man said that God was ". . . forgiveness, happiness, comfort. Probably mostly comfort." He added that he believed that Jesus was "God, or God's son, or God basically."

When we asked Marginal young people whether they believed in the afterlife and whether they thought that heaven was a real place, most expressed a belief in the afterlife and heaven, although some were a bit unsure. Fewer of them said that they believed in hell. Those who were more certain of the existence of heaven described it as "wonderful" or a place of rewards after having lived a good life. A 26-year-old Catholic woman said, "Yes, I believe in heaven and I believe in hell." When we asked what she thought heaven and hell were like, she replied, "I really don't have any idea, other than being taught and believing that heaven is better than you could ever imagine, just the most wonderful place ever. And hell was the opposite of that." Her understanding of how people get to either heaven or hell was typical of most Marginal responses:

I: How do you think people get to heaven or hell?

R: [*Pause*] I would say heaven, just . . . trying to be the best person you can be. And asking for forgiveness when you aren't the best person that you can be. See, hell, I guess, I would say ultimately, if you [*sigh*]. If you commit a lot, a lot of horrible sins, like murder or anything like that, and you're truly not sorry. 'Cause I have always been taught that if you murder, or even if somebody killed 20 people, but if they've asked for forgiveness, they will not go to hell.

This description of heaven and hell was typical among Marginals: heaven was consistently described as a pleasant or wonderful place of rewards for good deeds performed during one's life, while hell—if they actually believed in it—was a place of punishment, usually reserved for those who commit the most heinous acts such as murder or rape. A typical description comes from this 28-year-old Conservative Protestant:

R: I believe in heaven and hell.

I: What do you think heaven and hell are like?

R: I think . . . hell is a place for punishment, and heaven is a place where you're . . . you're rewarded.

I: How do you think people get there?

R: By the way your life was lived—good deeds and bad deeds.

This Jewish young woman has a similar view:

ɪ: Do you believe in heaven or hell?

ʀ: Not hell.

ɪ: And what is heaven like to you?

ʀ: Pleasant. It's, I mean, I haven't been there.

ɪ: Okay. How do people get to heaven?

ʀ: By working off their sins.

Finally, similar to the Disaffiliated, some Marginals were uncertain whether they believed in life after death, or what it might entail. This 27-year-old Catholic provides a good example of this uncertainty:

ɪ: Do you believe in life after death?

ʀ: I don't know.

ɪ: You don't have a sense of what might happen when we die?

ʀ: I mean the idea of life after death is nice, right? You know you could always, you know, continue on in heaven or wherever, but I don't know. Like, when a spider dies, does he go to heaven?

Like those of the Disaffiliated, the beliefs of the Marginals were marked by uncertainty. The uncertainty, though, was of a different character. For the Disaffiliated, there was an uncertainty about whether God, heaven, and hell exist. The Marginals were more certain that there is a God and that heaven exists. But they were not necessarily able to articulate exactly what that means; their uncertainty lies in the details and the implication of these beliefs, rather than in uncertainty about the existence of God and heaven or in the concepts themselves. It is as if, by acknowledging God's existence, it dawns on them that perhaps the existence of a supernatural being should be followed by some sort of response to this reality—that perhaps they ought to have some understanding about this God and the implications of the fact that God exists. But at the same moment, they also realize that the "so what then?" question that follows from acknowledging this existence is a hard nut to crack with the few theological tools they have at their disposal.

Centrality of Faith

When examining the importance of faith in the lives of Marginal emerging adults, we see more of a distinction between the Marginal and the Disaffiliated, though they are still very distinct from the Committed.

Almost half (45 percent) said that faith is very or extremely important in their daily lives. This compares with 26 percent of the Disaffiliated, on the one hand, and 87 percent of the Committed, on the other. Thirty-two percent reported feeling very or extremely close to God—about half the rate we see among the Committed. While the majority of them have remained the same religiously, more than one-fourth reported having become more religious since the last survey. One clear distinction between the Marginal and Disaffiliated is the role they envision religion playing in their future. While Marginals do not currently attend religious services very often, 61 percent said they expect that they will be attending services when they are 35 years old, compared with just 27 percent of the Disaffiliated.

Despite the obvious differences between the Marginal and Disaffiliated groups, each demonstrates at least some interest in religion, though not as a central part of their lives. Recall Maria, who, when we asked how important religion was in her everyday life, estimated its importance at "five percent" and said that "it doesn't really bother me . . . as long as I live my life the way I should . . . then I think I'm kind of okay." Other Marginal emerging adults described the role of religion and spirituality in similar ways, suggesting that it operates in the background of their daily lives. In other words, religion is something that can be accessed, but it remains mostly inactivated in their daily lives. A 26-year-old Catholic said that, for her, "it's not something I think about often, it's more so I just *do*—like, if I was to say a prayer, it's not something that I really so much realize that it's like a religious part of the day." A 25-year-old Jewish man responded similarly:

ɪ: How much would you say religion or spirituality is part of your everyday life?
ʀ: Some, a little bit.
ɪ: And what is that little bit?
ʀ: Because your religion not only shapes society if you're Judeo-Christian, but it kind of shapes the way that you grew up, and the way that you grew up affects your belief system. And your belief system makes you who you are.
ɪ: So, is this on a conscious level, or . . . ?
ʀ: Sometimes, sometimes.

While these responses were fairly typical of Marginal emerging adults, some claimed that religion is part of their lives but were not certain how to articulate the specific role that it plays. A 26-year-old Mainline Protestant woman said that for her, religion is "part of my life every day. Like, percentage-wise, or . . . I mean, like, every day. There's always something. I kind of think that it's something that helps guide my life, I guess, is a good way to put it." This young woman seems to be searching for the answer even as she tries to express her response to us. For Marginals like her, there is a sense that spirituality is a part of their lives and that they believe it should be, but they have not thought particularly intentionally about it and struggle to articulate an answer to the question about the role that religion or spirituality plays in their daily lives.

Religious and Spiritual Practices

As with each of our other groups, prayer is the most common spiritual practice among the Marginal respondents, with 38 percent saying that they pray at least daily and more than half saying they have experienced a specific answer to prayer in the last five years. Yet, what they mean by prayer, as most of them acknowledged, isn't necessarily a set-aside time of quiet contemplation and interaction with the divine. Rather, prayer for Marginals—as for the Disaffiliated and Not Religious who also pray—tends to be spontaneous and random, depending on what they are doing and experiencing. This 29-year-old, who occasionally attends a Unity Church, said that she keeps "a constant dialogue kind of internally." She continued, "Prayer, in like a literal definition, I don't know if I actually am praying, but it's kind of like a constant check-in, in how I feel and you could say I pray." Similarly, a 26-year-old Mainline Protestant woman said:

> I think that it depends on . . . gosh, I don't know. I feel like I . . . I think it kind of depends on what I might be going through as far as when I really sit down and say a true prayer. I think that I, you know, will make small prayers here and there, like, oh, you know, "Please God, don't let me get into a car accident" or things like that. I feel like that happens every day. But if . . . when I sit down and really, like, pray hard for something . . . it kind of depends on what's going on in my life.

Others, however, did try to have a regular time to pray, as this 27-year-old Catholic told us: "I try to pray every night, if I don't fall asleep first *[laughs]*." And a 28-year-old Conservative Protestant said that he tries to pray "at least a few times a week."

About one-fourth of the Marginal emerging adults said that they have read religious material in the previous year. But, as with prayer, this practice seems fairly irregular and more aspirational in terms of their thinking— that perhaps they should be reading religious books or other spiritually oriented material. A typical response to our question about reading the Bible came from a 26-year-old Catholic, who said, "Nowadays, no, not really, so actually in the future I hope to have more time to do that." Another said that yes, she reads the Bible, but not "as frequently as I should."

Attitudes about Organized Religion

Marginal emerging adults present a somewhat conflicted perspective on organized religion and its role in their lives. On the one hand, they are still connected to organized religion by way of their occasional attendance at religious services. On the other hand, however, their occasional attendance limits the likelihood that they are strongly connected to or identified with these religious organizations. As we might expect, then, their responses to these questions fall in between the Disaffiliated and the Committed. Two-thirds continue to have a lot of respect for organized religion, while only about one-fourth think that it is a big turnoff or irrelevant for most people their age. Moreover, 79 percent said they have positive feelings for the religious tradition they were raised in.

Overall, the young people in the Marginal group are not particularly antagonistic toward organized religion, and in fact seem favorable toward it, although they don't seem to have any particular need to become more involved in religious institutions. For example, Maria—introduced at the beginning of this section—told us that she could "get by" without religion, as could most young people, but that it was "nice to know that you have something out there other than yourself watching out for you." For Maria, going to church was, at best, a "slim option" for most young people.

This was a common sentiment among Marginals: while they profess no antagonism toward religious institutions, they simply do not seek, or need, any greater level of participation. A Conservative Protestant man told us, "I don't believe you have to go to church. You know, I believe Jesus Christ died for my sins, and if you repent, you'll be forgiven, accepted into heaven." And a Mainline Protestant woman expressed a common refrain, indicating a residual feeling of obligation that was not sufficiently intense to motivate her to increase her involvement:

> I think it's one of those things where I always say, like, "Well I should probably go to church," and then I just don't go. But I don't feel like it makes me a bad person that I don't go. And I don't think that it makes me any less of a religious person that I don't go. I don't know. I guess it's just . . . it's not like on the top of my list to make sure that I go to church.

However, some Marginals did express their dissatisfaction and disagreement with religious institutions, usually around issues like LGBTQ identity, abortion, and gay marriage. An example of this type of response came from a Catholic woman who told us that, while she agreed with most of what the Catholic Church taught, "There are certain things that they teach that I disagree with. One being the whole gay marriage thing. Another would probably be . . . certain things like birth control, things like that I also disagree with." This perspective is similar to what we heard from the Disaffiliated, who did not want to be told what to think and believe and how to act by religious institutions or religious authorities. Rather, they seem to want to engage with institutions on their own terms, attend when they feel like it, and believe and act how they see fit, rather than conform to a particular religious tradition or instructions from a formal religious leader.

In sum, Marginal emerging adults occupy the space between the Disaffiliated and the Committed, although they seem to be more like the Disaffiliated in their uncertainty, their difficulty articulating their beliefs, and their lack of any regular spiritual practice. They do, however, place greater importance on faith in their daily lives than do the Disaffiliated.

In this way, Marginals maintain a level of occasional attendance but resist a greater level of commitment. It is unclear whether they continue to attend services because of their commitment to the importance of religion, or if their occasional attendance is what serves to keep religion a presence in their lives. In any case, there seem to be two types of Marginals. The first are those who are simply hanging on with their marginal involvement in the hope that something about religion might prove to be true, perhaps providing answers to questions that they can't quite articulate, and thus potentially gaining salience in their lives. The second are those like Maria, who appear to be perfectly content to occasionally attend religious services without considering any greater level of commitment, either at church or in their personal practices. For these young people, religion functions as an occasional event and provides a little "something extra" in their lives. But religion does not make great demands of them; rather, it rounds out their lives without making too many waves.

Committed

Amber, a 26-year-old whose father is a pastor in a Pentecostal church, is in many ways a typical Conservative Protestant: she has remained committed to her Christian faith, although she now attends a non-Pentecostal church that emphasizes peace and justice in its theology. She graduated from an evangelical college with a degree in psychology and spent the next year working as a waitress while saving money for a two-year mission trip to Europe, where she worked with young women who had been victims of human trafficking. While on her mission, she maintained a long-distance relationship with her boyfriend, whom she married upon returning to the United States. When we interviewed her, she and her husband had just celebrated their one-year anniversary. She still lives near her hometown, which is also near where she went to college, so she has friends and family in the area. She looks forward to having children and being a stay-at-home mom.

When we interviewed Amber, it became evident that, for her, religion—while important in her life—operated simply as one of her responsibilities and commitments rather than as the core motivating factor in her life. She enjoys singing, so she sings in the worship band at her church. She said that she thinks of Christianity more as a "mindset" than a set of rules and said that she doesn't feel like her faith is necessarily obvious to others at her work, although she does want to influence them through how she lives her life. Although she attends church regularly, she is somewhat ambivalent about institutionalized religion, believing it to be a mix of good and bad: "When the church organizes, it has incredible potential for good, and when it organizes to just control people or just be greedy with money or whatever, it can be very bad." She does believe that churches have great potential to solve different social problems, such as hunger, poverty, or human trafficking, if only they "got together and really organized themselves." But, she added, "most Christians, me included, aren't doing their jobs."

As a group, emerging adults we label as Committed are those for whom religion is clearly a part of their lives. By definition, the Committed group includes those who are regularly attending religious services at least two or three times per month. We also see a variety of other ways in which religion plays a role in their lives. What all of the Committed share in common is that they have settled into their religion and appear to be carrying it into adulthood. Through the course of our interviews, however, we came to see that, within this group of young people that we consider to be religiously committed, there are two distinct subgroups.

The first is a smaller group of individuals—like Kristen, whom we met in Chapter 1—for whom faith is a driving force and a central motivator in their daily lives. These are the emerging adults who can clearly articulate what they believe and how those beliefs affect their daily lives, and who are regularly and intentionally involved in religious or spiritual practices. The second and larger group of Committed emerging adults are represented by Amber. These young people seem to have settled into a more routine approach to religion, in which it remains an important part of their lives on one level, yet appears to be just one more regular aspect of their lives, like commuting to work or going to the grocery store. For these young people, religion does not necessarily hold compelling authority in their lives, but rather is part of the larger package of "a good life" and is available for them when it serves to meet particular needs. Thus, in general, not unlike those in the Marginal and Disaffiliated groups (and to a much lesser degree the Not Religious), these Committed emerging adults draw on religion for their own well-being, though it does not make significant demands of them or their time.

In this section we examine the general trends among the Committed emerging adults, while keeping in mind the distinction between the different types of religious commitment we heard among this group.

Beliefs

In many ways, the Committed emerging adults are as we would expect when it comes to their religious beliefs, with most holding to conventional beliefs. Among the Committed, fully 98 percent believe in God, and 83 percent identify God as a personal deity who is involved in peoples' lives. Not surprisingly, Committed emerging adults are more likely than emerging adults in the other groups to say that they believe in heaven. Conversely, the Committed are less likely to believe that it is okay to pick and choose religious beliefs, or that many religions may be true—although roughly one-third of the Committed do agree with these statements. Yet, in the

context of our interviews, it became clear that there is significant variation among Committed emerging adults in how they are able to articulate
the particulars of their religious beliefs. In this articulation of beliefs, we
see the distinction between the religiously motivated and the religiously
routinized.

Amber provides an example of those Committed emerging adults who,
on the one hand, are fairly certain of their beliefs, but when asked to tell
us what they believe, tended to provide only general statements of belief
without too many specifics. When we asked Amber what she believes, she
replied, "Well, the Apostles Creed, I basically follow that. That's the gist of
it." When we asked what she believed about God, she said, "To me God
is good. He is compassion. He is all that is beautiful in the world. This
sounds really trippy, but [*laughs*] I don't know how to put it. He is just.
I mean there's a lot of words. There's a lot of words. Gracious. Merciful.
Lots of things."

A 28-year-old Catholic woman presented her beliefs with a similarly
general description:

i: Do you believe in God?
r: Yeah, absolutely. I believe he created the world. I believe he kind of has
    our path set for us. I think he does give you free will. That's the most
    important thing he gave you, you can make right decisions or you can
    make wrong decisions. That's still your decision.

This 25-year-old Unitarian woman is another example of those who provided a generalized description of their beliefs and, like some Marginals,
seemed to be struggling to understand the specifics that underlay the
generalities:

I believe people have souls, and I think it has to do with the way
that we're—I think it's people, and the way that we connect to one
another and also other living things. But life is really a force, and
I think that collective life is—there's something collective about the
way that we are alive together. I think that . . . people have spirit, and
there's something that is what enables us to connect to one another
that's not just, you know, neurons firing in a certain way.

In a similar manner, this 25-year-old Latter-day Saints (LDS) man responded that he believed that life "is a creation. And that it's just too,

it's too beautiful to be something by accident. And that . . . people do have a spirit about them. I find that some people are more in tune to different . . . feelings, emotions, spirits—stuff like that, rather than others."

As we noted previously, there are also Committed young people who are able to articulate their beliefs with greater precision. Kristen—mentioned earlier and in Chapter 1—is one of the most fluent about her beliefs among those we interviewed. Here, again, is her immediate response when we asked her to tell us what she believed:

> I believe that the Bible is true, that it's the word of God and it can be proved throughout history to be accurate. I believe that God is the creator. That he made man, that he made the earth, and I believe that God lives in heaven, where it's the perfect place. Nothing bad happens there, you always have health insurance [laughs], and . . . It's the perfect place.

She continued:

> I believe that God loves us. . . . I believe that there is sin, and I believe that there there's a payment for that sin. That none of us could pay because no one's perfect, although we try. So, I believe that God sent his son Jesus, who left his perfect home in heaven to come live here on earth and to pay the result of our sin, because he was perfect. So, I believe that Jesus paid for our penalty by dying on the cross. That he was dead and he rose again three days later. And that when we confess our sins, and that we choose to also believe in God, that he forgives us of our sins and so we have a new identity that once we were dead spiritually but now we're alive spiritually.

Very few of the Committed emerging adults had as much to say about their beliefs as Kristen, but they still have a firm grasp on what they believe. This 27-year-old Conservative Protestant was not as effusive about his beliefs as Kristen, but his response demonstrates a similar certainty and specificity that was missing in what we heard from the more routinized Committed emerging adults:

> I think that there is only one God. There is only Jesus, and he's the only . . . savior, so that's how I think that other religions are not

true. And so I think that Christianity is the only truth. I believe in the Trinity, and I believe that after you die, you either go to Hell or Heaven, and we're all going to be judged at one point and that Jesus is, is God. That's our only savior, true heaven. That's what I believe.

When we asked the Committed emerging adults to describe their beliefs about life after death, most were certain that there was an afterlife, although some were less certain about heaven and hell and how a person might end up in either place. For example, Amber told us that she believes in life after death, but that she has "no clue" as to what that might actually be. She told us, "I would never presume to say what that's like. Like, heaven, I don't think is this place with gold castles in the clouds. I don't know what it is. I just believe it, but I have no idea what the specifics are, and I'm kind of okay with it."

A 28-year-old Mormon woman told us that she believes in God and that she believes that "as long as you're a good person and make good choices, you will go to heaven. And by choices, I mean, like, you don't rob a bank or not even that because you can repent and be sorry for that. But maybe, like, don't kill anybody, and be nice [*laughs*]." A 28-year-old Catholic said that she imagined life after death as a "happy, quiet place that's very light and with friends and family that I'm no longer with." She added that she believes in heaven and hell but that "hell is not fire and brimstone, I believe it's just dark. I believe it's the absence of love—that's what I believe in."

The more religiously motivated Committed emerging adults gave responses that expressed more certainty, along with views about the afterlife that evince a deeper knowledge of their religious traditions. Kristen once again provided a more definitive response, saying, "I believe that there is a heaven and a hell, and that if you die not knowing Jesus, that you will spend eternity in hell. But if you die knowing Jesus, you will spend eternity in heaven." And this 28-year-old Conservative Protestant said: "I definitely think there's an afterlife and a heaven for those who have received salvation, and then hell and ultimately the circle of fire after, you know . . . the long haul of the revelation period and all that."

Thus, religious beliefs among the Committed are fairly conventional, if not always fully in agreement with finer theological points. And, despite the fact that they regularly participate in services at religious institutions, there are distinct differences in their ability to articulate their beliefs. Among those who are more motivated by their faith, we heard clearer and more confident statements of religious belief. By contrast, among the majority of Committed emerging adults for whom religion seems to be more of a routinized component of their lives, we heard more uncertainty, as they were unable or uninterested in clearly articulating specific beliefs. That relatively few of the Committed emerging adults we spoke with were able to clearly articulate their beliefs is something we have seen in each wave of this study, dating back to when they were teenagers. Yet, this inarticulateness does not seem to be specifically related to their age, as some reviewers suggested was the case when our respondents were teens. Rather, as they have grown up, their lack of ability to articulate their beliefs has remained, perhaps because there is no reason for them to have well-articulated beliefs. They have simply accepted their faith as they have experienced it throughout their lives.

Centrality of Faith

For further evidence about the centrality of faith in the lives of Committed emerging adults, we turn to the questions of religious salience. The emerging adults in the Committed group are more likely than those in other groups to say that faith is an important part of their everyday lives. Among the Disaffiliated and Marginal respondents, we saw that religion did not play a central role in their lives, with less than half of respondents identifying faith as very important to them. While they held some religious beliefs and had varying levels of connection to religious practices, religious faith was for the most part just not salient for them. In contrast, Committed emerging adults offer a view of how religion can be a more integral part of one's life. Eighty-seven percent of the Committed respondents said that faith is very or extremely important in daily life. For the religiously motivated Committed respondents, their religious faith is a core element of who they are and how they live. For example, one 27-year-old man replied, "I think it shapes a lot of my life. I mean the way that I live my life, to interact with other people. Decisions on hobbies and social gatherings . . . just the way that you treat people and your decision-making abilities." This type of response was most common among the religiously motivated Committed emerging adults. As a 25-year-old Mormon young man told us:

> It affects me a lot. It makes me the person I am, a lot of the time people find me to be a little bit different. I don't swear; some

people look at that as odd. I don't really drink anymore because of that . . . and some things that I do or practice, they find it different. They might not know why I do it, but they do notice it.

A 27-year-old Conservative Protestant woman answered, "How much is it? Pretty much it's who I am. I mean, I base decisions on my spirituality understanding and religion understanding, so yeah, it's pretty much who I am, so everything."

Yet, even as we see religious salience among the Committed in ways that we do not see it among the other groups, it is not universal within this group of young people. While few would deny that religion is important in their lives, our face-to-face conversations reveal variations in what they mean when they say that faith is important. For example, Amber told us that, for her, religion is "central at my core . . . but it's not central in every single thing I do. I live a pretty normal life, like my coworkers don't see me as this weird super Christian. I think I'm pretty normal. So it's central, but it's also not something that I'm always talking about." For Amber and other more routinized Committed emerging adults, faith exists as a more mundane part of their lives and is worked into their daily routine as the rest of life permits. Faith is important, but in the sense that it is one of many important factors that make their lives complete, not necessarily the central factor around which their lives revolve. A 28-year-old LDS woman provides an example of how issues of religion and faith are just one part of her family's life:

I think, I don't want to say it's a really big part, like we're . . . our days are not based on religion, if that makes sense. But it does, it does tend to come up, like over the dinner table or breakfast table or you know, sometimes even while we're doing our homework or something. Somebody asks a question or something, I guess if that makes sense. Like it's not like the center of our world.

Similarly, a 28-year-old Conservative Protestant told us that, for him, religion and spirituality were a part of his life "100 percent as much as feasible." He provided examples of how religion is just one of the routines in his life:

I mean, obviously, you know, sitting through traffic isn't necessarily a religious or spiritual experience. I mean, it could be if . . . depending on how bad it is [*laughs*]. But, yeah, I definitely think it's a part and I think since I work at a private university too that is, you know, Christian-focused . . . it's just involved I think in my work life as well as my home life.

And this 24-year-old Catholic woman suggested that, even though she was a regular church-attender, religion was a fairly limited part of her life. She said, "I wouldn't say it's part of my everyday life. It's part of, like, my couple days a month life [*laughs*]."

There is clearly a range of religious salience among the Committed emerging adults that we spoke with. But even among those who do not talk about their faith as central to their daily lives, there is a clear sense that religion and faith have a seat at the table and are a component of their identity, however compartmentalized that might be. This is distinct from even the Marginal emerging adults, for whom religion operates primarily in the background of their lives and is accessed only on demand, should the need or desire arise.

Another measure of religious centrality is how close Committed young people feel to God. While 87 percent reported that faith is very or extremely important in their lives, just 61 percent said that they feel very or extremely close to God. This is higher than other groups by almost double, but a much lower percentage than those who respond similarly about the importance of faith. The contrast between the responses to these two questions is telling. When respondents say that faith is important in their daily lives, this can mean that it is important on an internal emotional level, or at the instrumental level of playing an important role in their identity and the overall function of their lives. In our face-to-face interviews, we heard both types of responses. But asking respondents how close they feel to God taps into a component of religion that might be missed by the importance-of-faith question. This is more specifically a measure of their own felt connection to their faith—the internal emotional component that may or may not be part of the calculation when answering the question about the importance of faith.

Feeling close to God implies not only a connection to faith but also confidence in one's relationship to the professed faith. So, we find it noteworthy that among the group of our respondents who we label as religiously Committed, less than two-thirds reported feeling very or extremely close to God. While this alone does not tell a complete story, these survey findings lend further support to the notion that religious commitment takes different forms. That there are more Committed young people who profess to the importance of faith than who personally feel a close connection to God suggests that, for at least some of the Committed, the faith that they speak of may be more pragmatic than personal.

In addition to the salience of faith in the daily experience of Committed emerging adults, there is evidence to suggest that religious beliefs and practices will continue to be a core part of their lives—in whatever form it takes—into the foreseeable future. More than half of the Committed reported that they have become more religious over the past five years, while 93 percent reported that they believe they will be attending religious services when they are 35 years old. By their own accounts, then, there is momentum in the direction of continued religious engagement.

Religious and Spiritual Practices

As with each of the other groups discussed in this chapter, among the Committed respondents, prayer was the most commonly mentioned spiritual practice. For the Committed, however, prayer was a much more traditional practice related to the rest of their religious lives than for young people in the other groups. More than 70 percent of Committed emerging adults said they pray at least daily, although again, the particular form of prayer varied. Many have set aside time—whether daily or weekly—to pray, maybe read scriptures, and in general just recalibrate their lives. For a few respondents, prayer is very intentional and scheduled. For example, this 24-year-old Hindu woman detailed her daily prayer regimen:

I: Do you pray?

R: Yeah, I pray three times a day: when I wake up, every time I have a meal, and right before I go to bed.

I: Okay, and what kinds of things do you pray for or about?

R: When I wake up in the morning I pray to God, I thank him for giving me my mind back in the morning, because we believe that when you're asleep you don't know, you know, Bob from John, I don't know that I'm a daughter, I don't realize that I'm a student. There's no worries. But as soon as I open my eyes all of that comes back, and I thank God for that. I apologize to Mother Earth for stepping on her throughout the day. And then, when I eat, I thank God for turning the food that I eat, whether it's good for me or not, into blood that is useful to my body, for providing food that I do have. And then when I go to sleep I thank him for the day that I've had, regardless of whether it's good or not. And again, I apologize for stepping all over Mother Earth throughout the day, or doing anything wrong that I may or may not have realized.

Of course, the particular form and frequency of this young woman's daily prayers are at least partially linked to her religious tradition. But other Committed emerging adults show a similar commitment to regularly set aside a time of day to pray. For example, a 27-year-old Mainline Protestant told us that he prayed "three times a day. I pray for God's will to be done, I pray for moral help, I pray for specific life issues, and, you know, job, good place to stay, make a right decision, feel better, be able to help someone, have spiritual gifts, [and] have power to help other people."

Most, however—like this 28-year-old Conservative Protestant—have a somewhat more flexible version of a regular prayer time:

I probably set aside time for prayer at least once every other day. I'll do a lot of, like, quick prayers, like while I'm driving or whatever, that's usually if something pops in my head. I might pray for a friend if I think of something they told me about. But in the other times it's more prayer over maybe things that are coming up in the week or things that are going on either at work or at home, and kind of realigning myself, just like realigning my spiritual center to get back on track and kind of get rejuvenated for what's going on.

These responses suggest two types of prayer: regular time set aside for prayer and quick prayers in the midst of other activities. The latter form of prayer is what we heard more commonly from all four groups of emerging adults, including the Committed group. Many Committed respondents framed prayer as more of an ongoing part of their daily lives—a reflex almost—rather than a set-aside time or practice. Similar to the Conservative Protestant man quoted previously, this 28-year-old Catholic said:

I guess it depends. Do I sit down and have, like, long prayers? No, not really . . . probably not too often. But there's little things throughout the day, you know, like I said, if I'm late to work and the lights are green and, like, just thankful and I'll be like, "Oh thank you God that everything's working out well and I'm getting to work on time." But I don't, you know, it's not like a nightly thing where before I go to bed I say prayers.

These responses demonstrate a regular connection to prayer for Committed emerging adults, but it would be a stretch to say that prayer is an intentional spiritual practice in their lives. It would be more apt to say that it seems to be evidence of the general relationship to religion that we have found across each of our groups, where they draw on it for their own well-being, but it makes few demands of them or their time.

Committed respondents also reported other religious and spiritual practices at significantly higher rates than emerging adults in our other groups, such as having read religious or spiritual material in the previous year (58 percent), practicing a weekly day of rest (39 percent), or denying themselves something as a spiritual practice (36 percent). Those in the Committed group also reported religious experiences at much higher rates than other young people, with 77 percent saying that they had experienced an answer to prayer and 63 percent reporting that they had witnessed a miracle sometime in the last five years.

Overall, religious engagement among the Committed emerging adults takes a rather conventional form—in particular, public religious attendance and unstructured, reflexive prayer. We do find that the Committed are much more likely to be engaged in religious practices than their peers, by a significant margin. However, we do not find much evidence that intentional spiritual disciplines are being regularly incorporated into their daily lives.

Attitudes about Organized Religion

Among all of the emerging adults in this study, the Committed have the highest level of respect for organized religion, with 78 percent agreeing that they have a lot of respect. That leaves almost one-fourth of the Committed emerging adults who are at least somewhat disillusioned or otherwise dissatisfied with organized religion—although only 12 and 19 percent, respectively, go so far as to say that they think organized religion is a big turnoff and is irrelevant for most people their age. In comparison to respect for organized religion in general, Committed emerging adults are more positively predisposed to the particular religion in which they were raised, with 88 percent reporting positive feelings toward the religious tradition of their childhood.

When we asked about their feelings toward organized religion and religious institutions, Committed respondents tended to frame their answers from within their own religious traditions and experiences, often noting the limitations of these institutions, despite their overall acceptance of them. For some, similar to Marginals, their reservations about religious institutions centered around issues such as gay marriage or abortion—asserting, for example, their belief that churches or other religious institutions should not be able to tell people whom they can love or marry, or otherwise direct such personal aspects of members' lives. For example, a 28-year-old Catholic woman said that while she enjoys being Catholic, she thinks that "the Catholic Church is a little outdated, but they have . . . everybody believes in something different. So they have what they believe, whether it's gay marriage, whether it's abortion. To me, I don't think really anybody should be able to tell us who we can and cannot marry, if that's who makes you happy—that's who makes you happy."

Commenting more broadly about problems or scandals in religious institutions, a 24-year-old Catholic man suggested that, when individuals do bad things, the broader institution should not be tainted by their misbehavior:

> I mean there's always going to be controversy of things that swirl around it. [But] I trust mostly because [even though] I have had little bumps in the road about, like, certain priests doing things which aren't good, but at the end of the day . . . that shouldn't make me feel less joy when I go to Mass or do anything within the Catholic faith.

A 26-year-old Conservative Protestant woman similarly acknowledged the good and bad inherent in any institution, saying that churches and religion are "a mixture of good and evil," but also that religious organizations are positive influences in society "that do a lot for a lot of people. There are a lot of churches who have food banks and just even with their offerings and things give to the poor families."

When asked whether they thought religious institutions contribute anything good or helpful to American society, most Committed emerging adults said that they thought this was true. Some, like this 27-year-old Mormon man, framed their view in religious terms, saying, "I think more people need it right now. I know the trend is kind of declining for . . . at least practicing religion on a regular basis. And I think that's not going to be good in the future. I think—yeah, I wish it was going the other way." A 28-year-old Catholic woman answered similarly, saying that she thinks that religious institutions promote unity through their practices: "I believe in the idea of if you pray together, you stay together . . . you know, having some sort of union together, being grateful to something bigger than yourself."

Other Committed emerging adults framed their positive view of religious institutions in more practical terms related to the different kinds of assistance they provide. A 27-year-old Mormon woman emphasized the kinds of assistance that the LDS church is known for, such as responding to natural disasters, saying, "They do a lot of good . . . when natural disasters happen. Different things like that. Funding to help them, you know, with the tornados or with tsunamis that come up. I feel like churches are also ready to step in and help out." And a 28-year-old Conservative Protestant man asserted that, in his view, "churches do good deeds," giving the example of a program in his city where local religious groups come together to serve the city.

Religion—whether measured by attendance at religious services, religious beliefs, or different religious and spiritual practices—is much more a part of the lives of Committed emerging adults than any of the other groups discussed in this chapter. But there also appears to be a divide within this group. There are some for whom religion is the key motivating factor in their lives, driving their decisions and life choices. For many others, there is a clear commitment to religion and its importance in their lives, but it takes a different role. For these religiously Committed young people, religion takes a seat at the table of their lives. It connects with other parts of life in a supportive fashion, though it does not take over or dominate the whole; religion is always there and can be called on in a crisis to offer additional support without dominating all aspects of their lives. Religion is very much a part of the experience of the group of young people we call Committed. But in reality, only a small subset of these emerging adults are motivated by or particularly enthusiastic about its presence in their lives.

Excursus: Spiritual but Not Religious

Much has been made over the last several years about the apparent rise in individuals who describe themselves as "spiritual but not religious," particularly in relation to the increase in numbers of those who claim no religious affiliation.[11] This idea, while present in each of the four groups of emerging adults that we've been discussing in this chapter, is not a particularly prevalent or important part of how emerging adults are thinking about their religious and spiritual lives, regardless of where they are placed within our four groups. Yet, owing to the prevalence of this theme in both academic literature and popular media, it is worth taking a look to see how emerging adults think about the phrase "spiritual but not religious."

At its core, the notion of spiritual but not religious emerging adults is intended to evoke the idea that, although the individuals are not affiliated with any religious organization or particular faith tradition, they main-tain some sort of inner spiritual life in which they contemplate their own existence and the possibility of the sacred or divine. Thus, the concept of spiritual but not religious brings to mind images of spiritual seekers en-gaging in intentional sacred practices such as meditation or prayer as well as personal experiences that are interpreted as mystical or spiritual in na-ture. Recent research, however, indicates that identifying as spiritual but not religious takes on a variety of meanings for individuals, many of which are not consistent with this popular image of the spiritual seeker.[12] We find further evidence of this in our in-person interviews with the young people in our study.

We first asked these young people as teenagers if they had ever heard the phrase "spiritual but not religious." At that time, the overwhelming re-sponse was that they were unfamiliar with the idea. Only eight percent of Wave 1 survey respondents said that it was very true that the term "spiritual but not religious" described them. Our follow-up in-person interviews suggested that, of this eight percent, many were actually Conservative Protestants who used the term to refer to their personal relationship with Jesus (in contrast with rote religion), and their use of this term did not signify a rejection of traditional religion or an embrace of alternative spirituality.

Now in their 20s, the emerging adults in our study seem to have a better understanding of what that phrase might mean. The percentage of our respondents who said that the term "spiritual but not religious" is a *very true* description of themselves, while still not large, did increase from eight percent in Wave 1 to 17 percent in Wave 4. As expected, the emerging adults in the Committed group are the least likely to identify as spiritual but not religious—10 percent said it is *very true*—while the differences across the other three groups are minimal, ranging from 17 to 21 percent.

While more emerging adults now identify spiritual but not religious as a true description of themselves, their responses in follow-up inter-views still don't fall into the categories that we might expect, given the existing literature and how this terminology has become understood in more popular explanations.[13] Among the Not Religious, Disaffiliated, and Marginal, we heard very similar variations of two themes when it came to discussions about "spiritual but not religious" and whether that term accurately described their views. The first type of response was from emerging adults who did identify as being spiritual but not religious. They explained that, for them, it meant that they believed in God or some higher power. However, being spiritual but not religious was generally unrelated to any specific spiritual practices such as prayer, meditation, reading sacred texts or other religious material, or even a more general effort to seek out deeper meaning in their lives. Certainly there were those who, for example, said that they prayed; but in general, there was no significant or regularly pursued form of spiritual or religious practice associated with this concept.

For example, a 25-year-old man who identified as Not Religious responded, "I guess it depends on how you describe spiritual—like do I pray, or have crosses in my house? No. Do I believe in a higher power? I guess if that's spirituality versus religious, then yes."

In some of these cases, like this young man, emerging adults agree that they are spiritual but not religious, yet seem almost to be talking themselves into this identity as a response to our questions. This 28-year-old Disaffiliated woman seemed to come to her conclusion in the process of providing her response:

> I believe, definitely. I believe in certain things. I believe in the religious aspect, like, what they say is right and wrong. I agree with it. And I agree that there is God and I agree with all that stuff, but I'm not religious to the point where I go to church and I do those kind of things. So yeah, I guess the spiritual but not religious kinda makes sense.

Similarly, this 27-year-old Catholic woman works through her answer to conclude that she is spiritual, and this is largely attributed to her belief in a higher power:

R: I'm not religious. And I guess . . . a little bit spiritual.
I: You said you maybe consider yourself a little bit spiritual. What does that mean?
R: I believe in God. I believe in a higher power, but I don't necessarily believe in all the doctrine, the teachings of the Catholic church.

> I guess I'm spiritual and that I believe in a higher power, but not re-
> ligious in the sense that I am not a practicing Catholic or practicing
> anything else.

For these emerging adults who agreed that they were spiritual but not
religious, the term may not have immediately resonated, but on further
consideration, they were able to find themselves in the concept, seeing
how they could maintain the connection to spirituality without the connection to religion. It is our sense that the spiritual but not religious identity
among these emerging adults is often more a case of trying on the term to
see if it fits, rather than a clear identity that they held before our conversation with them.

A second theme that we heard across all four groups of emerging adults
was skepticism about the whole idea of spiritual but not religious. For
these young people, claiming to be spiritual but not religious sounded like
a dubious notion at best and, at worst, was an identity that had no substan-
tive meaning. One young man from the Marginal group told us that the
phrase "sounds like a Miss America answer" and added that, in his view,
"Spiritual and not religious is usually what people say to get out of having
these conversations revolving around the idea of religion." Similarly, a Not
Religious woman expressed a bit of contempt for the term, considering it
a meaningless concept:

> I can't stand that spiritual thing. What does that even mean? That's
> a non-answer to me. So no, I don't consider myself spiritual or re-
> ligious. I believe in God, which is something to me completely dif-
> ferent, because when you put the word religious, when you attach
> that to it, it means that man has been involved and put his two
> cents in.

Among the Committed emerging adults, skepticism often took the form
of finding the whole concept illogical. These young people either struggled to understand the idea or said that they were both spiritual *and* religious and that they couldn't see how one could exist without the other.
A 26-year-old Mainline Protestant man said, "I consider myself to be
both," while a 25-year-old LDS man replied, "I don't know the difference
between the two, so I wouldn't be able to answer it honestly." When we
asked Kristen if she would consider herself to be spiritual but not religious, she said:

I still don't really grasp the entire concept of that, so no, but I also wouldn't ever describe myself as religious and not spiritual. I would never say, "Hey, I'm religious." Like if someone said, "What are you?" I wouldn't say I'm religious, or if someone said, "What are you?" I wouldn't say I'm spiritual. I'd say I'm a Christian.

Across all four of the religious groups we have examined in this chapter, we find that spiritual but not religious is not an identity that is deeply held by many emerging adults. More of them are familiar with the term than in the past, and some are able to articulate how it might be an apt description of their own faith or worldview. But even when this is the case, their assent to the description is typically limited in scope to a belief in a higher power and does not encompass a wider ranging impulse toward spiritual seeking. With the decline of traditional measures of religion, the notion of young people embracing spirituality instead of organized religion has taken hold in the popular imagination. On the ground, however, spiritual but not religious does not seem to be a concept that is particularly meaningful for this group of emerging adults.

Conclusion

Any attempt to summarize the religious lives of a group of people will inevitably bump up against limitations and challenges. This chapter is no exception. There are many different ways to conceptualize and describe the lived religious lives of young people. However, in examining these young people through the lens of the Not Religious, Disaffiliated, Marginal, and Committed groups, we have arrived at a few general themes that help us to understand the changing role of religion in the lives of emerging adults.

Divergence

If we take a step back, what is the big-picture story here? In Chapter 3, we provided evidence of an overall religious decline and a general move away from organized religion. Yet, we also saw some evidence of polarization or divergence, with groups like the LDS and Conservative Protestants showing somewhat higher levels of commitment among their remaining adherents—while, at the same time, larger numbers of young people are identifying as not religious. Now in their mid to late 20s, our respondents seem to be settling into these religious identities. Among our sample, there was not much in the way of direct and adamant opposition to religion. Rather, young people are just not particularly interested in religion, and it does not seem particularly relevant to their lives. Of course, this is especially true among the Not Religious and the Disaffiliated, and this trend is evident within the Marginal group as well. But we also hear the echoes of this sentiment among those Committed emerging adults who have adopted the more routinized version of regular religious engagement.

As we saw in Chapter 3 and in this chapter, attendance is waning among emerging adults. On the one hand, this signals a movement away from organized religion. Another interpretation of this is that attendance at religious services has become much more voluntary. As young people get older, they become more independent from the religious expectations of families, and they are coming of age at a time when being not religious is more socially acceptable than it has been in recent memory. Whatever the reason, they feel freer to elect not to attend religious services.

If this is the case, the reverse is also true: those who are attending religious services are likely there of their own choosing. When attendance becomes more voluntary and less normative, those who are truly committed will continue, and the less committed will be more likely to drift away. Thus, while attendance at religious services may be lower, it may carry more meaning regarding the religious commitment of the attendees.

We see some evidence for this in the increasing connection between religious service attendance and the reported importance of faith in daily life. One measures public religious practice, the other private religious salience. Over the 10 years of this study, the correlation between attendance and importance of faith has gotten stronger at each time point. At Wave 1, the two variables were correlated with a Pearson's r of 0.49. This increased to 0.59 at Wave 2, 0.62 at Wave 3, and finally by Wave 4 the correlation between public and private religiosity was 0.68. The increasing strength of the correlation shows that, as young people get older, their public religious practice comes more in line with their personal religious salience.

This alignment happens at both ends of the spectrum, with those who say faith is not important no longer attending religious services, and those for whom faith is very important maintaining their religious service attendance at much higher rates than others. As we saw in Chapter 3, there seems to be a hollowing out of the religious middle, with growing numbers of Not Religious and a smaller but still present group for whom religion is a fixture in their lives.

Liminality

Another theme that arises from our assessment of these four groups of young people is that of liminality—of being in between. The Marginal and Disaffiliated groups each represent different versions of this in-betweenness. The Disaffiliated emerging adults occupy the liminal ground of maintaining some semblance of religious identity but having little if any meaningful connection to religious community or practice. They embody the uncertainty of those who, for all practical purposes, are ready to abandon religion, but their lingering doubts about the possibility of religious truth keep them from cutting the cord entirely. The Marginal emerging adults operate in their own version of uncertainty. They maintain some level of religious connection, but it is on their own terms and to their own ends. However, they seem somewhat uncertain about the deal they have struck. If there really is something to religion, they wonder if perhaps they should be more involved. But why do they continue to hang on if they can't really articulate how or why religion is relevant to their lives?

Their existence in this liminal space raises the question of their life-history trajectories. Will they make their home in this liminal space, or are they moving in one direction or the other? Consistent with the idea of a liminal space, these emerging adults could conceivably go either way—toward more involvement or toward less involvement. In other words, their liminal status could be the last way station on their journey completely out of religious involvement, or they could find a way back in. Given the very tenuous hold many emerging adults have on their religious faith, it is hard to imagine that they would return to religion in any significant or widespread way. Looking back over the previous survey data, it appears that those who occupied the liminal space at Wave 3 have moved into the Not Religious space by Wave 4. If this is any indication, we might interpret this in-between space as just a point on a trajectory leading away from religion among emerging adults.

It is also possible that this liminal space might be the new religious or spiritual location for emerging adults. It doesn't take a lot (if any) sort of commitment because whatever religiosity they evince is all on their terms, and they can increase or decrease their involvement as life situations change. As we saw with Maria, it might be that this existence fulfills whatever needs they have and thus suits them just fine. And, in fact, the next theme we discuss would fit well within this narrative.

Hanging On

Despite the general move away from organized religion, there remains among emerging adults a basic set of beliefs and practices that suggest that they are maintaining at least the possibility that there is "something else"—that is, something more than just secular or material life. Yet, even while they leave such a possibility open, this should not be interpreted to mean they are thinking long and hard about it. Overall, with the exception of the most religiously engaged, religion does not have a particularly important role in the lives of emerging adults; it is more of a constant but unremarkable presence.

As such, religion remains a theoretical or abstract option for them, but it just doesn't have the pull or attraction to really grab their attention as something to which they would fully commit. Many want to hang on to some form of supernatural or mystical belief. But even while they are hanging on, what they are hanging on to is taking on a more symbolic quality. One example would be those who continue to engage in prayer but acknowledge that they think of prayer as a way of talking out problems or connecting with others, rather than an active attempt at communicating with God.

Another example is the difference we see between believing that a divine being exists and professing belief in that divine being as salient to one's own life. This was illustrated earlier in this chapter by the Disaffiliated woman who said, "I believe that there is a God, I don't know if there's a specific one God." While these young people may be hanging on to general beliefs about religious propositions, this does not necessarily translate to embracing particular religious beliefs in their own lives.

The maintenance of some semblance of religious belief and practice suggests that they want to hang on to the possibility of religious reality, even if it is strictly on their terms. Perhaps this draws on the cultural impulse of tolerance and open-mindedness—not wanting to definitively say religion has no place in the world. But for all practical purposes, there is very little agentic impulse, particularly among the Not Religious and the Disaffiliated, to explore this possibility, and very little expectation that religion will ever be significant in their own lives again. They do have agency to choose the important elements in their lives, and religion is further down the list than other things like family, romantic relationships, and friends.

Throughout this chapter, we have explored the contours of the current religious lives of the emerging adults in our study. In Chapter 5, we widen our lens to consider the different pathways by which these emerging adults arrived at different places of religious engagement or disengagement. Looking across the full scope of the National Study of Youth and Religion, we map out the most common religious trajectories from adolescence to emerging adulthood as well as the factors associated with each of these trajectories.

Tables

Table 4.5 Beliefs about God

	Not Religious (%)	Disaffiliated (%)	Marginal (%)	Committed (%)	All (%)
Belief in God					
No	31	2	2	1	12
Yes	39	89	89	98	74
Unsure	30	9	9	1	14
Views of God					
A personal being	16	52	66	83	51
Uninvolved creator	5	6	5	3	4
Cosmic force	21	18	8	3	13
None of these views	27	22	19	9	20
Does not believe in God	31	2	2	1	12

Source: National Study of Youth and Religion survey 2013.

Table 4.6 Belief in Heaven

	Not Religious (%)	Disaffiliated (%)	Marginal (%)	Committed (%)	All (%)
No	40	4	5	2	16
Yes	32	80	81	94	67
Unsure	28	16	14	4	17

Source: National Study of Youth and Religion survey 2013.

Table 4.7 Beliefs about Religious Exclusivity

	Not Religious (%)	Disaffiliated (%)	Marginal (%)	Committed (%)	All (%)
Truth in Religion					
Only one religion is true	5	21	27	61	27
Many religions may be true	54	73	67	37	55
Very little truth in any religion	41	7	6	2	17
Okay to pick and choose religious beliefs without having to accept teachings of faith as a whole					
Disagree	31	35	49	71	46
Agree	69	65	51	29	54

Source: National Study of Youth and Religion survey 2013.

Table 4.8 Centrality of Faith

	Not Religious (%)	Disaffiliated (%)	Marginal (%)	Committed (%)	All (%)
Importance of Faith in Daily Life					
Not at all important	56	8	3	0	22
Very unimportant	15	15	4	1	9
Somewhat important	25	51	48	11	31
Very important	3	17	28	31	18
Extremely important	2	9	17	56	21
Feeling Distant or Close to God					
Extremely close	4	8	10	18	10
Very close	5	19	22	43	21
Somewhat close	16	34	41	29	28
Somewhat distant	12	22	18	7	14
Very distant	7	8	4	1	5
Extremely distant	6	4	1	0	3
Does not believe in God	50	5	4	2	20

Source: National Study of Youth and Religion survey 2013.

Table 4.9 Past and Future Religion

	Not Religious (%)	Disaffiliated (%)	Marginal (%)	Committed (%)	All (%)
Self-reported religious change over past 5 years					
Became more religious	7	12	27	54	25
Became less religious	28	25	17	6	19
Stayed about the same	65	63	57	40	56
Plans to attend church at age 35					
No	61	11	6	0	24
Maybe	34	61	34	6	31
Yes	5	27	61	93	45

Source: National Study of Youth and Religion survey 2013.

Table 4.10 Religious Practices and Experiences

	Not Religious (%)	Disaffiliated (%)	Marginal (%)	Committed (%)	All (%)
In the past 12 months, respondent:					
Practiced religious or spiritual meditation	19	15	15	19	17
Read religious or spiritual book other than the scriptures	12	17	26	64	30
Tried to practice a weekly day of rest or Sabbath	3	6	11	41	15
Fasted or denied self something as a spiritual discipline	4	11	15	37	16
Witnessed a miracle in the past five years					
Yes	14	33	44	63	37
Maybe	12	20	17	17	16
No	73	47	39	20	47

Source: National Study of Youth and Religion survey 2013.

Table 4.11 Prayer

	Not Religious (%)	Disaffiliated (%)	Marginal (%)	Committed (%)	All (%)
Frequency of praying alone					
Multiple times a day	3	8	18	44	18
About once a day	4	18	20	27	16
A few times a week	7	19	23	16	15
About once a week	4	8	8	5	6
One to two times a month	7	15	12	4	9
Less than once a month	14	16	13	3	11
Never	61	15	6	1	25
Experienced answer to prayer or guidance from God in the past five years					
Yes	16	39	52	81	45
Maybe	15	24	23	13	18
No	69	36	26	6	37

Source: National Study of Youth and Religion survey 2013.

Table 4.12 Attitudes about Organized Religion

	Not Religious (%)	Disaffiliated (%)	Marginal (%)	Committed (%)	All (%)
I have a lot of respect for organized religion in this country					
Strongly agree / agree	25	57	67	78	54
Don't know / unsure	12	14	14	10	12
Strongly disagree / disagree	63	29	19	12	34

Table 4.12   Continued

	Not Religious (%)	Disaffiliated (%)	Marginal (%)	Committed (%)	All (%)
I have very positive feelings about the religious tradition in which I was raised					
Strongly agree / agree	28	71	79	88	62
Don't know / unsure	17	12	8	3	10
Strongly disagree / disagree	27	15	9	4	15
Does not apply	22	4	3	3	10
Most mainstream religion is irrelevant to the needs and concerns of most people my age					
Strongly agree / agree	50	33	28	19	34
Don't know / unsure	24	19	17	12	18
Strongly disagree / disagree	27	48	54	69	48
Organized religion is usually a big turnoff for me					
Strongly agree / agree	72	36	20	12	38
Don't know / unsure	9	9	14	9	10
Strongly disagree / disagree	20	55	67	79	52

Source: National Study of Youth and Religion survey 2013.

Table 4.13 Spiritual but Not Religious

	Not Religious (%)	Disaffiliated (%)	Marginal (%)	Committed (%)	All (%)
Very true	21	20	17	10	17
Somewhat true	44	52	50	36	44
Not true at all	35	28	34	54	39

Source: National Study of Youth and Religion survey 2013.

5

How Did They Get There?

RELIGIOUS TRAJECTORIES IN THE LIVES OF EMERGING ADULTS

(with Jonathan Hill)

THROUGHOUT THIS BOOK, we have met several of the young people who participated in our study. Each has a unique story to tell; yet, among them we can find common threads of experience related to their religious and spiritual journeys. On the surface, Kristen—the highly religious woman we met in Chapter 1—and Josh, the nonreligious young man we met in Chapter 4, appear to have very little in common. Yet, both are examples of young people whose religious journeys are marked by consistency and stability.

Kristen was raised in a home where her evangelical faith was a daily presence—in family interactions, practices such as church attendance, prayer and Bible reading, and her schooling. Overall, across each interview, Kristen demonstrated a commitment to understanding and living her life by the teachings she first learned while a child. Mapped as a trajectory, her story reflected consistently high religiosity from adolescence to adulthood. Josh also had a consistent religious trajectory, although at the other end of the spectrum from Kristen. Josh was raised in a home where religion was not present at all—neither of his parents were religious—although he was encouraged to pursue any interests he might have about religion while growing up. Throughout each of four interviews with Josh, his responses to our questions about religion remained remarkably consistent: he was curious about religion, particularly whether the claims could be rationally "proved," but in the end, nothing he ever investigated met his criteria for truth.

Many of the emerging adults in our study have similar stories—religious lives that have remained relatively stable over time. But for other young people, their religious journeys include shifting toward or away from religion and doing so in gradual or (less often) dramatic fashion. We met Heather in Chapter 1. Taking a snapshot of the religiousness of Heather and Josh at Wave 4 would reveal similar levels of religious practice and commitment, in that neither of them is religious nor professes any connection to religion at this point in their lives. However, taking the longer view of their stories and the paths that led them to where they are today illustrates some of the different religious trajectories that young people follow from adolescence into adulthood. Heather's life started out looking more like Kristen's, with a religiously devoted mother, regular attendance at religious services, and socialization into the faith, resulting in confirmation in the Catholic church. But when she got older, Heather jettisoned the religious practices and commitments of her Catholic upbringing and adopted a nonreligious identity. In doing so, Heather illustrates one of the most common religious pathways among emerging adults—that of religious decline over time.

Thinking about Kristen, Josh, and Heather, we can see that in order to fully understand the religious experiences of emerging adults, we have to account not just for where people started religiously and where they are today but also for the path they followed to get from one point to the other. In this chapter, we sketch a picture of the various paths—or, more precisely, the religious trajectories—that young people follow as they move from adolescence to their mid-20s. We explore the most common trajectories and examine the factors associated with each type of spiritual journey.

Often, trends are represented by showing changes in the average of a given measure over time. For example, if we want to document how religious service attendance changes between adolescence and emerging adulthood, we can examine the mean of our measure of service attendance at each wave of the National Study of Youth and Religion (NSYR) (Figure 5.1). Alternatively, we could examine how a proportion changes over time. For example, we might want to know what percentage of all young people attend church at least weekly at each wave of the NSYR (Figure 5.2). Both of these data points tell us something important about the overall shape of religious practice associated with young people as they age.

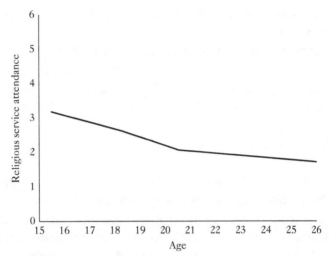

FIGURE 5.1 Mean change in religious service attendance by age, weighted.
Source: National Study of Youth and Religion surveys 2002, 2005, 2008, 2013.

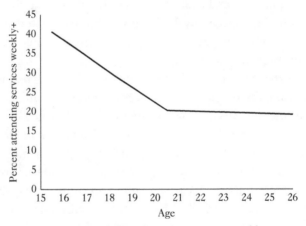

FIGURE 5.2 Percentage attending religious services weekly or more by age, weighted.
Source: National Study of Youth and Religion surveys 2002, 2005, 2008, 2013.

While this type of analysis is helpful, it is remarkably easy for the reader to be left with the impression that the "typical" young person will follow a similar trajectory. But this simply isn't the case. A brief thought experiment will illustrate. The first figure *could* consist of three types of young persons: The first attends religious services every week and never deviates from this in all four waves of the data. The second type is like the first, except never attends religious services. The last type begins like the first, but at some point along the way, stops attending religious services altogether, and ends up like the second group. Such a pattern *could*, hypothetically, produce the first figure we examine (although we know, from examining the data, that this is not the case). Figure 5.1 could also be produced by everyone following exactly the same pattern and attending religious services less frequently at each wave. But which one is correct? Distinguishing between these scenarios is certainly important if we want to accurately understand the patterns of religiousness and spirituality from adolescence onward.

Parsing out the common and uncommon trajectories requires a different approach. In this chapter we use a method known as growth mixture modelling (GMM), which sorts individuals into various groups based on similarities in their trajectories.[1] In other words, it's a method designed to distinguish between the different scenarios that might produce the same overall mean-level or proportion-level changes over time. While not everyone will fit perfectly in one group or another, this approach attempts to find a balance between the complexity of individual cases and the (over) simplicity of single-trajectory summaries.

To begin, we calculated a simple summary measure of religious service attendance, frequency of prayer, and self-rated importance of faith at each wave of the NSYR. This measure, although not perfect, is consistently captured at all four waves of the NSYR and taps into different dimensions of religious faith (public practice, private practice, and personal salience). Each measure is weighted equally and then added together to create a scale of religiousness that ranges from zero to 12. The mean level scores at each wave are reported in Figure 5.3.

The GMM analysis tells us that the mean-level trajectory in Figure 5.3 is *not* the typical pathway for most. Rather, our analysis suggests there are six different "typical" religious pathways from adolescence into emerging adulthood, and young people do not all take the same pathway (Figure 5.4).[2] While the overall means at each wave suggest declining religious practice and salience, the picture in this figure complicates a simple story of religious decline. It would be more accurate to say that decline occurs in different ways. Of the three trajectories that exhibit some sort of downward trend, only one indicates a complete disengagement from religion.

This steep decline from high to low accounts for about 13 percent of the young people in our study. This group averages a moderate to high religiousness on our 12-point scale at the beginning, but ends more than seven points lower, with a religiousness score comparable to the fully

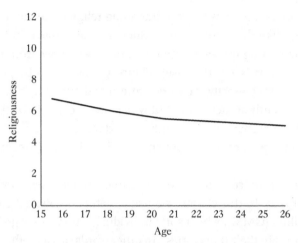

FIGURE 5.3 Mean change in composite religiousness measure by age, weighted.
Source: National Study of Youth and Religion surveys 2002, 2005, 2008, 2013.

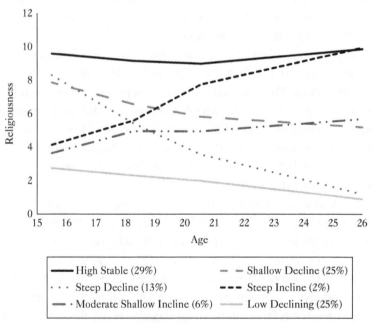

——High Stable (29%)	– – Shallow Decline (25%)
· · · Steep Decline (13%)	– – – Steep Incline (2%)
— · Moderate Shallow Incline (6%)	—— Low Declining (25%)

FIGURE 5.4 Results from growth mixture model of six class trajectories by age, weighted.
Source: National Study of Youth and Religion surveys 2002, 2005, 2008, 2013.

disengaged group. The other two decline trajectories are less severe. One group starts at a moderate level (a little below eight on our 12-point scale) and ends at a moderate-low level (a little above five on the same scale). This group makes up about one-fourth of the young people. The other group starts near the bottom, at less than three, and ends at less than one. This group is disengaged religiously throughout the timeframe of the study, but still shows some movement, from a smattering of religiousness for some of them to virtually nothing by their mid-20s. This group also makes up one-fourth of the sample.

The most stable trajectory reflects young people who exhibit moderate to high religiousness throughout their late teens and 20s. This group is also the largest, at 29 percent. The remaining two groups are the smallest of the six, and both show a general movement toward increased religiousness over time. The smallest group, at only two percent, shows a substantial incline, moving from relatively low levels of religiousness (slightly above four on the 12-point scale) to relatively high levels (slightly below 10). The other group begins with a similar increase, but levels out and ends up with a moderate level of religiousness (a little less than six on the scale). This group represents six percent of the young people in our study. Table 5.1 describes each of the various trajectories in terms of where they begin and end.

Stepping back for a moment, it is worth noting how little drastic religious change occurs for most young people. Four of the groups, comprising 85 percent of all young people, show some sort of stability or incremental change that never exceeds more than three points on our scale.[3] Although the more typical trend is still downward overall, they are not experiencing a radical shift in their religious life one way or the other (at least using these particular measures). For the 15 percent who do undergo substantial shifts in religiousness, the vast majority belong to the group that is becoming less religious (13 percent) rather than more religious (two percent).

Establishing typical and atypical religious trajectories is useful at a purely descriptive level; however, we also want to dig a little deeper into the nature of these trajectories. Just who are the people in these different groups? Are there factors in adolescence that seem to set the stage for belonging to one group versus the others? And what about the consequences of these trajectories? Does belonging to one or another of these groups make any difference in the life of young people in their mid-20s? It is to these questions that we now turn.

Table 5.1 Median Values of Religion Measures for Each Class Trajectory at Waves 1 and 4

	Where They Begin (Wave 1 Medians)	Where They End Up (Wave 4 Medians)
High Stable (29%)	Attends church once a week Faith is very important Prays about once a day	Attends church once a week Faith is extremely important Prays about once a day
Shallow Decline (25%)	Attends church two to three times a month Faith is very important Prays a few times a week	Never attends church Faith is somewhat important Prays a few times a week
Steep Decline (13%)	Attends church once a week Faith is very important Prays a few times a week	Never attends church Faith is not important at all Prays a few times a year
Steep Incline (2%)	Attends church many times a year* Faith is very important Prays one or two times a month	Attends church once a week Faith is very important Prays multiple times a day
Moderate Shallow Incline (6%)	Attends church a few times a year Faith is somewhat important Prays one or two times a month	Attends church a few times year Faith is somewhat important Prays a few times a week
Low Declining (25%)	Attends church a few times a year Faith is not very important Prays less than once a month	Never attends church Faith is not at all important Never prays

*"Many times" a year is the category that falls between a "few times a year" and "once a month."

Source: National Study of Youth and Religion surveys 2002, 2005, 2008, 2013.

Demographics and Family Structure

We begin this exploration by looking at the demographic factors of gender, race, and social class. Figures 5.5 through 5.7 show the proportion of each class trajectory that is female, persons of color, and from

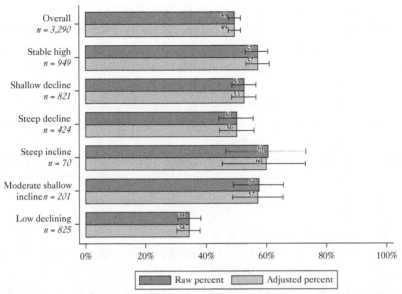

FIGURE 5.5 Raw and adjusted percentage who are female by class trajectory, weighted.

Source: National Study of Youth and Religion surveys 2002, 2005, 2008, 2013.

Notes: N = 3,290. Error bars display 95 percent confidence interval of estimate. Adjusted percent represents the average marginal effect from a logistic regression after controlling for parents' income, education, family structure, region of residence, teen race/ethnicity, and age.

higher socioeconomic strata, respectively. Because we use similar figures throughout the remainder of this chapter, it is worth pausing for a moment to explain the interpretation of the figures.

Taking Figure 5.5 as our example, the top bar of the graph shows the overall proportion of adolescents at the first wave who are female. In fact, there are two bars grouped together. The top one is the "raw" percentage estimate—this is just the straightforward statistic based on the NYSR sample (adjusted for the usual survey weights). The second bar is the adjusted percentage estimate. This is the estimated percentage after other factors like family income, educational attainment of parents, family structure, region, race/ethnicity, and age are statistically controlled (for most graphs, we also statistically controlled for gender, but this would not be appropriate for Figure 5.5). We will typically refer to the raw estimate, but occasionally we point out the adjusted results, when there are differences worth noting between the two.

The top bar serves as a reference for the other bars. The bars below are the estimates for survey respondents in each of the six growth curve groups. Each bar also includes error bars. These show the 95 percent confidence interval for each estimate. In other words, they show the range we might expect the true value to reasonably fall within. They also help gauge whether we can be confident that one group is different from another. For example, we can clearly see from Figure 5.5 that the Stable High group is disproportionately female (57 percent) and the Low Declining group is disproportionately male (34 percent female). We can also be pretty confident that these two groups are different from one another statistically and that they are different from the overall percentage estimate for females (49 percent).[4]

A similar pattern emerges when examining the racial/ethnic composition of the religious trajectory groups. People of color are more likely to be found in the groups characterized by higher levels of religiousness. In Figure 5.6 we see that people of color make up more of the religious categories (both those who are stable and those who increase), with about

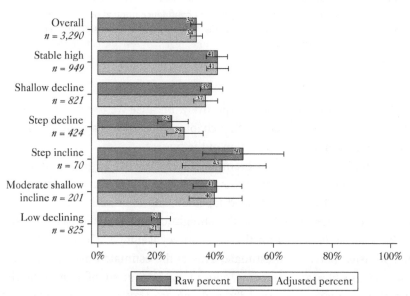

FIGURE 5.6 Raw and adjusted percentage of people of color by class trajectory, weighted.

Source: National Study of Youth and Religion surveys 2002, 2005, 2008, 2013.

Notes: N = 3,290. Error bars display 95 percent confidence interval of estimate. Adjusted percent represents the average marginal effect from a logistic regression after controlling for parents' income, education, family structure, region of residence, gender, and age.

four out of 10 adolescents in these groups being people of color. The Steep Decline group, and especially the Low Declining group, are more likely to be white (with only about two out of 10 being nonwhite in the latter). Here, we also see that, unlike the estimates for gender, when we adjust for other factors (especially parents' income and education), some of the differences between the groups are less dramatic—particularly in the Steep Decline and Steep Incline groups.

Directly examining parents' education and income corroborates this (Figure 5.7). High socioeconomic status is similar across most of the trajectory groups, with the exceptions of those in the Steep Incline and Steep Decline categories (with a rather dramatic difference in the former).[5] While 23 percent of teens can be classified as being raised in households with relatively privileged economic and educational capital, fully 30 percent of those in the Steep Decline group, and only five percent of those in the Steep Incline group, meet these criteria.

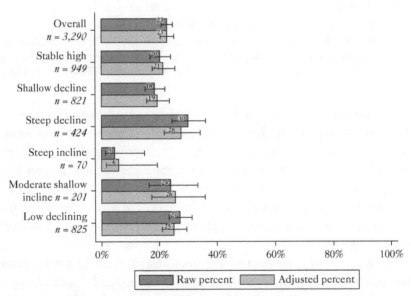

FIGURE 5.7 Raw and adjusted percentage living in a high socioeconomic status (SES) household in adolescence by class trajectory, weighted.

Source: National Study of Youth and Religion surveys 2002, 2005, 2008, 2013.

Notes: High SES households have one or more parents with a college degree and had a household income of at least $80,000 in 2002–3.

N = 3,290. Error bars display 95 percent confidence interval of estimate. Adjusted percent represents the average marginal effect from a logistic regression after controlling for family structure, region of residence, race/ethnicity, gender, and age.

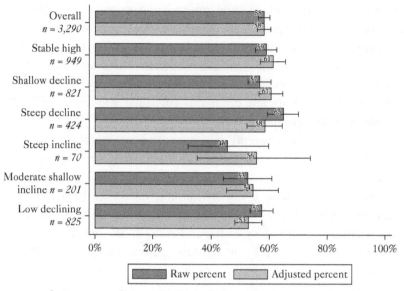

FIGURE 5.8 Percentage living with biological or adoptive parents by class trajectory, weighted.

Source: National Study of Youth and Religion surveys 2002, 2005, 2008, 2013.

Notes: N=3, 290. Error bars display 95 percent confidence interval of estimate. Adjusted percent represents the average marginal effect from a logistic regression after controlling for parents' income, education, region of residence, teen race/ethnicity, gender, and age.

Finally, we include a basic measure of family structure (Figure 5.8). Here we are examining the percentage of young people who, as teens, were raised in homes with two biological or adoptive parents. The differences here are fairly minor, with those in the Steep Incline category less likely to be in such households (although the adjusted percentage shows that this is at least partially due to the differences in socioeconomic status shown in the previous figure—single parents have, on average, fewer economic resources).

Let's pause for a moment to take stock of what these first few figures tell us. The emerging picture relates to social location and resources. Men, whites, and those with high socioeconomic status are overrepresented in groups that end up ranking low religiously in emerging adulthood. This includes those who measured high on our religion scale as teens (the Steep Decline group) and those that were low to begin with (the Low Declining group). Those without these markers of social advantage are more likely to stay religious and are much more likely to be overrepresented in the group that becomes substantially more religious in emerging adulthood, even though this group is relatively small. Family structure, in and of itself, is relatively unimportant compared with gender, race, and social class.

These findings align with a variety of views that suggest religion may serve as a social or psychological resource for individuals with less material, social, and cultural capital. Religious congregations have often been cited as places that can function as social safety nets, provide venues to teach civic skills, extend social networks across status barriers, and provide a site for the arts to flourish.[6] At a psychological level, religion has been cited as a source of comfort and stability when "existential security" is low or as a source of help from a superhuman power.[7] While we don't want to read too much into these few variables—after all, we are not using any direct measure of social or psychological deprivation—we do find that the general picture that emerges is consistent with approaches that emphasize these factors.

Religious Environment in Adolescence

Although there are clear fault lines along race, class, and gender, demographics are obviously not destiny. The religious environment in which the teen is raised, perhaps unsurprisingly, remains the most powerful predictor of the various religious trajectories we document. In this section, we use various measures of this environment to investigate how they map onto the trajectories.

The next four figures (Figures 5.9 through 5.12) are measures of the most common religious traditions (measured by the affiliation of the congregation the teen attended or identified with). Figure 5.9 breaks down the proportion of Conservative Protestants in each of the trajectory groupings. The pattern is striking. Moving down the figure, each group has progressively fewer Conservative Protestants. Although Conservative Protestants account for three in 10 young people in the NSYR, they make up more than four in 10 (42 percent) of those who remain consistently religious as they move into emerging adulthood. However, Conservative Protestants are also well represented in the two categories that decline religiously. This tells us that belonging to a Conservative Protestant tradition does not somehow ensure that teens will stay strong in their faith commitments as they get older. It *does* mean that Conservative Protestant teens are overrepresented in the trajectories that begin with moderate to high rates of religious service attendance, prayer, and importance of faith in daily living.

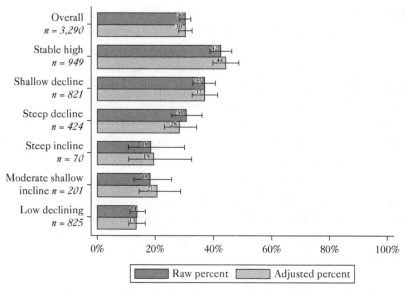

FIGURE 5.9 Percentage Conservative Protestant during adolescence by class trajectory, weighted.

Source: National Study of Youth and Religion surveys 2002, 2005, 2008, 2013.

Notes: N = 3,290. Error bars display 95 percent confidence interval of estimate. Adjusted percent represents the average marginal effect from a logistic regression after controlling for parents' income, education, family structure, region of residence, race/ethnicity, gender, and age.

On the other hand, Conservative Protestants are relatively unlikely to be found in the groups that begin with moderate to low levels of religiousness in the teenage years. At the very bottom of the figure, only 14 percent of those in the Low Declining category were Conservative Protestants as teens. In groups that show some level of increase in religiousness over time, about two in 10 could be classified as Conservative Protestants at the first wave of the NSYR.

Black Protestants, although often similar to Conservative Protestants on certain theological positions, reveal a pattern that diverges somewhat from that of their theological cousins (Figure 5.10). While they are nearly twice as likely to be found in the Stable High group as in the general population (19 vs. 11 percent), they are much less likely to be found in the decline groups—particularly the Steep Decline category (five percent). Like Conservative Protestants, they are quite unlikely to be found in the Low Declining category (three percent). Unlike Conservative Protestants, however, they are also well represented in the categories that show an upward

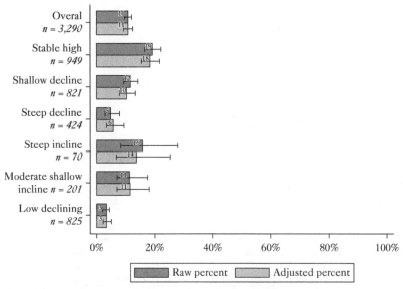

FIGURE 5.10 Percentage Black Protestant during adolescence by class trajectory, weighted.

Source: National Study of Youth and Religion surveys 2002, 2005, 2008, 2013.

Notes: N = 3,290. Error bars display 95 percent confidence interval of estimate. Adjusted percent represents the average marginal effect from a logistic regression after controlling for parents' income, education, family structure, region of residence, gender, and age.

religious trajectory over time. There are nearly as many Black Protestants in the small Steep Incline category as Conservative Protestants (16 and 18 percent, respectively), despite the fact that Conservative Protestants outnumber Black Protestants almost three to one in the NSYR sample.

Turning now to Figure 5.11, Mainline Protestants make up the same proportion of young people in the first wave of NSYR as Black Protestants. Despite this, their faith trajectories are quite different. For most categories, Mainline Protestants are not particularly overrepresented or underrepresented. They are equally likely to be in the Stable High category as the Low Declining category (both nine percent). Even a category where they appear underrepresented, the Steep Incline group, reveals that the differences are not so dramatic after our statistical controls are introduced (four percent without controls and seven percent adjusted for controls). There is one clear exception: there are nearly twice as many Mainline Protestants in the Steep Decline category (21 percent) as in the overall sample. So, while Black Protestants are half as likely to be found in this category, Mainline Protestants are nearly twice as likely.

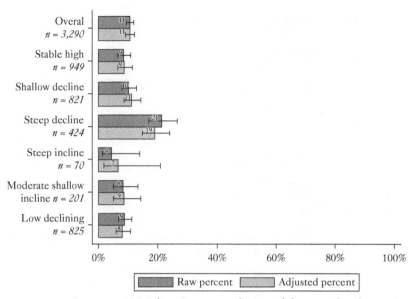

FIGURE 5.11 Percentage Mainline Protestant during adolescence by class trajectory, weighted.

Source: National Study of Youth and Religion surveys 2002, 2005, 2008, 2013.

Notes: N = 3,290. Error bars display 95 percent confidence interval of estimate. Adjusted percent represents the average marginal effect from a logistic regression after controlling for parents' income, education, family structure, region of residence, race/ethnicity, gender, and age.

The final religious tradition we examine is Catholic (Figure 5.12). A little more than one in four teens were Catholic in Wave 1 of the NSYR. And, in most of the trajectories we've mapped out, Catholics make up about the same proportion of each group (ranging from 27 to 32 percent). Like Mainline Protestants, there is an exception. This time it is the High Stable group that stands out: only 18 percent of this group is Catholic. Again, this doesn't mean that there are no Catholic teens that continue to go to Mass, pray, and say that their faith is important as they transition into their 20s. But we do see that Catholics are underrepresented among those young people who are maintaining their religious faith into adulthood.

In summary, religious traditions are not equally represented in the different faith pathways. While Conservative Protestants and Black Protestants make up about four in 10 teens, they make up more than six in 10 teens who stay religious as they get older. And they account for only 17 percent of the young people who appear to be consistently disconnected from or uninterested in religious faith (the Low Declining group).

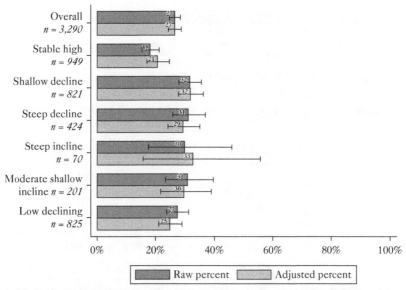

FIGURE 5.12 Percentage Catholic during adolescence by class trajectory, weighted.

Source: National Study of Youth and Religion surveys 2002, 2005, 2008, 2013.

Notes: N = 3,290. Error bars display 95 percent confidence interval of estimate. Adjusted percent represents the average marginal effect from a logistic regression after controlling for parents' income, education, family structure, region of residence, race/ethnicity, gender, and age.

Mainline Protestants and Catholics also make up nearly four in 10 teens, yet they make up more than half of the young people we would classify as exhibiting a steep drop in measures of religious faith and practice. In addition to this, they only account for around one-fourth of the group that remains at least moderately religious throughout the four waves of the NSYR (the High Stable group).

The connection between religious traditions and the different religious pathways is not surprising, given our analysis of individual measures of religion in Chapter 3. As we noted in that chapter, the general pattern of declining religious engagement includes movement in both directions. And the solidification of religious commitment appears to be happening most commonly among those young people who hail from more conservative or culturally distinct religious traditions.

Moving beyond religious traditions, we now investigate several more direct measures of household faith and practice. The next two figures (Figures 5.13 and 5.14) examine reports of the religious service attendance of respondents' parents. Forty-four percent of the parent respondents in

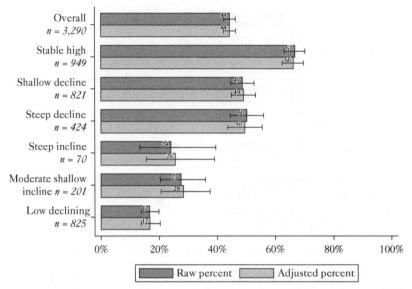

FIGURE 5.13 Percentage with parents who reported attending services weekly by class trajectory, weighted.

Source: National Study of Youth and Religion surveys 2002, 2005, 2008, 2013.

Notes: N = 3,290. Error bars display 95 percent confidence interval of estimate. Adjusted percent represents the average marginal effect from a logistic regression after controlling for parents' income, education, family structure, region of residence, teen race/ethnicity, gender, and age.

the first wave of the NSYR reported that they attended church weekly or more. Two-thirds of the parent respondents of youth in the Stable High category reported weekly attendance, and about half of parent respondents reported this in the two categories that exhibit religious decline. As would be expected, regular worship attendance by a parent was much less common for those teens who started out less religious. About one-fourth of those in the categories that later saw increases in religion had a parent who attended weekly, and only 17 percent of young people who were consistently low on religious measures had a parent who attended church regularly.

The pattern is similar if we examine whether the teen and parent attend religious services together at Wave 1. This is not a measure of how frequently either parent or teen attends, but rather if they attend services at the same religious congregation. About two-thirds reported that they did. While this result is highest in the Stable High category (87 percent), it is not dramatically higher than the two declining categories (78 and

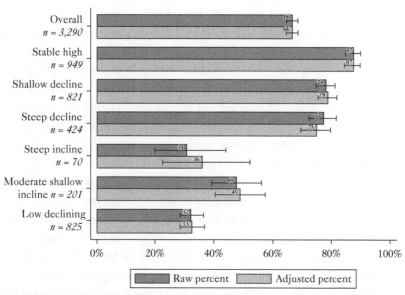

FIGURE 5.14 Percentage with parents who reported attending services with teen by class trajectory, weighted.

Source: National Study of Youth and Religion surveys 2002, 2005, 2008, 2013.

Notes: N = 3,290. Error bars display 95 percent confidence interval of estimate. Adjusted percent represents the average marginal effect from a logistic regression after controlling for parents' income, education, family structure, region of residence, teen race/ethnicity, gender, and age.

77 percent). It is less common in the other categories, the lowest being the Low Declining group (32 percent) and the Steep Incline group (31 percent).

For the sake of space, we have not included a number of other analyses of household religious faith. The story is largely the same for all of them, however. We examined how often the parent prays for the teen, whether married parents belong to the same faith (religious homogamy), and how important faith is in the daily life of the parent. In each case, we saw a clear step-like pattern, with descending percentages in each category moving down the figure. In other words, teens who stay religious are the most likely to have parents who measure high on religious measures, and parental religious commitment becomes increasingly less likely as we move to the Low Declining category at the bottom of the figures.

Most of these measures of household religious environment do not dramatically distinguish which teens remain religious and which teens decline in religiosity. None of these measures seem to be the "key" to keeping teens in the faith. However, there was one exception. In Wave 1, the teens were asked how frequently their family talked about God, sacred texts, prayer, or other religious or spiritual things together. We examine these responses by religious trajectory in Figure 5.15. About one-third (34 percent) of teens said that their family talks about these religious matters at least a few times per week. Those who are in the declining groups (Shallow Decline and Steep Decline) are roughly similar to this overall rate. However, teens who stay religious into emerging adulthood are much more likely to report their family talking about matters of faith (62 percent). We will return to this finding shortly.

First, though, we want to end this section with two figures that measure youth-focused church programming. The first (Figure 5.16) measures youth group participation and the second (Figure 5.17) religious mission trips. Although youth group participation is more common, the pattern is similar. In both figures the Stable High group has the largest proportion who participated in church programming. The most noticeable gap, however, is between the top three classes and the bottom three.

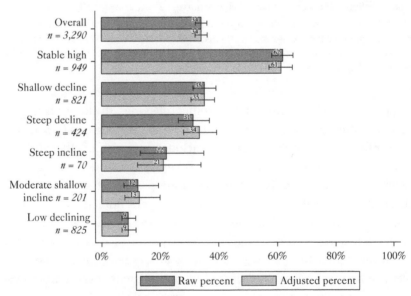

FIGURE 5.15 Percentage who reported religious talk in home a few times per week or more as teen by class trajectory, weighted.

Source: National Study of Youth and Religion surveys 2002, 2005, 2008, 2013.

Notes: N = 3,290. Error bars display 95 percent confidence interval of estimate. Adjusted percent represents the average marginal effect from a logistic regression after controlling for parents' income, education, family structure, region of residence, teen race/ethnicity, gender, and age.

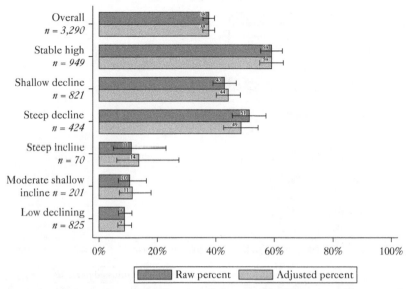

FIGURE 5.16 Percentage attending a religious youth group in adolescence by class trajectory, weighted.

Source: National Study of Youth and Religion surveys 2002, 2005, 2008, 2013.

Notes: N = 3,290. Error bars display 95 percent confidence interval of estimate. Adjusted percent represents the average marginal effect from a logistic regression after controlling for parents' income, education, family structure, region of residence, teen race/ethnicity, gender, and age.

Again, it does not seem to be the case that either of these—youth group or mission trips—clearly distinguish who stays religious and who does not over time.

In sum, the nature of the religious environment matters. Young people who have parents who say their faith is extremely important, attend church regularly (and with their teen), belong to the same faith tradition, pray regularly for their teen, and talk regularly about religious or spiritual matters in the household are all disproportionately represented in the Stable High category and underrepresented in the Low Declining category. We suspect this is capturing how deeply integrated religious faith is in the teen's household. The extent that religion is a regular part of the day-to-day goings-on of family life has an influence on whether a young person continues with the faith as they enter emerging adulthood.

The measure of religious talk in the household also helps to explain some of the differences in religious traditions we discussed at the beginning of this section. Nearly half of Conservative Protestants (47 percent)

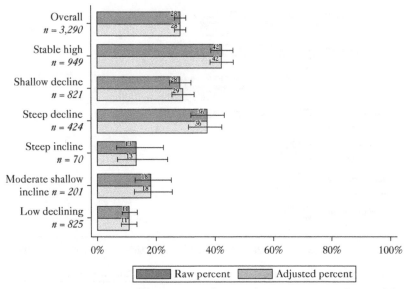

FIGURE 5.17 Percentage who participated in a religious mission trip in adolescence by class trajectory, weighted.

Source: National Study of Youth and Religion surveys 2002, 2005, 2008, 2013.

Notes: N = 3,290. Error bars display 95 percent confidence interval of estimate. Adjusted percent represents the average marginal effect from a logistic regression after controlling for parents' income, education, family structure, region of residence, teen race/ethnicity, gender, and age.

and more than half of Black Protestants (56 percent) reported religious talk at least a few times per week. The equivalent statistic is only 23 percent for both Catholics and Mainline Protestants. Running a statistical model that controls for the frequency of religious talk in the household accounts for nearly half of the advantage Conservative Protestants have over Catholics and Mainline Protestants in keeping young people in the Stable High category, compared with one of the categories of religious decline.[8] In other words, the fact that Conservative Protestants are more likely to remain religious may be explained by the integration of faith into household life that is more common within this religious tradition.

Adolescent Relationships

We now turn from explicit measures of religion to other relational factors that might matter during the teenage years. The next few figures examine how the relationship with parents and peers might influence the religious trajectory of teens as they move into emerging adulthood. Let's begin by considering how close the teen was to his or her parents. The first wave of the NSYR contains numerous measures of the parent-teen relationship. We created a composite index from the various measures.[9] Figure 5.18 shows what percentage of each group scored in the top 30 percent of the index. In other words, these teens tend to score higher than the average in terms of feeling close to their parents, talking to them about personal subjects, and doing various activities together. The Stable High group is disproportionately made up of young people who were close to their parents as teenagers (37 percent), while the inclining classes and the Low Declining class all have lower than average numbers of respondents who were close to their parents. The Shallow and Steep Decline classes are close to the mean at 31 percent in each.

Next, we used a similar technique to measure the degree to which parents monitor what their teen does and who she or he spends time

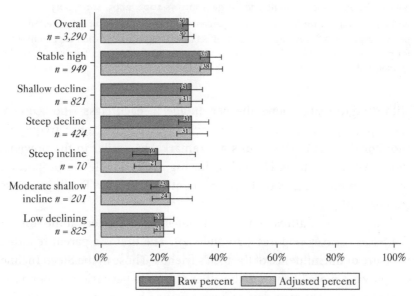

FIGURE 5.18 Percentage who felt close to parents as teens (top one-third of composite measure) by class trajectory, weighted.

Source: National Study of Youth and Religion surveys 2002, 2005, 2008, 2013.

Notes: N = 3,290. Error bars display 95 percent confidence interval of estimate. Adjusted percent represents the average marginal effect from a logistic regression after controlling for parents' income, education, family structure, region of residence, teen race/ethnicity, gender, and age.

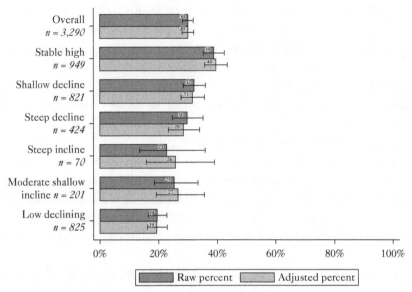

FIGURE 5.19 Percentage whose parents monitored their activities and friends closely as teens (top one-third of composite measure) by class trajectory, weighted.

Source: National Study of Youth and Religion surveys 2002, 2005, 2008, 2013.

Notes: N = 3,290. Error bars display 95 percent confidence interval of estimate. Adjusted percent represents the average marginal effect from a logistic regression after controlling for parents' income, education, family structure, region of residence, teen race/ethnicity, gender, and age.

with.[10] Figure 5.19 shows the percentage in each class who score in the top 30 percent (high scores mean that parents more frequently monitor the teen). The results are remarkably similar to the previous figure, with the Stable High class having about double the proportion of high monitoring parents (39 percent) as the Low Declining class (19 percent).

The next two figures examine relationships with peers at the time of the Wave 1 survey (Figures 5.20 and 5.21). The first is a parent-reported measure of the influence of the teen's friends. Those in the Steep Incline category are more likely than the other groups to have friends whom the parent respondent considers to have a very or somewhat negative influence (22 percent in this group compared with 13 percent overall). The differences between the various groups is still relatively small. Figure 5.21 includes the teen's assessment of how important it is to fit in with what other teens think is cool. This is designed to be another measure of peer influence, this time from the teen's perspective. In this case,

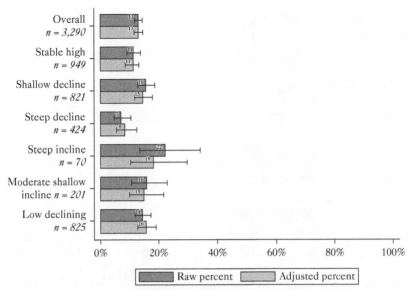

FIGURE 5.20 Percentage whose parents reported friends are generally "very nega-tive" or "somewhat negative" influence in adolescence by class trajectory, weighted.

Source: National Study of Youth and Religion surveys 2002, 2005, 2008, 2013.

Notes: N = 3,290. Error bars display 95 percent confidence interval of estimate. Adjusted percent represents the average marginal effect from a logistic regression after controlling for parents' income, education, family structure, region of residence, teen race/ethnicity, gender, and age.

the Low Declining group includes disproportionate numbers of those who said it is "not important at all" to them. However, like the previous measure, differences in peer influence are not that dramatic between the various groups.

Although this is not an exhaustive analysis of the influence of parents and peers, we do find that the religious trajectories young people travel are more strongly influenced by their relationships with parents than with peers. Having close, warm relationships with parents who regularly spend time with their teen and monitor the teen's activities and relationships is most associated with the Stable High category and least associated with the Low Declining category. While the previous section helped to identify what religious activity in the home might be associated with certain tra-jectories, these graphs show that what matters is not simply the content of the religious environment but also the quality of relationships. How parents invest or do not invest in their teens' lives has consequences for their religious faith as they transition into adulthood.

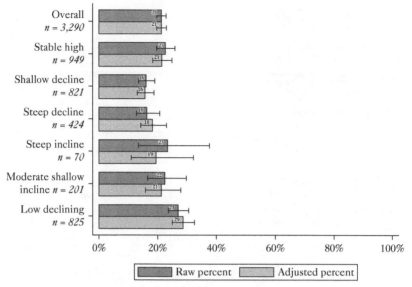

FIGURE 5.21 Percentage who reported it is "not important at all" to fit in with what teens think is cool by class trajectory, weighted.

Source: National Study of Youth and Religion surveys 2002, 2005, 2008, 2013.

Notes: N = 3,290. Error bars display 95 percent confidence interval of estimate. Adjusted percent represents the average marginal effect from a logistic regression after controlling for parents' income, education, family structure, region of residence, teen race/ethnicity, gender, and age.

Postadolescent Life Events

Finally, we want to move away from the teenage years to consider important life events that occur after adolescence. In some ways, this means we are thinking less about the factors that might shape future trajectories and more about the way that some religious trajectories might be more (or less) likely to be accompanied by important educational, occupational, and familial changes in life.

Let's begin with education. Figure 5.22 looks at the percentage of the NSYR sample respondents who have graduated from college with at least a bachelor's degree by the fourth wave. Overall, this is 41 percent of the emerging adult sample. The measure of education is not noticeably different across religious categories, with one exception. Only 20 percent of the Steep Incline group have a bachelor's degree. Controlling for our standard set of variables, however, changes this substantially. After additional factors are accounted for (especially parents' income and education

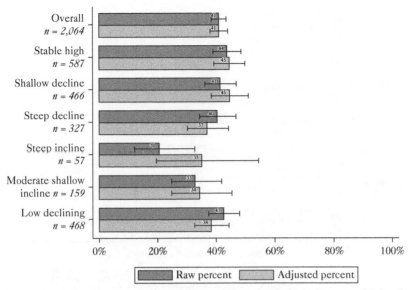

FIGURE 5.22 Percentage who reported receiving a bachelor's degree or higher by Wave 4 by class trajectory, weighted.

Source: National Study of Youth and Religion surveys 2002, 2005, 2008, 2013.

Notes: N = 2,064. Error bars display 95 percent confidence interval of estimate. Adjusted percent represents the average marginal effect from a logistic regression after controlling for parents' income, education, family structure, region of residence, teen race/ethnicity, gender, and age.

measured in adolescence), we could expect this group to have a degree acquisition rate of closer to 35 percent. To be clear, this is *not* the rate of college completion this group has; rather, it is simply what we might expect if socioeconomic status were similar across these religious trajectories. In other words, the lower educational attainment among the Steep Incline group can be explained in part by the socioeconomic background of the young people in this group.

The next three figures focus on marriage and romantic partnerships. Figure 5.23 shows the percentage of emerging adults in each group who have never married by Wave 4. This tends to be relatively low for the Stable High group (45 percent) and the Steep Incline group (49 percent) and relatively high for the Steep Decline (67 percent) and the Low Declining (69) groups. Another way to put this: those groups that *end up* being less religious by Wave 4 are also less likely to have ever been married. It appears to matter less where one starts religiously during the teenage years and more where one ends up in their 20s. As we will see in the next chapter,

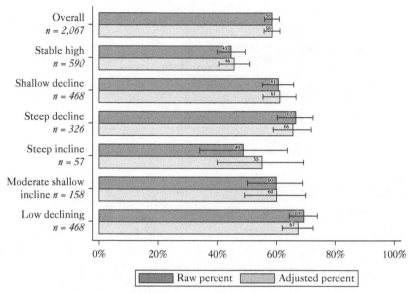

FIGURE 5.23 Percentage who reported having never married at Wave 4 by class trajectory, weighted.

Source: National Study of Youth and Religion surveys 2002, 2005, 2008, 2013.

Notes: N = 2,067. Error bars display 95 percent confidence interval of estimate. Adjusted percent represents the average marginal effect from a logistic regression after controlling for parents' income, education, family structure, region of residence, teen race/ethnicity, gender, and age.

marriage and religious faith are mutually influencing factors in the lives of young people.

The next figure is restricted to those who have been married or are currently married (Figure 5.24). Here, we examine whether any of the religious trajectories are associated with higher or lower rates of divorce or marital separation. Among those who have ever been married, about 17 percent reported a divorce or separation. Most religious trajectories are similar, and in fact the lower sample size means our estimates are less precise (notice the range of the error bars). Still, we can be fairly confident (statistically speaking) that the Stable High group has lower rates of divorce and separation than other trajectories.

Our last measure of marriage and relationship status includes only those who have never married, who are divorced, or who are currently widowed (Figure 5.25). Here, we are investigating how many are currently living with their partner in a marriage-like relationship (cohabiting). Overall, the data suggest that about 13 percent are currently cohabiting at

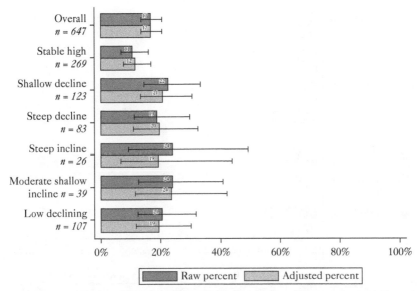

FIGURE 5.24 Percentage who reported having had a divorce or separation at Wave 4 (includes only those who reported having ever married) by class trajectory, weighted.

Source: National Study of Youth and Religion surveys 2002, 2005, 2008, 2013.

Notes: N = 647. Error bars display 95 percent confidence interval of estimate. Adjusted percent represents the average marginal effect from a logistic regression after controlling for parents' income, education, family structure, region of residence, teen race/ethnicity, gender, and age.

Wave 4. Here, again, we find a relationship with the various religious trajectories. The cohabitation rate is lowest among those who are currently the most religious (seven percent in the Stable High and six percent in the Steep Incline groups) and highest among those who are the least religious (16 percent in the Steep Decline and 18 percent in the Low Declining groups). In other words, we find precisely the opposite relationship that we found when examining marriage.

Next, we want to explore political identification. The last decades of the 20th century saw a realignment of conservative politics with religious faith, especially among Protestants.[11] Do we see a similar association among emerging adults? Figure 5.26 displays the proportion of emerging adults in each group who identify as politically conservative at Wave 4. The differences are striking. While 28 percent of all emerging adults identify as politically conservative, fully 46 percent of the Stable High emerging adults identify as such. The Steep Decline and Low Declining groups

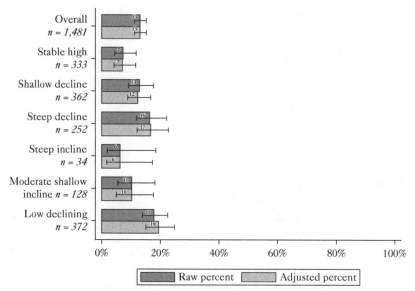

FIGURE 5.25 Percentage who reported currently cohabiting with partner at Wave 4 (includes only never married, divorced, or widowed) by class trajectory, weighted.

Source: National Study of Youth and Religion surveys 2002, 2005, 2008, 2013.

Notes: N = 1,481. Error bars display 95 percent confidence interval of estimate. Adjusted percent represents the average marginal effect from a logistic regression after controlling for parents' income, education, family structure, region of residence, teen race/ethnicity, gender, and age.

stand out in sharp contrast to this. Here, only 14 percent (Steep Decline) and 18 percent (Low Declining) identify as politically conservative.

To what extent might this be due to how they identified as teens? Unfortunately, we don't have such a measure from Wave 1, but we do have the political identification of the parent respondents. We ran the models again, this time including parents' political identification as a control factor in the adjusted results (not displayed). The findings remain virtually unchanged. Emerging adults in the Stable High group are much more likely to be politically conservative, while Steep Decline emerging adults are much less likely to be so. This suggests that young people are at least partially defining their political identities in ways that fit the religious trajectories they are traveling.

In the previous section, we saw that young people who were close to their parents as teens were more likely to fall into the Stable High religious group. What does this look like later in life? Figure 5.27 uses the Wave 4 report of closeness to parents. There are some striking differences between

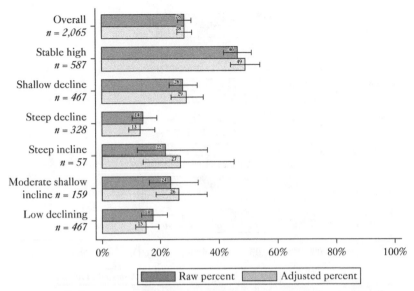

FIGURE 5.26 Percentage who reported they consider themselves politically conservative at Wave 4 by class trajectory, weighted.

Source: National Study of Youth and Religion surveys 2002, 2005, 2008, 2013.

Notes: N = 2,065. Error bars display 95 percent confidence interval of estimate. Adjusted percent represents the average marginal effect from a logistic regression after controlling for parents' income, education, family structure, region of residence, teen race/ethnicity, gender, and age.

this and the previous measure. The Steep Decline and the Low Declining groups feel less close to their parents than the other groups (43 percent and 45 percent, respectively, compared with 54 percent overall). On the other hand, the Steep Incline and the Moderate Shallow Incline respondents are nearly as close to their parents, on average, as the Stable High group (58 and 59 percent for the two incline categories, compared with 64 percent for Stable High). In the previous figure, the Steep Incline cohort had the *lowest* levels of closeness to parents as teens. Again, this tells us that higher religiousness, at the time of reporting, tends to come packaged with closer relationships to parents. The small group of respondents who started off relatively low religiously, and relatively less likely to report being close to their parents, became both more religious and closer to their parents over time.

The last measure we include is an overall assessment of life at Wave 4 (Figure 5.28). Respondents were asked to agree or disagree with the following: "In most ways your life is close to ideal." More than six out

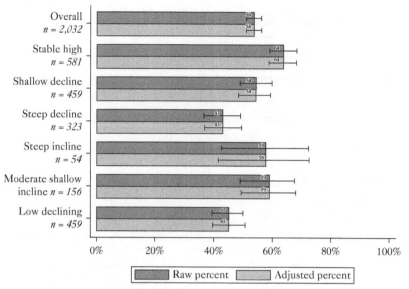

FIGURE 5.27 Percentage who reported being very or extremely close to parent(s) in Wave 4 by class trajectory, weighted.

Source: National Study of Youth and Religion surveys 2002, 2005, 2008, 2013.

Notes: N = 2,032. Error bars display 95 percent confidence interval of estimate. Adjusted percent represents the average marginal effect from a logistic regression after controlling for parents' income, education, family structure, region of residence, teen race/ethnicity, gender, and age.

of 10 emerging adults agree with this statement. Those in the Stable High group are the most likely to agree with this statement (69 percent), while those in the Steep Decline group are the least likely (53 percent). The differences between these groups are not large, but they do fit a clear pattern and are significantly different from a statistical perspective.

What can we say about how the religious trajectories that we have been exploring relate to where young people end up in life by their 20s? In general, we see that those who are in the Stable High religious trajectory are more likely to have a college degree, be married (and less likely to be divorced or cohabiting), feel close to their parents, and be generally satisfied with the direction their life has taken them. They are also much more likely to be politically conservative. Many of these factors, particularly the marital and relational ones, are also associated with those who become more religious by their mid-20s (particularly the Steep Incline group). Notice that we are *not* arguing that there is something causal going

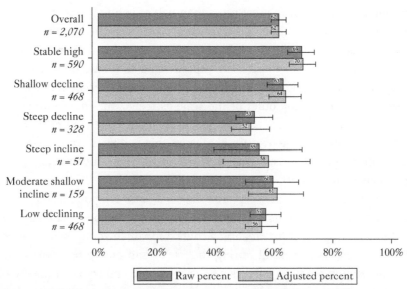

FIGURE 5.28 Percentage who agreed with the statement, "In most ways, [my] life is close to ideal," at Wave 4 by class trajectory, weighted.

Source: National Study of Youth and Religion surveys 2002, 2005, 2008, 2013.

Notes: N = 2,070. Error bars display 95 percent confidence interval of estimate. Adjusted percent represents the average marginal effect from a logistic regression after controlling for parents' income, education, family structure, region of residence, teen race/ethnicity, gender, and age.

on here. We are simply noticing that several of these factors—education, marriage, relationships, politics, and life satisfaction—tend to be part of the package of some religious trajectories.

Conclusion

In this chapter, we analyzed the complex pathways of religious faith that young people travel as they move from their teens to their 20s. Instead of looking at overall mean-level change for everyone, we used a technique (GMM) that separated out the most dominant trajectories in the data. We found that, although the general trend is downward on measures of religious service attendance, prayer, and importance of faith, a not insubstantial number of young people (nearly three in 10) remain moderate to high on these measures as they transition into adulthood. Moreover, about one-fourth of young people remain low on these measures throughout the four waves of the NSYR (although they continue to trend slightly downward

throughout). This means that more than half of young people are not exhibiting substantial religious shifts—at least as measured by these three
factors—as they move into adulthood. Moreover, those that are experiencing changes are not necessarily experiencing dramatic ones. Another
30 percent are experiencing small to moderate shifts over time, beginning
toward one end or the other of the scale as teens, but ending up somewhere in the middle. This means that only about 15 percent exhibit dramatic religious change over time. Most of this is downward (13 percent),
becoming less religious, but a small group becomes substantially more
religious (two percent).

The rest of the chapter explored the social and religious factors associated with these various trajectories. Household religious factors appear
to be most important for creating a context in which young people maintain religious engagement during their teen and emerging adult years.
Having highly religious parents who are invested and active in the life of
their teen is associated with a stable religious trajectory moving into adulthood. In particular, we found that teens who report regular discussions in
the household about God, prayer, scripture, or other religious things are
much more likely to stay religious themselves over time. We think this
measure is likely capturing how faith is integrated into daily living and
routines in some households. We also found that this factor was substantially different across religious traditions and helped at least partially to
explain why Conservative Protestants and Black Protestants were much
more likely to see their teens continuing to practice their faith into the
emerging adult years.

Attempting to understand who takes up religious faith and practice as
they enter emerging adulthood is a little more challenging. To begin, only
a very small number (about two percent) of young people fit the Steep
Incline trajectory. The data seem to suggest that those who do experience increased religious engagement are more likely to come from positions of social or economic disadvantage. Women, people of color, those
without college-educated parents or middle-class incomes, and those who
do not have particularly warm relationships with their parents are all
overrepresented in this Steep Incline group. It is possible that, for these
young people, their life opportunities may make a religiously upward trajectory appealing. Instability in the household, lack of resources, culturally marginal status, less support from mainstream institutions—all of
this leads to greater than typical chances of turning to faith communities
during the transition to adulthood.

The chapter finished by examining how various life outcomes related to these trajectories. We found that those who ended up more religious by the fourth wave, and especially those who stayed religious throughout the years measured in the NSYR, were more likely to be married, college educated, close to parents, and satisfied in life. They were also much more likely to identify as politically conservative.

In addition to revealing the correlates and covariates of religious trajectories, the pathways examined in this chapter provide another lens through which to see the big picture of the religious lives of emerging adults. Consistent with the previous two chapters, we acknowledge that, taken together, there is aggregate religious decline among emerging adults in our study.

However, parsing out this larger trend reveals distinctly different lived experiences among these young people. While many are moving away from religious engagement, there are distinct pathways by which they are making these shifts. Combining the quantitative analysis of the typical trajectories of religious change with the stories that emerge from our qualitative interviews, we see that there is a group of young people who are gradually drifting away from religious communities and practices that no longer seem relevant for their lives, while a smaller group seems to have shifted away from religion in a more intentional and decisive way. This chapter also highlights, however, the story of the emerging adults who are not drifting away from religion, but rather are maintaining or increasing their religious commitment. Examining the distinct trajectories by which emerging adults live their religious lives, we see again the pattern of polarization toward the religious and not religious ends of the continuum and a hollowing out of the religious middle.

6

Faith and Family

THE INSTITUTIONS OF family and religion are intimately intertwined in the United States. Although ties to both institutions appear to be loosening, the nuclear family arrangement, despite its numerical decline, continues to be closely linked to religious identity. Given the interwoven relationship, understanding current patterns of family formation is particularly important for understanding religious trends during emerging adulthood.[1] In this chapter we explore the various ways that marriage and parenthood are tied to religiousness among the young people in our study.

One hope of our research has been to understand the trajectories of young people's lives as they move from adolescence into adulthood. This transition to adulthood is changing dramatically, shifting with the rapidly changing tides of society. Understanding how current emerging adults are navigating their entrance into adulthood tells us much about their lives, but also about society itself as well as the forces that are at work in shaping the next generation. Along the path to adulthood, most individuals make some kind of transition from their family of origin to establishing partnerships, having children, and forming their own families. Recent decades have brought significant changes to the timing and sequencing of these transitions into life partnerships and parenthood, and we can envision several different pathways into family formation.

There are multiple factors that predict or influence the particular pathways that people follow. And after they opt for one of those different pathways, their lives evolve in distinct and meaningful ways. In this chapter we explore how perspectives and expectations about marriage and family life differ across religious groups. We introduce six different stages of family formation: married with children, married without children, cohabiting with children, cohabiting without children, single with children, and single without children. We then examine how religious identity is related to which stage young people find themselves in, and in turn how these different stages of family formation affect the religious lives of the young people in our study.

The median age of first marriage has been rising steadily over the past several decades. In 2012, the median age of first marriage was 29 for men and 27 for women.[2] Marriage continues to be a desired and significant life goal for the majority of young people. But for a variety of reasons, the transition into marriage has been happening steadily later in life since the 1950s. It is not just a delay in marriage, however, that has been noted by social scientists. There have also been significant changes in the landscape of who gets married and who does not. Rather than the first step toward adulthood, marriage is now often seen as a capstone experience, the culmination of other life achievements, and, for many, a status symbol. Understanding marriage as a marker of "success," some scholars have noted the growing gaps in marriage rates across different socioeconomic groups and have identified marriage as—increasingly—a status of privilege, easily available to the elite and often escaping the grasp of those at the bottom end of the socioeconomic ladder.[3]

When it comes to marriage rates, just over one-fourth of the respondents in our study are currently married. Another 5 percent have been married at some point previously but are either separated, divorced, or widowed. Table 6.1 shows the marital status of the emerging adults in our study. Altogether, approximately 30 percent have been married at some point, and another 10 percent are currently engaged to be married. Two percent reported that they are in a civil union, registered domestic partnership, or common-law marriage. The remaining 58 percent have never

Table 6.1 Wave 4 Marital Status

Never married	58%
Currently engaged	10%
Currently married	25%
Civil union	2%
Separated or divorced	4%
Widowed	<1%
Total	100%

Source: National Study of Youth and Religion survey 2013.

been married. This is not entirely surprising, considering that the age range of our respondents, 23 to 28, does not include the median age of marriage for men (at 29) and only barely captures the median for women (27). So, those in our sample who are married are on the early side of the curve when it comes to marriage timing. The emerging adults in our study have a slightly lower marriage rate than we see in other nationally representative data, though it follows the general trend of low marriage rates among people in their 20s.[4]

Similar to marriage, the average age at which women have their first child is also increasing. In 2000, the average age of first-time mothers was 24.9 years. By 2009, this average age at the time of a first birth had increased to 25.2 years, and five years later in 2014, it was up to 26.3 years. This increase can be attributed both to a decline in the rate of teen pregnancies over the same time period and the fact that more women are waiting until they are older than 30 to have their first child. In 2000, 23.9 percent of first births were to women older than 30, and in 2014, these women accounted for more than 30 percent of first-time births.[5] These statistics confirm that the transition into family formation has been delayed across the population.

Given the age range of our respondents—from 23 to 28—we would expect that many of them have not yet transitioned into parenthood. Nationally, the percentage of women who have had a child during this age range has been decreasing steadily over recent decades. In 2000, 50 percent of women ages 23 to 28 had already had at least one child, while 50 percent had not had any children yet. By the year 2010, only 45 percent of women ages 23 to 28 had at least one child, and 55 percent were still childless. Compared with these general US statistics, our sample is less likely to have transitioned to parenthood. Sixty-six percent of the young women in our study have not given birth to any children, while 34 percent reported having given birth to at least one child at the time of the Wave 4 survey. If we include nonbiological children, such as adopted children or stepchildren, then slightly less than 40 percent of the women in our sample reported having at least one child. About half of the parents in our study have only one child, while the members of the other half of the parent cohort each have more than one child.

Expectations and Plans for Marriage

There is a well-established body of literature documenting that religious identity is related to earlier transitions into marriage and parenthood.[6]

Scholars have proposed many possible reasons that religious young people transition into family formation at younger ages than their peers. Religious congregations are often a context where young people will hear pro-family messages and see family life as the normative standard in their communities. Early transitions into marriage and parenthood are often encouraged and supported by religious groups. In addition to the pro-family messages that encourage marriage and parenthood, religious communities can also create a context that discourages behaviors that might otherwise make it possible to postpone marriage.

The increasing social acceptance of nonmarital sex and cohabitation before marriage allows young people to engage in romantic partnerships that can, in turn, delay marriage. Work by Manning and colleagues found that, while the median age of first marriage has increased, the median age at which people create their first union or romantic partnership has remained stable.[7] In other words, for many people, cohabitation has replaced marriage as the first step toward family formation. Religious individuals, however, are more likely to oppose nonmarital sex and cohabitation. Without cohabitation as an option during the emerging adult years, religious individuals may be more likely to transition directly into marriage. And earlier marriage is often correlated with earlier timing of having children.

People's attitudes and intentions offer helpful, if imperfect, predictors of their future behavior. Researchers have found young people's attitudes about gender and marriage to be predictive of their future behaviors and transitions into marriage.[8] Similarly, we expect that how emerging adults view marriage and form their expectations about the timing of marriage will be important factors in their decisions about whether and when to marry. Further, we expect that these attitudes and expectations will be shaped by the context of emerging adults' lives, and religious communities that encourage marriage while discouraging nontraditional family arrangements are an important part of this context.

We collected both quantitative and qualitative information about what young people expect regarding marriage, as well as the criteria that inform their decisions to marry. In the survey, respondents were asked, "What do you think is the ideal age to get married?" In addition, we asked a series of questions about the things they might want to accomplish before getting married. The common stem of this series of questions was, "People have different ideas about what should be accomplished before one is ready to marry. Please tell me how important it is or was to you, personally, to

accomplish each of the following things before getting married." This was
followed by a series of statements:

· Complete your education before getting married.
· Establish your career before getting married.
· Buy a home before getting married.
· Live on your own for a while before getting married.
· Date enough other people before getting married.
· Live with the person you are thinking of marrying before getting
  married.
· Travel or have adventures.
· Enjoy a long time without commitments or responsibilities.

Respondents were asked to rate the importance of each of the above items
with the following response options: extremely important, very important,
somewhat important, not very important, not at all important, I do not
want or plan to get married. These questions allow us to assess the goals
and expectations that young people have about marriage and the timing of
the decision to marry.

Regarding the timing of marriage, Table 6.2 shows a linear relationship between religious engagement and notions about the ideal age of
marriage. Those who are not religious reported an ideal age of about 27
and a half. In contrast, the regularly involved religious respondents reported that 25 and a half is an ideal age to marry.[9]

When asking about the criteria for marriage during our in-person
interviews, the common refrain is that they are seeking to be "ready"
for marriage. What does this mean? For some it is a nebulous personal
readiness—know who you are and what you want; be emotionally stable
and ready for a commitment. But for many, "readiness" is more practical.

Table 6.2 Ideal Age to Marry

	Mean Age (years)
Not Religious	27.6
Disaffiliated	27.2
Marginal	27.0
Committed	25.7

Source: National Study of Youth and Religion survey 2013.

Complete your education, establish a career or job path, and most important, be financially able to support yourself and a family. This is not a new story. It resonates with much of what has been written about marriage trends in recent years.[10] Emerging adults place significant emphasis on the goal of financial stability before committing to marriage. Yet, this goal is growing ever more elusive. Scholars have argued that the increasing challenge of obtaining financial stability is a significant driver in the delay of marriage in general.[11] Religiously motivated young people are not necessarily less likely to believe in the importance of being financially prepared for marriage. It was not mentioned as frequently in the qualitative data but was still a common sentiment among the religious and nonreligious alike.

Religious and nonreligious young people have similar aspirations for marriage when it comes to traditional milestones such as completing education, establishing a career, owning a home, and living on their own (i.e., apart from their parents). Comparing the four religious groups introduced in Chapter 4, the survey data do not reveal large differences in the priority given to accomplishing these things before marriage. However, we see greater differences in the less traditional measures: dating enough other people before getting married, living with a partner before marrying the partner, having time for travel and adventure, and enjoying a period of time in life without significant responsibilities or commitments. For each of these four statements about things young people might like to accomplish before marriage, the religiously Committed reported them to be significantly less important to accomplish before marriage than the other three groups (Marginal, Disaffiliated, Not Religious). These four expectations regarding marriage align with the tenets of emerging adulthood and fit well with the idea of this life stage as a time of uncertainty, self-exploration, and identity formation. And these mores of emerging adulthood seem to have taken hold more strongly among the less religious when it comes to their criteria for marriage readiness, while more religious emerging adults are less likely to be embracing these ideals as prerequisites to marriage.

So, while religious and nonreligious young people have similar expectations when it comes to education and careers, they have different expectations about the life experiences they want to have before settling into marriage. It is possible, then, that one reason why religious individuals marry younger is that they are less likely to prioritize having a lot of premarital relationship experience such as dating multiple partners or living with a partner for a period of time before committing to marriage. They are also less likely to say they would put off marriage for a time of self-exploration, as indicated by their responses to questions about travel, adventure, and responsibilities.

Another consideration in understanding marriage timing is the underlying motivation or desire for marriage within each group of young people. The young people in our survey were asked to tell us how they might feel if they did not end up marrying. The question was: "Suppose your life turns out so that you never get married. Would that bother you a great deal, some, a little, or none at all?" In the responses to this question about their future, we see clear differences by religious category. Table 6.3 shows that respondents who do not identify as religious are by far the least likely to anticipate being bothered by never getting married. Only 26 percent of the Not Religious said that this would bother them a great deal, and one-fourth said it would not bother them at all. In contrast, about 40 percent of the other three groups anticipated that it would bother them a great deal never to marry.[12] This is true even of the Disaffiliated, who never attend religious services but still carry some religious identity. So, as a life goal, those who are the most disconnected from religious institutions also seem to be least attached to the idea of participating in the institution of marriage. In contrast, young people with a connection to religious institutions express more anticipated disappointment with the idea of never getting married. To the extent that motivation or desire for marriage drives marriage rates, it would not be surprising, then, for religious individuals to marry at younger ages than nonreligious individuals.

Table 6.3 Would Be Bothered if Never Married

	Not Religious (%)	Disaffiliated (%)	Marginal (%)	Committed (%)	All (%)
Bothered a great deal	26	41	41	43	36
Bothered some	27	25	27	29	27
Bothered a little	22	16	16	14	17
Not at all bothered	25	18	16	14	19
Total	100	100	100	100	100

Source: National Study of Youth and Religion survey 2013.

Marriage versus Companionship

Although a sizeable number of respondents reported that never getting married would not bother them, this does not mean that they do not desire committed, long-term relationships. We heard in the qualitative interviews that most respondents do aspire to having a long-term committed partner, and for the vast majority of them, this is likely to mean marriage.

However, there are differences in their visions of the form that this relationship will take. Among those who are more religious, the desire for a committed, long-term relationship clearly implies marriage. This is not surprising, given that most religious groups in the United States encourage marriage as the desired and normative context for adult life. As noted previously, young people who are involved in religious congregations have likely been exposed to a variety of pro-marriage and pro-family messages. Among our respondents, this appears as a theological bent toward marriage—that is, the understanding that marriage is something ordained by God and therefore part of the ideal package for a whole life. This is illustrated by an exchange with this 27-year-old Conservative Protestant young man:

INTERVIEWER: How likely is it that you'll get married someday?
RESPONDENT: Yeah, pretty likely, I hope so.
I: And why do you want to get married?
R: Yeah, like the whole thing of creating a family and passing your values onto the next generation of your children and . . . I think, like, God says . . . I mean you need a helper, you can't just do this all on your own. You can't go through life on your own. So, like, I think that's another important part.

This 25-year-old Black Protestant woman also believed that marriage was an important part of life according to her faith:

I: Is there a certain age or point in life when people should take dating more seriously and date to find a spouse, or not necessarily?
R: I think as soon as possible. I don't think there's a specific age. As soon as possible. You stick to that one person. Make it work— especially if you love and care for them. There should be nothing to break you up.
I: And if people didn't really want to date, didn't really want to get married, should they anyway? Is there one goal for everybody?

R: You're supposed to.

I: Okay. And why are you supposed to?

R: Jesus. He said so.

Although not particularly forthcoming with the details of this theological mandate, she is clear that Jesus desires people to be married.

The connection between companionship and marriage is not as clear-cut for those who are not religious. The rising acceptance and occurrence of cohabitation has contributed to an openness to considering alternatives to traditional marriage. Among the Not Religious respondents, marriage is still the most likely scenario, but it is not the only possibility. This group seems to privilege the relationship, in whatever form it takes, over the marriage itself. For example, this 24-year-old Atheist is not married in the legal sense, yet he had this to say about his current relationship:

> Oh yeah, I feel like we're already married. Yeah, I would do the same thing a married guy would. I take care of her and cook for her and all that stuff, so you know, we're married. I mean, why do you have to have a piece of paper and a ceremony to say you're married?

This sentiment about marriage being "just a piece of paper" was echoed by other nonreligious respondents as well. This is what we heard from a 25-year-old Not Religious woman on the subject:

I: Do you think you want to get married someday?

R: Maybe. I don't know.

I: And what do you think it would be like to live with somebody you're married to versus living with them when you are not married?

R: I really don't think it would be any different. Like, my family doesn't believe in, like, the whole you wait to live with them 'til you're married and stuff like that. My mom was with my stepdad for years and years and lived together before they got married, and so I don't see that big difference. Like, it's just a piece of paper or a ring. I don't think it'd be any different.

I: And do you want to get married someday?

R: Hmm, I think. I mean it's not, like, *that* important. I—we're talking about marriage not just a relationship right? Yeah, I don't—I mean if you have someone, you have somebody.

I: And how likely do you think it is that you'll get married?

R: It's a 50/50 chance at this point [*laughs*]. I don't know.

While the majority of the young people we spoke with believe they will marry eventually, the sense of necessity for marriage was stronger among those who identified themselves as religious. Although marriage was certainly valued by religious and nonreligious respondents alike, those who are not religious were more likely to be open, at least in theory, to alternatives to formal, legal marriage and less likely to be disappointed in the event that they never marry.

Attitudes about Nonmarital Sex

When considering the religious differences in attitudes about marriage and openness to alternative forms of relationships, one important component is attitudes toward nonmarital sexual behavior. Religious affiliation and belief have been linked to more conservative attitudes about nonmarital sex and delayed sexual activity among adolescents.[13] The emerging adults in our survey were asked, "Do you think that people should wait to have sex until they are married?" Half of all respondents answered, "Not necessarily" to this question. Twenty-one percent said yes, people should wait, and 29 percent said no, people do not need to wait for marriage to have sex. Examining responses across the four religious groups, we found that among the Committed emerging adults, 58 percent agree with the proposition that people should wait to have sex until one is married, and 16 percent of the Marginal emerging adults hold this belief. In contrast, only 2 percent of Not Religious young people and 6 percent of the Disaffiliated think that sex should be saved for marriage.

There is quite an ideological gap between the religiously Committed and the rest of the sample when it comes to views about sex before marriage. While these beliefs about nonmarital sex do not perfectly predict the decisions young people will make about their own sexual activity and relationships, research shows that disapproving attitudes toward nonmarital sex are linked to starting sexual intercourse at a later age.[14] Those who are more religiously engaged are more likely to believe in delaying sex until marriage, and these beliefs may encourage some young people to enter into marriage sooner.[15]

Cohabitation

Cohabitation is also an important part of the larger puzzle of emerging adult relationships and the transition into marriage. Whether emerging adults themselves realize it or not, cohabitation offers a viable alternative to marriage for those who are ideologically open to such an arrangement, and it has the potential to influence their timing of marriage. As with attitudes about sex before marriage, there is a gap across religious groups when we consider attitudes about cohabitation.

We asked respondents who had not already lived with a partner whether they would consider doing so in the future. Among the Committed emerging adults, just 42 percent said they would be willing to cohabit. More than 80 percent of the Marginal and Disaffiliated respondents expressed that willingness, while 93 percent of the Not Religious agreed that they would consider cohabiting in the future. Table 6.4 shows the percentage of each religious group that has, in fact, cohabited with a partner, and their behavior appears to line up with the attitudes they reported about cohabitation. The Committed emerging adults reported the lowest rate of cohabitation, at 36 percent. Among the remaining three groups, more than half have cohabited, including 66 percent of the Not Religious emerging adults.

Attitudes about cohabitation are not simply theoretical, and they are also linked to future marriage patterns. The question about willingness to cohabit in the future was also asked in the Wave 3 survey, and those who said they would cohabit are much less likely to be married five years later, compared with those who are not willing to cohabit with a partner in the future. Of those who were already cohabiting or who said yes, they would consider cohabitation in the future, 21 percent were married by the time we surveyed them in 2013. However, this is significantly less than those who at Wave 3 said that they would not consider cohabitation; 32 percent of these young people are married by Wave 4.[16] In other words, holding proscriptive ideology about cohabitation is linked to higher rates of marriage among these emerging adults.

Table 6.4 Ever Cohabited

Not Religious	66%
Disaffiliated	57%
Marginal	57%
Committed	36%
All emerging adults	55%

Source: National Study of Youth and Religion survey 2013.

The act of cohabiting is also associated with marriage patterns, as seen by comparing emerging adults who have lived with an unmarried partner at some point in the past with those who reported that they have never lived with a romantic partner to whom they were not married. Among those who have never cohabited, 33 percent are now married. However, among those who reported cohabitation, less than 20 percent are currently married.[17] So, among the emerging adults we studied, cohabitation is inversely correlated with being married before age 30.

The causal arrow surely runs in both directions here: Those who marry young have less opportunity for cohabiting relationships. On the other hand, those who enter into cohabiting relationships seem less likely to end up married before age 30. We must proceed with caution in our interpretation because many of these young people have not yet reached the average age of marriage in the United States. So, we can't comment on the long-term marriage prospects of respondents, or how cohabitation influences their marriage trajectories in the long run. What we *can* say is that cohabitation does not appear to correlate with marrying on the younger side of the age continuum. This is consistent with research that suggests that the rise of cohabitation may be contributing to the overall delay in marriage, and this is most common among those who are not religiously opposed to cohabitation.[18] On the other hand, when highly religious young people find themselves in a romantic relationship, proscriptive beliefs about nonmarital sex and cohabitation may provide a stronger incentive to marry earlier, compared with their peers for whom marriage is not a requirement for the initiation of sexual activity and living together.

Religion and Family Status

Marriage and childbearing have become more disconnected in recent decades, and a single trajectory of "marriage then children" no longer fits for large portions of the population. Recent work by Amato and colleagues highlights the need to consider both marriage and parenthood in the study of transitions into family formation.[19] Yet, examining these two issues separately does not account for the ways in which marriage and parenthood interact on the path to family formation. The impact of becoming a parent is different within a marriage context than if one is parenting children without a partner. Similarly, marriage often takes on different meaning when it is paired with parenthood.

The emerging adults in our study are at different stages of their family formation trajectories. There is much more variation and complexity than can be captured in a single chapter on this topic. Of specific interest in this section, however, is whether we find in our data support for previous research that suggests that religion is associated with earlier transitions into family formation. For our purposes, we will focus on six main categories of family status with regard to partnership and parenthood, as mentioned earlier in this chapter. To account for the different configurations of marital status and parenthood, we will focus on the current status of each respondent at the time of the Wave 4 survey: married with children, married without children, cohabiting with children, cohabiting without children, single with children, and single without children.[20] The family status indicators, shown in Table 6.5, only measure the respondents' reported relationship status and parent status at the time of the Wave 4 survey. Although we do not account for the timing of the birth and/or marriage, we can assume that the starting point for these family statuses occurs at some point before the Wave 4 measure of religion. The separation of unmarried respondents into single and cohabiting categories acknowledges that cohabitation continues to be a liminal status in terms of family transitions, serving as a precursor or alternative to marriage for some young people, while also potentially delaying marriage. In addition, as discussed

Table 6.5 Family Status by Wave 1 Religious Tradition

| | All (%) | Religious Tradition Wave 1 (Ages 13–17) | | | | | | |
		CP (%)	MP (%)	BP (%)	RC (%)	J (%)	LDS (%)	NR (%)
Married with children	14	18	11	11	9	9	30	14
Married without children	12	17	13	3	9	6	13	9
Cohabiting with children	6	6	5	7	6	0	7	9
Cohabiting without children	11	9	15	5	12	4	7	16
Single with children	11	10	6	36	10	0	4	8
Single without children	46	40	50	37	54	81	39	45
Total	100	100	100	100	100	100	100	100

BP = Black Protestant; CP = Conservative Protestant; J = Jewish; LDS = Latter-day Saints; MP = Mainline Protestant; NR = Not Religious; RC = Roman Catholic.

Source: National Study of Youth and Religion surveys 2003, 2013.

previously, cohabitation is often discouraged within religious communities. Choosing to remain single as an early emerging adult does not run counter to pro-family religious norms in the same way that cohabitation might. Therefore, these two family stages are examined separately because their relationships with the religious lives of young people likely follow different patterns.

Early family formation is linked both to religious tradition or institutional affiliation and to personal religious practice and belief. We examine the relationships between adolescent religion (i.e., the religious identity of emerging adults when they were teens) and future transitions to marriage and parenthood that appear in our data. Looking first at the broad categories of religious traditions, we see that emerging adults who identified as Mormons, Conservative Protestants, or Black Protestants in their teenage years are the most likely to have made family transitions by the time we survey them for Wave 4 (Table 6.5). Among the respondents who were Latter-day Saints (LDS) in their teens, 30 percent are currently married with children, 13 percent are married without children, and 11 percent are cohabiting or single with children. Only 46 percent of those who were Mormon as teens have not experienced either marriage or parenthood. Among the emerging adults who are identified as Black Protestant or Conservative Protestant at the time of the first survey, only 37 and 40 percent, respectively, are single with no children. Thirty-five percent of the Conservative Protestants are currently married, and 34 percent have children at the last survey. Including the 7 percent who reported a previous marriage (not shown), 42 percent of Wave 1 Conservative Protestants reported having gotten married at some point during the course of the study.

Measuring religious salience from the teenage years tells a very similar story. Table 6.6 compares Wave 4 family status by levels of importance of faith at Wave 1. Among those for whom faith was very or extremely important as adolescents, 32 percent are married by the time they reach their 20s, and 36 percent have children. In comparison, just 18 percent of those who as adolescents said faith is somewhat important and those who said it is not very or not at all important are married at the final survey, while 28 and 22 percent are parents, respectively. Thus, among emerging adults for whom faith was important as teenagers, less than half have not yet transitioned into either marriage or parenthood. For their counterparts for whom faith was less important as youth, more than 60 percent are still awaiting these transitions.[21]

Table 6.6 Family Status by Wave 1 Importance of Faith

	Not Important (%)	Somewhat Important (%)	Very/Extremely Important (%)
Married with children	9	11	17
Married without children	9	8	15
Cohabiting with children	5	7	6
Cohabiting without children	16	14	8
Single with children	8	11	12
Single without children	53	50	41
Total	100	100	100

Source: National Study of Youth and Religion surveys 2003, 2013.

Religious affiliation is certainly not fixed, and many of our respondents change their religious affiliation or identity over the course of the study. This warrants an examination not just of early religion on future marriage but also of current religious identity as it relates to current marital status. Looking at Wave 4 religious tradition, the pattern is similar to the Wave 1 analysis (Table 6.7). Among the emerging adults who identified as LDS in the Wave 4 survey, 42 percent are married with children and 15 percent are married without children, meaning that 57 percent of this religious group is currently married, compared with just 26 percent of the entire sample of respondents. Another nine percent have children but are unmarried, leaving just 34 percent of current Mormon emerging adults who have not experienced either marriage or parenthood by the time they reach the ages of 23 to 28. Conservative Protestants have the next highest family transition rate, with 56 percent who are married and/or have children. This means that 44 percent of the current Conservative Protestants are unmarried and without children.[22] Mainline Protestant and Jewish respondents have marriage rates of less than 30 percent each; 25 and 20 percent, respectively, of these two groups have children, either within or outside of marriage.[23] While a relatively low number of Black Protestants are married (19 percent), they have the highest rate of respondents with children; 58 percent of Black Protestants have had children either within or outside of marriage.[24] The lowest rates of marriage are for the Catholic and Not Religious groups of emerging adults, each with only 17 percent currently married.[25] The low marriage rates are somewhat offset by higher rates of cohabitation among Catholics and Not

Table 6.7 Family Status by Wave 4 Religious Tradition

	All (%)	CP (%)	MP (%)	BP (%)	RC (%)	J (%)	LDS (%)	NR (%)
			Religious Tradition Wave 4 (Age 23–28)					
Married with children	14	20	13	14	8	12	42	9
Married without children	12	21	16	5	9	16	15	8
Cohabiting with children	6	6	2	9	7	8	4	6
Cohabiting without children	11	5	8	4	12	12	2	18
Single with children	11	9	10	35	7	0	5	8
Single without children	46	38	51	33	57	52	32	50
Total	100	100	100	100	100	100	100	100

BP = Black Protestant; CP = Conservative Protestant; J = Jewish; LDS = Latter-day Saints; MP = Mainline Protestant; NR = Not Religious; RC = Roman Catholic.

Source: National Study of Youth and Religion survey 2013.

Religious. However, even if we consider marriage and cohabitation together, just 36 percent of Catholic young people are currently partnered—less than any other group—while 41 percent of the Not Religious have partners through marriage or cohabitation. The differences in marriage rates across religious traditions are consistent with other research findings on this topic.[26]

When we examine family status by the four categories of religious engagement, we see a large difference between those who are regular attenders and those who are not (Table 6.8). Emerging adults in the Committed group are the least likely to be single without children: just 38 percent fall in this category. They are also the group least likely to be cohabiting without children, at just three percent. By comparison, 46 percent of Marginal attenders, and half of the Disaffiliated and Not Religious respondents, are single without children, while the rate of cohabiting without children ranges from 10 to 18 percent for these three groups. Among the Committed emerging adults, 44 percent are currently married, while 23 percent of the Marginal attenders are married. Disaffiliated and Not Religious emerging adults are married at rates of 16 and 17 percent, respectively.[27] The Committed emerging adults are also the most likely to have children: 38 percent reported being a parent, and the majority of these regularly attending parents are currently married. Among each of

Table 6.8 Family Status by Religious Group

	Not Religious (%)	Disaffiliated (%)	Marginal (%)	Committed (%)
Married with children	9	8	15	23
Married without children	8	9	8	21
Cohabiting with children	6	7	8	4
Cohabiting without children	18	13	10	3
Single with children	8	14	13	11
Single without children	50	50	46	38
Total	100	100	100	100

Source: National Study of Youth and Religion survey 2013.

the other three groups, the percent who are unmarried with children is higher than those who are married with children.

By each religion measure examined previously, young people who are more religious, both as teenagers and emerging adults, are more likely to be married or have children in early emerging adulthood than those who are more disengaged from religion. Given the age limitations of our sample, we note that we cannot predict the eventual marriage or parenting status of those in our study. But what we *can* say is that religion is associated with earlier transitions to marriage and parenting among this group of emerging adults. In all likelihood, this will also translate to higher rates of marriage and parenting over the life course, but that is a conclusion that can't be drawn at this time from these data.

Family and Future Religion

The National Study of Youth and Religion (NSYR) sample is consistent with other research that finds that religious individuals generally transition to marriage and parenthood at an earlier age, on average, than those who are less religiously engaged.[28] A parallel question that is of considerable interest is whether the transitions to marriage and parenthood have implications for the ongoing religious lives of young people. That is, does the causal arrow run in the other direction as well? Although religious individuals are more likely to get married and have children in the first place, is it the case that marriage and parenthood act to increase religious engagement for those who make early family transitions? Previous research has found some evidence for increased religious participation among those who are married or have children.[29] In the following section we turn to these questions, looking at how not just religious participation but also self-identified religious salience and change are shaped by new family relationships.

The short answer is that there is still much we do not know about the long-term effect of marriage and parenting on the religious lives of emerging adults. The emerging adults in our study are between the ages of 23 and 28. As we noted previously, this means that many of them have not yet approached the average age of first marriage for people in the United States. Among the respondents in our final sample, just one-fourth are currently married, and another four percent have been married but are currently divorced, separated, or widowed. This means that, for almost 70 percent of the sample, we do not yet know when they will marry or whether marriage will affect their future religious lives. Likewise, just more than 30 percent are parents, leaving a sizeable portion of our respondents yet to experience the impact that children might have on religious belief and practice. However, examining the lives of those in our study sample who have already made the transition to marriage or parenting can offer some insight into the relationship between early family transitions and religious engagement.

Among those who are already somewhat religious, family commitments may encourage more regular attendance at religious services. Figure 6.1 compares the current religious service attendance of the six family groups, and we see that marriage appears more closely related to attendance than does having children. Married emerging adults reported attending religious services more than those who are not married, regardless of whether they have children. About 35 percent of both groups of married respondents attend weekly or more, and a similar percentage reported that they never attend.

In contrast, among the cohabiting and single emerging adults, weekly attendance ranges from just 3 percent to 16 percent. And reports of never attending religious services are much higher among the unmarried compared with the married respondents. Cohabitors without children have the highest rate of saying they never attend religious services, at 73 percent, with the other three groups falling just above or below the 50 percent mark. While the presence of children was not associated with differing levels of attendance among the married respondents, parenthood is more closely associated with attendance for those who are not married. Among both

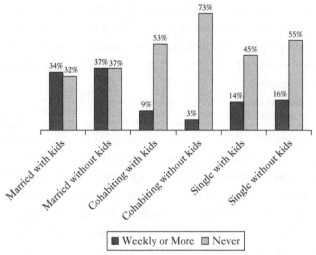

FIGURE 6.1 Wave 4 religious service attendance by family status.
Source: National Study of Youth and Religion survey 2013.

single and cohabiting emerging adults, those who have children are some-what less likely to say they never attend religious services compared with their counterparts who do not have children. Fifty-five percent of single re-spondents without children say they never attend, while among those with children, this drops to 45 percent. Among cohabiting young people, the gap is even larger. When children are present in cohabiting relationships, reports of never attending services drops from 73 to 53 percent.

Weekly attendance at religious services has declined, on average, across all groups of the emerging adults in our study. And while there appears to be a strong association between family status and attendance, we have established that individuals who are already religious are more likely to get married and have children sooner than their nonreligious peers. So, while the association between family status and attendance seen in Figure 6.1 is telling, the question of whether marriage and parenthood have a direct impact on the general decline in religious participation deserves further examination. To address this question, we focus on those respond-ents who were weekly attenders at Wave 3. Among this group of religiously engaged young people, is marriage or parenthood associated with whether they maintained their religious participation when we interviewed them again at Wave 4?

Figure 6.2 includes only those young people who attended religious services weekly at Wave 3. Among this group of regularly engaged young people, we can see that those who are married were far more likely to remain weekly attenders by Wave 4 than any of the other emerging adult family status groups. Approximately two-thirds of those who are married maintain weekly attendance from Wave 3 to Wave 4. Those least likely to maintain weekly attendance are the emerging adults who are in cohabiting relationships without children, with only 11 percent still saying they regularly attend religious services.

Emerging adults who are cohabiting without children are those who have not made a transition to marriage or parenthood, more conventionally approved family statuses within religious communities. Instead, they are engaging in a relationship pattern that is often discouraged by religious groups. So while these individuals were weekly attenders at Wave 3, they are no longer regularly engaged in a religious congregation. The implication here is that while marriage appears to help young people maintain their religious engagement, cohabitation may serve as a barrier to participation in religious communities. It is possible that individuals in cohabiting relationships no longer feel welcome or comfortable attending religious services. It is also possible that individuals who have disengaged from religion for other reasons find themselves less bound by religious proscriptions against cohabitation and pursue those relationships more readily.

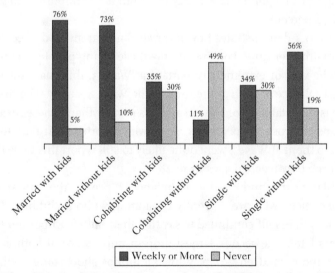

FIGURE 6.2 Wave 4 religious service attendance if weekly attender at Wave 3.
Source: National Study of Youth and Religion surveys 2008, 2013.

Whatever the causal direction, it is clear that the trajectories of family formation among emerging adults are intertwined with their ongoing religious participation. Given that cohabitation is becoming much more common, this could signal yet another factor that is related to the overall decline in religious service attendance among young people.

Attendance at religious services demonstrates one facet of religious engagement. In addition to the public religious practice of service attendance, however, another way to measure religious engagement is to consider the extent to which religion is salient and meaningful in people's lives. Marriage and parenting may reinforce the practice of religious service attendance, but does it change the role of faith in the personal lives of individuals?

Again, we compare reports from the young people in six different stages of family relationships. Figure 6.3 shows the percentage of each group who reported that faith is very or extremely important to them as well as those who said it is not important. Looking at the numbers for very or extremely important, we see the highest percentages among those who have family commitments: married with children, married without children, single with children, and cohabiting with children. Emerging adults who are cohabiting or single without children reported that faith is significantly less important compared with the married with children group. These two groups who are not married and do not have children have the most respondents who say that faith is not important to them, at 48 and 36 percent.[30]

Figure 6.4 demonstrates how marriage and parenthood affect the salience of faith over time. Looking at only those young people who reported faith to be very or extremely important at Wave 3, this chart shows their reported salience of faith at the time of the Wave 4 survey. The first thing to note is that stability for this measure is greater than for the measure of attendance. Across all six groups, those who reported their faith to be important to them at Wave 3 were quite likely to still report this to be the case by the time they reached ages 23 to 28.

Similar to the findings for attendance, however, the largest change is among those who are currently cohabiting without children. For this group, less than half continued to say that their faith is important to them five years later. The second largest drop in importance of faith is for the single without children group. While all groups show some decline, this decline is the greatest for emerging adults who have not yet married or had children.

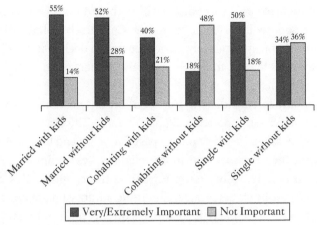

FIGURE 6.3 Wave 4 importance of faith by family status.
Source: National Study of Youth and Religion survey 2013.

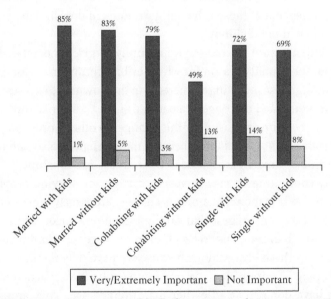

FIGURE 6.4 Wave 4 importance of faith if very/extremely important at Wave 3.
Source: National Study of Youth and Religion surveys 2008, 2013.

Marriage and parenting may not necessarily create an increased importance of faith. However, they do appear to stabilize the faith that emerging
adults already have. In other words, when it comes to the personal salience of religious faith, it seems that transitioning into family life has a
stabilizing effect. Marriage and parenting are not necessarily causing a

significant increase in the importance of faith, but family responsibilities may help to solidify its place in their lives. Conversely, cohabitation is the family status that is most closely associated with a decline in religious salience and appears to have the most disruptive impact on the religious lives of emerging adults.

Another way to consider the impact of family relationships on religiosity is to look at self-reported religious change. The emerging adults in our study were asked to reflect on the past five years and to report whether they thought they had become more religious, less religious, or stayed about the same religiously. Figure 6.5 shows the results of this question across the six family status groups. Emerging adults who are married with children are the most likely to report becoming more religious (41 percent) and least likely to say they became less religious (11 percent) during the past five years. In contrast, those least likely to report becoming more religious are the emerging adults who are not married and do not have children: 18 percent of those cohabiting without children and 21 percent of those single without children.

Respondents were offered the opportunity to give an open-ended answer about the primary reason for why they had become more or less religious. Among those reporting an increase in their own religiousness, about 13 percent mentioned marriage or a partner, and 27 percent identified their children as the primary reason for this change. In other words, 40 percent of the respondents who said they became more religious also said that the change can be primarily attributed to their family relationships.[31]

Family commitments may serve as a catalyst for drawing people back to religion.[32] While the results of our analysis are largely consistent with this expectation, we suggest that family transitions encourage religious *stability* more than religious *revival*. Caution is necessary in drawing conclusions from these observations because we have only the first scene in multi-act play. The individuals in our sample who have married and had children have done so at an earlier than average age. They are a select group of individuals who we know were already predisposed to be more religious than their peers. We do not want to overstate the claim that marriage or becoming a parent creates a religious awakening. That is more dramatic than what appears to be taking place. Rather, we think marriage and parenting create a context in which individuals may find support for their existing religious identity and practices.

This 23-year-old Conservative Protestant illustrates this point when he discusses the effect of marriage on his church attendance:

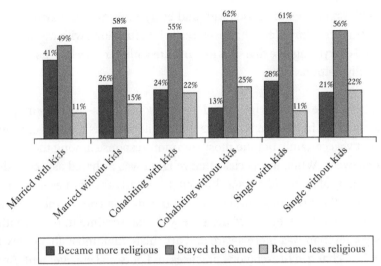

FIGURE 6.5 Wave 4 self-reported religious change by family status.
Source: National Study of Youth and Religion survey 2013.

I wasn't too good about going to church when I was in college; I wish I had done a better job with that. I had a church, but there wasn't any church that I really felt I connected with. . . . A lot of it probably was just me trying to want to sleep in on a Sunday or whatever. But it's gotten better, because now that we're a couple and we're in a different city, we wanted to meet more people, so we're . . . being intentional about that—joining groups and stuff like that. And so . . . that's brought a whole lot more to the church and everything, which has been great.

For this young man, having a partner with whom to share the process of seeking out church involvement made a difference in his regular attendance pattern. And while relocating often creates a disconnect from religious communities, in this case, the relocation created an opportunity for him and his wife to get involved in church.

In addition to the practical motive of wanting to meet people, some respondents spoke of the role their marriage played in encouraging them in their faith and keeping them engaged at a personal level. The young man quoted previously went on to say:

I can't imagine being married to someone who didn't share my beliefs, because it would be tough not having someone to go to church

with or, like, go to classes with and everything. So just having that
influence in my life . . . has been really helpful, along with my family
and everything like that. But just my life with her now has just been
really helpful.

There were others who shared similar sentiments—that their spouse
was a partner in religion as well as life. While this was not uncommon to
hear, it was certainly not the most common response among the married
interviewees. While it was clear that religion was a shared aspect of their
lives, many of them did not speak about it as clearly as this or even acknowledge that their marriage influenced their religious commitments in any
way. It is not that they would disagree with that sentiment, per se; rather,
this young man was more aware and articulate than most about how his
marriage changed his religious practices and personal engagement. As we
have seen in other areas of our study of these young people, they are often
unaware of the social forces that are operating in their own lives.

A common refrain across the long arc of the NSYR has been that a
lack of awareness on the part of the participants does not mean that religion isn't operating at some level in their lives. In this case, the survey
data suggest that marriage and parenthood serve as agents to solidify the
religious engagement of young people. We do not think they spin people
full circle—that is, they are not turning atheists into attenders. More accurately, we think marriage and parenthood stem the tide of religious decline.
If young adults marry someone who shares their religious commitments,
then that partnership makes it more possible for young people to remain
religiously engaged in ways that being single might not. Likewise, when
people become parents, they are more likely to want to remain connected
to those institutions that offer support and guidance for them as they raise
their children. In other words, formal family commitments, whether marriage or parenthood, reduce the likelihood of drifting away from religious
engagement.

The other story worth noting here is the impact of cohabitation. Across
the analysis of public religious participation, private religious salience, and
self-perceptions of religious change, we see that emerging adults who are
cohabiting without children experience the most distance from religion,
as measured by our survey items. It is evident that cohabiting relationships do not reinforce or support religious engagement in the same way
that marriage seems to. Rather, it appears that cohabitation moves young
people further from their faith than other family arrangements.

While the causal direction and mechanisms of influence are not specified by our data, this is a trend that is worth paying attention to. Cohabitation has been rising steadily in recent decades and is now the most common pathway to marriage.[33] At the same time, it seems that emerging adults who are involved in these cohabiting relationships are becoming more distant from communities of faith. Discerning the reasons that cohabitors are less likely to remain religiously engaged may be a key factor in understanding the future landscape of the religious lives of this population.[34]

Ashley and Carla

In contemplating the relationships between marriage, parenthood, and the continuation of religious faith, two young women that we interviewed stand out. Their stories are salient not because they are necessarily representative of the larger group of interviewees—in fact, their stories were not common. But they resonate as examples of the potential connection between religious engagement and marriage and parenting, and perhaps as a counter-example to the more common story of the way that marriage and parenting can hold people in their faith. For Ashley and Carla, marriage might be the thing that keeps them from returning to the faith of their youth.

Some readers may recall Ashley—the Abider from *A Faith of Their Own*. At that time, she was generally quite committed to her Christian faith, although she had some clear ambivalence about the church. In our final interview, Ashley and I met for coffee on a summer afternoon in the Northwest.[35] She told me that life was going well for her and filled me in on the changes in her life since we had last seen each other. She experienced a traumatic breakup with a long-term boyfriend during her last year of college. She had been diagnosed with depression while she was in high school, and this breakup sent her into a significant depressive episode. During this time, she started spending time with a friend she had met during her first year of college. He was supportive of her during her recovery from the breakup. They eventually began dating and are now married. She has decided to return to school to earn a master's degree and was excited to be starting that program in the coming months.

Ashley seems happy in her marriage. Although they had a rough start to their dating relationship, she describes their current relationship in very positive terms; she says they get along very well and that he is good for her, noting that she has not had a depressive episode in a very long time and that life is pretty stable right now. As the interview progressed, we turned

to the topic of religion. I asked Ashley how she would describe herself religiously and she responded:

> Religiously, I guess, I'm a Christian who doesn't attend church. So
> I still have the fundamental beliefs . . . but it's been awhile. And
> I don't identify as well, like, with the church as well. Like, I never
> identified terribly well. But I still really believe, like, the core beliefs,
> in like God and Jesus.

Ashley expresses something akin to regret over the fact that she is not currently connected with a church. She sees the value in that connection and
senses the loss of not being part of a church community. But she always
had a hard time fitting in at the churches she attended and says it is hard
to get motivated to attend church when it is not a place where she feels
comfortable. Despite this, she has not ruled it out of her future. I asked
what she thinks she will be like religiously at age 40, and she says, "I hope
to be more serious about religion. Like, not necessarily in my parents'
church but, you know. To find a community who think similarly to me and
be able to spend time with them would be really nice." So, while she is not
currently attending church, she contends that her beliefs are still the same
and she hopes to find a church community again in the future.

Ashley reported that her husband is not particularly religious. He was
raised by Southern Baptist parents, but they stopped attending church
years ago. While he identifies as a Christian, he does not attend church
and has no interest in doing so. Ashley reported that he was a philosophy
major in college and "he's not as firm in a lot of the more traditional, like,
doctrine." I asked Ashley if she were to decide to start attending church,
whether he would attend with her. Her response was, "Maybe once in a
while. But I couldn't rely on him to, like, happily attend with me." When
I asked how she felt about this, she said, "I mean it's not thrilling. But it
is what it is. It's like, something I knew going in and, so, I can't really be
angry with him now. But it would be nice if he was like, 'okay, let's go to
church.' But, I'm hoping, you know, we'll see how things progress. I mean
he's open to it, but yeah, it'd be tricky."

A few weeks later, I am sitting in the corner of a noisy Mexican restaurant in the Southeast talking with Carla. As a self-proclaimed introvert,
she admits that she is nervous about the interview and was hoping the
restaurant would have been less crowded. She is hesitant throughout the
interview, but lights up when we start talking about her fiancé. They have

dated for eight years and recently got engaged. She is convinced he is the one for her and is very excited about finally getting married.

During the course of the interview, my questions about religion bring an interesting response. Carla "shoulds" herself a lot: I *should* know more about my faith, I *should* go to church more, I *should* be more involved with my congregation. She lacks confidence in her own knowledge about her faith and repeatedly seems embarrassed that she is not more conversant in this area. Her fiancé is not religious, and Carla does not think that he would consider himself a Christian. In fact, it seems that she struggles to defend her faith against his skepticism and doubt, and while she wants to express her faith to him, she feels intimidated by her lack of knowledge and conviction about religious topics. She says she thinks he will want to raise children in church with her. But I am not sure she really believes this (and I certainly am not convinced, either).

Ashley and Carla both strike me as individuals for whom marriage and parenthood have the potential to bring about renewed religious engagement. Both express some level of regret over their current lack of religious engagement and acknowledge that their disconnect from church is a consequence of competing priorities. There are many demands on their time, and attending church is not compelling at this stage of their lives. They both report that they would like to attend more or be more involved in a religious congregation, but they have not taken the steps to do so. In addition, they both acknowledge that, in an ideal world, they would hope to raise their children in the same faith tradition they were raised in. In fact, they both see the presence of children as a possible motivator for renewed religious engagement. Here, Ashley speculates on the effect that having children might have on her own religiosity:

I: Do you see it getting any easier or more difficult to maintain your religious faith in the future?

R: I think, I'm guessing if we have kids, it'll be easier. Because that whole thing, like, "Oh, get your kids into church, get your kids into Sunday school." But I'm not sure that's really the right reason to do things. But I think that will make it easier [*laughs*] even though I think that's really sort of hypocritical.

Carla also wants religion to be a part of her children's lives. However, before we hear her assertion of this fact, she spends time fumbling through an attempt to explain her fiancé's position on this issue:

I: If you were to have children, would you raise them in a particular religion or faith tradition?

R: It's also something that I've discussed with my fiancé, and I think since he wasn't in church a lot growing up, since he was raised by a single parent and no father. . . . I guess in his house, he sees things a little bit differently. He . . . said he wants to go to church, it's just—God, what did he say the other day?—but yes, I do—I do want to raise my kids. I don't want them to just go to. . . . I want them to, you know, to go to church with someone with morals and values, what's right and wrong.

While both women talk about their future children and the importance of raising them in church, they also acknowledge that this will pose a challenge with a husband who is not as committed to the idea of raising children within a religious community. Ashley says that her husband is open to the idea in theory but has no interest in attending church himself. Ashley seems resigned to her husband's lack of interest, though she acknowledges that their religious differences affect her more than him:

I don't think that [our differences] bother him. Because for him, it's. . . . I feel like he's kind of on the easier side, like not believing, being more casual about a religion and being with someone who's more serious doesn't affect him probably as much as me being with someone who is more casual. Because I want him. . . . You know, he doesn't really care that I'm more serious. Whereas I would like him to be more serious.

While she says she is content with her current situation, she indicates that the religious disconnect between her and her husband may be more of an issue in the context of thinking about the future and the possibility of returning to church once she has children. I ask whether her husband's lack of religious interest might prevent her from being as religious as she would like to be, and she responds:

R: I think I am okay with where I am. I don't know if, down the road, like I see it as something that may be a problem at some point. . . . But as of right this moment, it's okay.

I: Okay, and it might be a problem because of children or something else?

R: Just if I really decide I want to get reconnected, I will want him with me, just because he's my partner. And so it'll be difficult if that's something he really isn't willing to do.

Although Ashley expresses some regret about her current disconnect from church, and she says she wants to take her children to church in the future, she does not sound optimistic about having the support of her husband. As for Carla, she tells a similar story of a fiancé who is not opposed to her taking their future children to church. Just after telling me that her fiancé would not identify himself as a Christian, she proceeds, unprompted, into the following remarks:

R: I hope in the end that doesn't become an issue when I do get married and have kids, but I mean it's stuff I've talked about. You know, like, look I'm getting married to you. This is something [*chuckles*], you know, we got to think about ahead of time. So if we have kids—but you see, he's not, he's not opposed to the idea. He does want our kids to be, you know, in church, around, you know, the right crowd of people. . . .
I: So, he wouldn't be opposed to you if you chose to take them to church?
R: No. Guess I'd go by myself, if I'd have to [*laughs*]. Nah, he would, he would probably go too. I think he's up to, you know, trying new things and learning new things.

She ends by saying that she thinks he would go with her if she chose to take the children to church. She is telling me with her words that this is something that he will be on board with. But sitting across the table from her, I see her nervous laughter and hear the doubt in her voice. At the conclusion of the interview, I wrote the following in my field notes: "I got the impression that our conversation seemed to make her consider in a new light the fact that she was marrying someone who is not religious and the potential problems that might cause in the future."

Religion shapes (or doesn't shape) the path to marriage and creates a trajectory that continues to operate in people's lives. Ashley and Carla are examples of women who were raised in religious homes and married at relatively young ages. Ashley married her husband at age 24. At 27, Carla is a little older than Ashley, though it is clear that she has been anticipating and planning for her marriage for a very long time. The timing was constrained by socioeconomic factors as well as the fact that it took her and her fiancé a long time to work their way through college. Carla's brother and twin sister are already married with children, and she is anxious to "catch up" with them now that she has graduated.

Neither Ashley nor Carla is particularly involved in religion currently. On the one hand, we see the influence of their religious upbringing in the way that the tendency toward early marriage is still operating in their lives. However, stepping away and taking a break from religion shifted their trajectories when it came to selecting a marriage partner. And their choice of a partner, rather than bringing them back to the faith of their youth, will likely solidify their movement away from it, at least in their practice and active engagement, even if not in their core beliefs or personal desire for a future faith for their children.

The stories of Ashley and Carla are not meant to represent the majority of the individuals we talked to. Statistically speaking, we have shown that marriage and parenthood do, on average, create a buffer against religious decline. However, their stories illustrate the potential for marriage to work in the opposite direction. In the same vein as "my marriage partner provides encouragement to my faith," being partnered with someone who is not religious can present obstacles to remaining engaged in one's faith. To be fair, Ashley and Carla were already disconnecting from religion when their relationships began. And this disconnection seems to have been a factor in their decision to move forward in a relationship with someone who did not share their faith (we see among the strongly religious more commitment to religious homogamy). But, once that trajectory is set, it makes it even less likely that the forces within marriage or parenthood that could potentially lead them to re-engage will do so, in their case.

The stories of Ashley and Carla stuck with me long after I had completed the interviews that summer, perhaps because of the uncertainty and regret that were just under the surface as they spoke. Or the recognition that this situation was the result of their own choice, unlikely to change, and something they hadn't really considered much before. It was that sense of the weight of the choices we make as young people that carry implications beyond what we can fathom at the time. Perhaps it was because I could see down the road something that they couldn't as well; as a social scientist, I am aware of the statistical probabilities that await them. And I feel their ambivalence and their sense that maybe they had missed something.

Conclusion

Throughout this chapter, we have looked at the often reciprocal relationship between religion and family formation. People who are more religious are more likely to transition into family formation sooner in life. Through their religious engagement, they are likely to hear pro-family messages and see family life held up as the normative standard in their religious communities. This social context encourages earlier transitions to marriage and childbearing. In turn, those young people who marry and have children may be looking to religion as a source of support during this life transition. Religious congregations and personal religious faith can offer solidarity and encouragement for the challenges of marriage and parenting. So, young people who are entering into new family relationships are more likely to stay engaged in the religious life that offers support for and normalizes their family choices.

There are those who see the precipitous decline of religion among young people and reassure themselves that they will come back to the church once they get married and have children. We caution that this interpretation of the data may be too generous. The significant delay in marriage and childbearing means that, for many emerging adults, by the time they make these family transitions, they may be so far removed from their previous religious identity that they will not have the kind of connection to religion that would support that renewal of faith. We do not yet have evidence to suggest that those who completely defect will return to religion upon marriage or even parenthood. However, when marriage or childbirth happens while they are still religiously committed, those life transitions can solidify their faith and keep them engaged.

Conclusion

EMERGING ADULTS AND THE FUTURE OF
RELIGION—MAKING SENSE OF IT ALL

EMERGING ADULTS ARE, overall, moving away from formal religious beliefs, practices, and participation in religious institutions. Even for those
emerging adults who maintain a place in their lives for religion, it tends to
be treated as just one part of their lives among many, not necessarily more
important than any other. One explanation of their changing religious and
spiritual ideas, beliefs, and practices is that this is part of their "identity exploration" resulting from their in-between status—no longer adolescents,
not quite adults. For emerging adults, religion just doesn't fit particularly
well with who they understand themselves to be.

The young people in our study do express almost unbridled optimism
about their own ambitions to pursue opportunities and dreams, however
unrealistic these may be. Recall, for example, John and Raymond from
Chapter 1, who each seem to have an optimistic outlook that is disconnected from the reality they are living. This applies to religion, too, as
we heard from emerging adults who are no longer religious but held out
the option that "anything can happen," whether a return to church, an
interest in meditation, or a self-styled spirituality. They are hopeful that
there is a life after death, but they are uncomfortable with the idea of hell.
As Heather said, "I don't really do hell." Yet, digging a little deeper exposes
their general lack of interest in actually doing anything related to religion
and spirituality.

The five characteristics of emerging adulthood that we outlined at
the beginning of the book—(1) identity exploration, (2) a period of instability, (3) a time of intense self-focus, (4) a time of transition or "feeling

in-between," and (5) a time of possibilities—at least imply that emerging adults are thinking deeply about their lives and trying to determine who they are and who they might become. And some emerging adults do pursue such introspection and personal development. Yet, we do not think this is the norm for emerging adults. Rather, they tend to be mostly prag-matic in their dream-making, whether about a career, marriage, kids, or religion—they ask, "Does this work for me?" They are not as self-aware as those five characteristics might lead one to believe, particularly as they think about and enact their religious and spiritual lives.

This is not to say that these different characteristics fail to capture the context within which emerging adults are living. Rather, emerging adults are largely passive in how they approach their "identity work," particularly in how they think about the role of religion and spirituality in their lives. Thus, contrary to the claims made by some scholars that emerging adults are "spiritual but not religious" or "postmodern pilgrims" who are actively seeking out new spiritual experiences, practices, and communities, we find that they are not, on average, pursuing any sort of spiritual quest or pilgrimage.[1]

Despite the general decline and move away from religion among emerging adults, they do not seem so much opposed to religion or to re-ligious organizations, at least in the abstract, as they are uninterested in religion, at least as they have experienced it. In general, they simply find it inconsequential in their lives. This is certainly true for those who identify as Not Religious, but we can also hear echoes of this among those who re-main committed and active in their faith.

Emerging adults who consider themselves Not Religious are the most obviously disengaged from religion. Yet, they are not all completely "sec-ular." For some, the religion of their youth still operates at a residual or background level, as evidenced by belief in God or an impulse to pray when they feel as though they need help or guidance at a particular mo-ment. This is not to say, however, that religion has any sort of real presence in their lives. Rather, they are open to and acknowledge the possibility of religion, while maintaining a personal distance from any religious tradi-tion or community. Thus, religion remains largely irrelevant; they are nei-ther for it nor against it. For the Not Religious, to the degree that religion exists in their lives at all, it is as a more or less theoretical or abstract op-tion, but one that they are unlikely to ever choose for themselves.

Disaffiliated emerging adults are those who maintain a religious iden-tity but are otherwise uninvolved with religion. They maintain a peripheral

connection to religion, more as a cultural identity marker than as a meaningful spiritual commitment. They often expressed "hope" that there
might be something beyond this life, and given this glimmer of possibility,
they are not willing to completely reject their religious beliefs or identity.
Many think religion *should* be part of their lives, even though it isn't—as
opposed to the Not Religious, who don't seem to feel the same regret.

Overall, these emerging adults do not have strong negative feelings
toward organized religion. Yet, despite their generally positive feelings
and their maintenance of a vestigial religious identity, they exhibit no
personal interest in having any involvement with religion or religious
institutions. Religion doesn't really affect or benefit their lives in any
direct, practical, everyday sense. Religion occupies a residual space for
them, where it would "be nice" if religious claims were true, but most
likely they aren't, so it is not worth the investment of time and energy
to pursue. Although they may participate in some limited forms of spiritual practice, these tend to be specific and idiosyncratic to the individual and his or her background.

The group of emerging adults who have a Marginal involvement
with religion seem best understood as occupying the space between the
Disaffiliated and the Committed, tending more toward the former than the
latter. However, they are distinct from the Disaffiliated emerging adults in
that they put more importance on faith than do either the Disaffiliated
or the Not Religious. We can divide the marginally committed into two
further types. First are those who are "hanging on," thinking that religion might ultimately prove true, and if so, might gain greater meaning
in their lives. At present, however, religion is given a low priority in their
lives, and it seems likely that as they move into the more regular routines
of adult work and family commitments, religion will become even less of a
priority for them, ultimately losing out to the other demands of their lives.
Thus, these emerging adults seem more likely to become Disaffiliated in
the future.

There are others in the Marginal category, however, who seem content
with the limited presence of religion in their lives and for whom it adds
something, whether spiritual or social, that seems important enough to
maintain. Perhaps they are looking for a place to feel whole or fulfilled, or
to have some sort of experience, or possibly to find answers to questions
they can't quite articulate. Many in this group of the marginally religious
have had some previous experience in religious institutions, which has
somehow kept them connected to religion. They seem likely to maintain

their current level of religious commitment until whatever benefits they receive from it cease to be an important part of their lives.

Of course, it is possible that either of these two groups of marginally religious emerging adults *could* increase their commitment levels at some point in the future. Their connections to religious communities, however tenuous, position them to respond to challenging life events or experiences in ways that could activate their religious commitment. But for emerging adults who already have one foot out the door of their religious traditions, this seems unlikely to happen.

Finally, there are the emerging adults we have identified as religiously Committed. These emerging adults evince more religious engagement and spiritual practice than their peers, and they acknowledge the importance of religion in their daily lives. They are going against the dominant trend of decline, and in some ways it appears that their involvement and commitment may have actually increased since their teenage years. For a subset of them, religious faith is a significant driver in their lives, shaping their decisions and life trajectories.

For most Committed emerging adults, however, religion is less a driving force than it is a routine part of their lives, not dissimilar from work or family obligations. Religion seems to fit into their lives as one among many other obligations—or perhaps preferences—as they are settling into adulthood. It is part of the overall package of their adult lives. For example, recall that the religiously committed are more likely to be married, which in many ways requires a set routine with demands from work, home, kids, and the like. Religion is simply one more of these life obligations.

For these young people, religious practice and engagement take a rather conventional form, mostly through attendance at religious services and unstructured, reflexive prayer. They do not show much evidence that they are developing intentional spiritual practices. They tend to draw on religion for their own individual well-being, while keeping it in a place in their lives where it makes few demands of them.

Despite the general trend away from religion among emerging adults, there seem to be varying degrees of "hanging on" to a very basic set of beliefs, along with some individualized spiritual practices that suggest they are maintaining at least the possibility that there is "something else" beyond material life. In some cases, this amounts to hedging their bets, to greater or lesser degrees, about whether religion might really be true and, if so, whether it should or could be a part of their lives. Of course, that implies that they are giving significant thought to issues of religion or spirituality, which for most does not seem to be the case. Indeed, in our interviews, many seemed to consider religion only because we were asking about it, not because these issues regularly occupied their thoughts. Thus, even though emerging adults may remain open to the possibility that God exists and that prayers might be answered, for many of them, religion ranges from being inconsequential in their lives to being, at most, an unremarkable presence. Religion remains something in which they *could* believe or to which they *could* belong, but it doesn't have the pull or attraction to gain their attention as something to which they might actually commit in any significant way.

The maintenance of various levels of belief and practice does suggest that they want to hang on to different parts of religion that they find to be beneficial in their lives—but strictly on their terms. They are exercising the agency to choose the important things in their lives, and religion is further down the list than other things like family, romantic relationships, and friends. It seems that what emerging adults are trying to figure out is a more general self-identity, rather than a specific religious identity. And, for some of them, this search for self-identity includes the question of whether to include any of their religious upbringing in the identity they are crafting for themselves as they enter adult life.

Inarticulacy of Beliefs

Throughout our conversations with emerging adults, most spoke about their lives, their relationships, their hopes and dreams, and even their failures in articulate and insightful ways. Yet, the ability to fully express how they viewed their relationships and their lives in general did not extend to their ability to talk about religion or spirituality. This inarticulacy is something that has been noted over the life of this research project, starting when they were teens.[2] In the intervening years, their ability to articulate religious teachings and exactly what they believe doesn't seem to have improved in any significant way.

Certainly, emerging adults from some traditions—Conservative Protestants and Latter-day Saints, for example—were better at articulating the teachings of their faith than others. Yet, even for these groups, the norm was a lack of religious literacy even of their own tradition. In general, emerging adults had difficulty expressing what they know about their religion—including their own religious beliefs—in response to our questions about faith, God, heaven or hell, or any number of other issues related to their religious and spiritual lives, regardless how religiously committed they were. Yet, emerging adults are not alone in this; several studies have shown the limited state of religious knowledge among Americans in general.[3] How can we explain this inability among emerging adults—and perhaps, more broadly, among Americans—to provide articulate answers to questions related to their religious and spiritual beliefs? In our view, there are three likely explanations that are each present, in different degrees, for different people.

First, and perhaps most obvious, there is a lack of knowledge about religion in general and their own religious traditions in particular. As Smith and Denton argued in *Soul Searching*, attaining religious knowledge is no different from learning other things; it takes an explicit effort. In short, religion needs to be taught. Many emerging adults told us that their parents were "open" to religion. However, it was not something that parents actually required or encouraged, assuming instead that emerging adults would pursue it on their own if they were interested. We've also heard the emerging adults in this study talk in the same way about how they want to approach religion with their own children. The end result, then, is that to the extent that emerging adults have picked up on religious knowledge, it is in an incomplete way, and the knowledge they do have is tailored to their own interests and needs.

Second, as we have shown throughout this book, religion just isn't all that important to most emerging adults and competes with other responsibilities and commitments in their lives. Even for those who are otherwise religiously committed, the tendency is to maintain a level of commitment that is less demanding of their time and effort.[4] Thus, as a completely voluntary institution, and one that can often require time and effort, religion loses out to more pressing demands for their time and attention. In turn, the less they are involved in religious institutions, of whatever sort, the less opportunity and interest they have to develop a bank of religious knowledge.

Finally, for those emerging adults who have maintained some relationship with religion, whether Committed, Marginal, or Disaffiliated, religious knowledge is simply a part of their consciousness that doesn't really need to be explained. In our view, this is related to the way that emerging adults approach moral issues. Recall that emerging adults consistently frame their moral decision-making as something they "just know" or "feel." In other words, an act or decision is right or wrong based on "tacit knowledge" that is felt rather than rationally articulated.[5] Similarly, while they may be fairly certain of their religious beliefs, they are only able to express the general contours of their beliefs, without too many specifics. Thus, as they have reached emerging adulthood, their beliefs remain "taken for granted" or an assumed part of their lives, and they are more or less accepting their faith as they have experienced it growing up. As part of the general context of their lives, ideas about God and faith are things they "just know." With some notable exceptions, emerging adults see no need to develop well-articulated beliefs because they are just an intuitive part of the world in which they have always lived.

The Cultural Spirituality of Emerging Adults

Despite their inarticulacy about specific religious beliefs, emerging adults do maintain a kind of generalized religious or spiritual life perspective through which their particular beliefs are filtered. That is, emerging adults share a more or less coherent view of the world that references the supernatural in its explanations and rationalizations of activities, which helps them understand and organize their experiences in the world. This perspective can be described as a "do it yourself" religious or spiritual outlook, in which they both borrow and develop beliefs and morals from different religious traditions and larger cultural currents. They do so, however, without any need for greater involvement in or commitment to any particular religious tradition or for any actual coherence with these traditions.[6] They have picked up on cues about religion from their youth and how they were raised, as well as from the larger culture, which are then cobbled together into a highly individualized religious/spiritual perspective that is tailored to their own needs. For most emerging adults, this perspective operates mostly as a background assumption of their daily lives, but nonetheless informs how they understand the world.

Thinking about the many ways that emerging adults have expressed this cultural spirituality, we have identified seven core tenets of this outlook: (1) Karma is real, (2) Everybody goes to heaven, (3) It's all good, (4) Religion is easy, (5) Just do good, (6) Morals are self-evident, and (7) No regrets. These basic tenets are defined and combined in somewhat different ways, depending on the individual, their life experiences, and their relationship to religion, but are present among most emerging adults, regardless of where they could be classified, from religiously Committed to Not Religious.

Karma is real. In our interviews, many emerging adults explicitly referenced their belief in karma, while others expressed a similar idea, such as "everything happens for a reason," or some related perspective that suggests that they believe in a "spiritual" or perhaps undefinable supernatural force that generally works to make for a just and ordered world.[7] Their view of karma is a popularized version that is not particularly true to its actual religious meaning. For emerging adults, it is a way to explain how they try to act toward others in the world and a way to explain how both the bad things and the good things that happen in their lives tend to balance out. In reality, the concept of karma that operates in the lives of most emerging adults is something along the order of "what goes around, comes around." In this sense, karma operates as a quasi-moral code that provides them with some sense of the necessity to treat other people well, or to otherwise do good (or at least not harmful) things in the world. It also serves as an explanation—a nonreligious theodicy of sorts—for why good people ultimately end up having good things happen to them and bad people end up having bad things happen to them.

Everybody goes to heaven. For most emerging adults, going to heaven is generally a result of how you act in the world, rather than being related to any specific religious teachings about heaven, hell, or the afterlife. On the one hand, emerging adults tend to express a belief that people go to heaven because of their good works on earth, which they often link to their perceptions of religious teachings about the afterlife. But, in reality, what they actually believe is that it is the rare person who does *not* go to heaven. Thus, rather than there being some sort of ledger that weighs a person's good actions against their bad actions—such as in their version of karma—for emerging adults, being kept out of heaven is determined by whether a person performs actions that are unforgiveable. And, as we've seen, this punishment is mostly reserved for murderers, rapists, or those who have hurt another person in a significant way.

Just do good. The golden rule for emerging adults is to be good to other people and to treat them fairly. This is related to their beliefs about karma and who goes to heaven as well as the conviction that the most important moral code is not to hurt anyone. If you treat people well, you increase your odds of going to heaven. But, more than this, being good to others is an expected way to live and act, although the particular elements of "treating others well" are largely undefined. This outlook has persisted throughout the course of this 10-year study, as exemplified most memorably when one teenager told us in Wave 1 that his perspective on life boiled down to, "You know, don't be an asshole."

It's all good. We've all heard the saying, "it's all good," usually as a replacement for saying something like, "everything's okay," or "don't worry about it." Yet, this term also highlights how emerging adults strive to live their lives as nonjudgmentally as possible. For emerging adults, "it's all good" means that other people can believe whatever they want, or act how they want, and as long as they aren't hurting others, it is seen as no problem: "It's all good." For emerging adults, then, two key tenets of life, tolerance and acceptance, are exemplified in this approach. It doesn't matter if they agree with others on religion, politics, whatever; it's all good.

Religion is easy. According to most emerging adults, maintaining one's religious life is "pretty easy," primarily because their understanding of religion imposes no significant demands on them. For emerging adults, one takes what one wants from religion and leaves behind anything that is irrelevant or inapplicable to one's life or that goes against one's own sense of what is right or wrong. Emerging adults don't want religious organizations to tell them what to do or believe, particularly on issues such as gender identity, sexuality, abortion, marriage, and the like. Further, religion and spirituality constitute just one part of life, and not necessarily the most important one. In the end, you get—or take—what you want from religion. Again, some people are more religious, some more spiritual, but overall, whatever they are, it's all good. And that equanimity is easy to maintain.

Morals are self-evident. Emerging adults adhere to the idea that morals and values are self-evident—you just know or feel what is right and wrong—even though they're all relative. In some ways, this is related to emerging adults' perspective on the ease of maintaining their religious and spiritual lives. That is, because morals and values are self-evident, they ultimately don't present any sort of dilemma when confronted with making a moral decision—you just know. Things just feel right or wrong. This all sounds pretty relative, and in some ways it is, although there are limits. Emerging adults also say that it is not okay to cheat in order to benefit personally. But this, too, is self-evident for emerging adults because it would go against their commitment to treating others well.

No regrets. If "it's all good" is one mantra of emerging adults, a related one is "no regrets." In fact, having regrets is something that most emerging adults at least imply would be a negative thing in their lives. This seems to be related to their belief in karma, in that there is some force or cosmic logic that evens things out and helps make sense of the inequities and bad things that happen to a person. Thus, all of the life experiences a person has had are what have made them who they are, and if any of those were changed, they would be a different person. Certainly, some acknowledge decisions and choices they may have made that weren't great, or some things that didn't work out, or opportunities they wish they had pursued. But, taken together, all of those experiences and decisions make a person who they are, and nobody wants to be any different from who they understand themselves to be. In turn, this helps to explain the preference among emerging adults for religion with no demands; such a religion would require a person to confess or repent of sins, or otherwise change their choices or behavior in many circumstances.

In sum, the cultural spirituality of emerging adults operates at an implicit or "felt" level in their lives. It would be a mistake to suggest that these various components have somehow been systematized into a set of coherent beliefs and practices, but, taken together, this loose set of tenets does provide a basic perspective from which they live their lives. Further, although there is remarkable similarity in how this general outlook is expressed across a wide range of emerging adults—from religious to not religious—each element tends to be tailored individually, with certain elements playing larger or smaller roles in each person's life. In the end, this cultural spirituality makes no particular demands on the individual because each individual decides how one's life is to be lived based on one's own needs and desires.

Moralistic Therapeutic Deism 2.0: The Pocket God

In *Soul Searching*, the book that reported on the religious and spiritual lives of these emerging adults when they were adolescents (ages 13 to 17), Smith and Denton described the religion of American teens as "Moralistic Therapeutic Deism" (MTD), in which their basic beliefs could be summarized as the following: (1) God created and watches over the world; (2) God wants people to be good, nice, and fair to other people; (3) the main goal in life is to be happy; (4) God does not need to be involved in one's life other than to resolve problems; and (5) Good people go to heaven when they die.[8]

Much of what these emerging adults told us aligns with the MTD they expressed in their teenage years, including what we have framed as their cultural spirituality. Yet, there have also been some significant changes—most important, in how emerging adults conceive of God and what, exactly, they expect or want from God. Most emerging adults still believe that God exists, although there is significant variation in how they may define and conceptualize God. But, in general, there is not a strong sense that God is or should be involved in their lives. Further, there is a definite lack of interest in pursuing any questions about God and the role he could possibly have in their lives.

As teens, their view of God was that he was "there," more or less waiting around like some cosmic butler to help the teen who might ask for assistance. As emerging adults, however, God is no longer understood in such a proximate and powerful way. Instead, the idea of God seems to represent their belief, or perhaps hope, that there *might* be something greater than themselves in the universe. This seems to be true even for those emerging adults who think of God as a personal being—while he is generally acknowledged as "being there," he is otherwise irrelevant and neutral in most instances. Or, perhaps more precisely, while emerging adults may ask God to help them out, they do not necessarily have any real expectation of a response. Rather, it is the process of asking that is helpful to them. Recall the young people who said they prayed not to a specific person or deity, but in order to articulate a need or to process their thoughts because the act of praying itself brought them comfort. Or those who were more traditionally religiously committed and said that they would routinely perform a "quick prayer" whenever they thought about it. In each instance, we see a traditional spiritual practice—prayer—that is essentially a therapeutic device that is activated through the ritual act.

Thus, God is increasingly remote from emerging adults' everyday concerns and rarely enters their thinking or occupies any real place in their lives. When they do entertain ideas about God, it is primarily on the terms and conditions that are set by each individual. God is thus controlled by the individual and reduced even further from any previous conception they may have had of such a being as a "creator" or "cosmic force." But even this implies the existence of a God who is waiting around to be called on to do something that emerging adults might ask him to do. While emerging adults have personalized and "reduced" God to serve their own idiosyncratic needs and desires, they don't seem to have much need for even this reduced idea of God.

To the extent that emerging adults *do* think about God, it is a God that is easily controlled, but has the potential to provide answers for them should the need ever arise. In many ways, the MTD God that exists beyond is now a personal "Pocket God," who occupies the same place in emerging adult lives as do the apps on their smart phones. On the one hand, they always have their phones in their back pocket; but, on the other, like the apps on their phones, God is reduced to just one thing among many other things in their lives. Like an app on the phone, he is accessible but has limited functionality. Moreover, the individual can control the extent to which their Pocket God has any access to and impact on their lives. Individuals access their Pocket God only when they need what he is designed to do, and they can control how he interacts with them. They can allow their Pocket God to know where they are and to provide them with notifications, or not. They can turn him on or off as needed or desired, or even delete him if he is no longer of use to them. In general, the Pocket God performs whatever task he is designed to perform, yet is not particularly useful beyond that singular function.

Thus, while MTD still operates in the lives of emerging adults, it now exists in a heightened form of individualization, customization, and singular functionality in their lives. Emerging adults are not looking for much in the way of help from or interaction with God. Rather, God seems more like an unseen companion that they can interact with whenever they desire and do it on their own terms. MTD 2.0 is really more of the comfortable feeling that emerging adults have when they know their Pocket God is with them, close at hand but safely stowed out of sight.

Will Emerging Adults Return to Religion?

When we talk about our research, we are inevitably asked whether we think that emerging adults will return to religion at some point. Most of the time, underlying the question is the assumption that young people will return to a more fully engaged religious faith after they marry and have children. There is some evidence for this pattern, at least for previous generations.[9] The idea is that when people have children, they want to expose them to religious teachings, which in turn will serve as some sort of moral foundation for their lives. Among the emerging adults in this study, we did hear echoes of this perspective. Some told us how they wanted their children to be exposed to religion for moral teachings or to expand their knowledge of religious worldviews.

Other observers argue that after people have left religion, they are unlikely to return.[10] These researchers maintain that the increase in the

number of emerging adults who are moving away from religion is mainly
a result of unanswered doubt about God or religious teachings, or that they
"just stopped" believing, or they have a negative view of religious institutions. Thus, emerging adults are not likely to return to religion, mainly
because they've already made up their minds and have rejected religious
beliefs.

This question of whether young people will eventually return to religion in any significant fashion is a pressing one. In our view, whether
emerging adults who have left religion will ultimately return is likely a bit
more complex and contingent than the notion that they want their children to be exposed to religious and moral teachings, or that they experienced doubt as teens and therefore decided to chuck it all in response
to their unanswered questions. The young people in our study are at the
beginning of their journey into adulthood, and it would be irresponsible
to claim that we can definitively address this issue with the data at hand.
What we can do is make some observations about the trends we see in the
data so far and the implications those trends might have for the future religious lives of emerging adults.

At each wave of the National Study of Youth and Religion project, we
have identified a group of religiously committed young people. These are
the respondents for whom religion plays a central role in their lives, and
we have seen some evidence of increasing religious ownership and commitment among these emerging adults. When asking the question, "will
they return to religion?" then, we are not asking about these particular
young people. They seem to be securely rooted in their religious lives.

Among the remaining respondents, the question of religious return
needs to be contextualized within two significant themes from our years
of research. The first is that, over the 10 years of the study, the aggregate
trend is one of declining religious engagement and a move away from involvement with religious institutions. While we have uncovered nuance
and variation along the way, religious decline has been the consistent trajectory for our respondents as a whole. Second, although our research has
focused on the causes and correlates of religious change, those patterns of
change are set within a larger context of general stability. As a whole, the
young people we studied have not experienced dramatic or unexpected
changes in their life trajectories, including their religious lives. Certainly,
at the individual level, there are plenty of examples of instability and dramatic life changes. At the aggregate level, however, the lives of the young
people in our study have progressed in generally stable and predictable

ways over the course of our research, and the trend of gradual religious decline has remained consistent for the duration of the project.

As we look back over the past 10 years of their lives, we consider how the inertia of these two trends—general stability and relatively gradual religious decline—might inform our expectations about young adults' future religious re-engagement. To this point, we have not seen any evidence that the way these emerging adults have arranged their lives will, at some point, lead them to shift course and re-engage with religion. While many expressed an openness to the possibility of future religious faith, very few expected to take any active steps in this direction.

Recall from Chapter 4 the young people who spoke about a return to religion as something that might "happen to them," but not as something that they would seek out on their own. Sociologically, we know that while individual agency alone is not a sufficient predictor of life events, it is unlikely that full-fledged engagement in a voluntary social institution such as a religious congregation will spontaneously impose itself on our respondents at some point in the future.

The inertia of their lives points toward a continued drift away from organized religion. But what about the introduction of marriage and children? These are the life events that observers point to as a potential impetus for a religious return—the point at which young people will reevaluate their lives and return to religious faith. And, as noted, there is evidence that, in generations past, marriage and parenthood have brought people back to religion. As we showed in Chapter 6, we do find that religious emerging adults are marrying and having children earlier than their peers, which in turn acts to slow down the rate of exit from religion.

This offers support for the close link between family formation and religious engagement and suggests that young people who are starting families of their own may in fact seek out the support of religious communities during this life stage. It is certainly possible that emerging adults will make more significant efforts to seek out religious faith after they marry and have children. Given that the median age of our sample is still younger than the median age of marriage in the United States, our data are not suited to clearly assessing this possibility. However, we can make some observations about this expectation, based on what we know about the lives of emerging adults in our current social context.

Previous work from the NSYR found that the drift away from religion begins in late adolescence.[11] At the same time, entrance into marriage and parenthood continues to be pushed later in the life course, and overall rates of marriage and childbearing in the United States are declining.[12] Thus, compared with generations before them, current emerging adults will experience an extended period of time between the onset of religious decline and starting their own families. It is during this same period that emerging adults are said to be engaging in self-focused identity explora-tion and transitions, crafting identities, and making life decisions that set them on various paths for the future.[13] So, these processes of identity for-mation and life decisions are likely to be informed only marginally, if at all, by religious ties and sentiments.

We did hear from emerging adults who say that they hope to raise their children in a religious community in the future, even though they are not currently religiously active. What we did not hear, however, was a clear conviction that they would be able to successfully act on this desire. The stories of Ashley and Carla from Chapter 6 illustrate how the conflu-ence of religious drift, delayed family formation, and the characteristics of emerging adulthood may create obstacles to a return to religious engage-ment when marriage and children are on the horizon. Both Ashley and Carla have drifted away from the religious faith in which they were raised, though they continue to identify as religious and express a desire to one day raise their children to be religious as well. During their own hiatus from active religious involvement, they have continued to move forward in other areas of their lives, completing educations, figuring out careers, and selecting partners whom they will marry and with whom they hope to have children. Both women are now partnered with men who do not share their desires for a religious upbringing for their children. And, during the course of our interviews, they both grappled with the implications of being married to a nonreligious spouse and the potential challenges this would create for returning to religion after they have children.

Selecting a marriage partner is just one example of a life choice made during emerging adulthood that has the potential to shape one's prospects for a future return to religion. We also heard young people talk about con-structing their daily lives through decisions about educational pursuits, careers and employment, geographic relocation, and other similar life events. Rarely did we hear them consider whether these pursuits would leave space in their lives for religious engagement. On the contrary, we often heard that their lives were constructed in such a way that religion was squeezed out or moved to the bottom of the list of the many demands for their time and attention. And the more distant their current lives are from religious ties, the more challenging it will be to reactivate those ties and forge a path back to a religious community.

So, what will happen when marriage and children are introduced into these lives that are constructed around priorities other than religious faith, and where ties to religious communities are tenuous? While marriage and parenthood may create the desire for religious re-engagement, the practical constraints of a life that has not already made space for religious engagement will raise the bar and make a religious return more difficult. In the case of Carla, she still lives near family and remains connected to her religious congregation. She can at least imagine where she would return if she did decide to raise her children in a church. Ashley, however, is far enough removed from her own religious identity and tradition that, even if she were to decide to return, she is not confident that she has a religious home to return to. Like many emerging adults we spoke with, her ties to the religion of her youth are stretched thin, and the path back to religious engagement does not seem clearly marked.

There have always been people who move away from religion for a time and then return again. This will continue to be true for these emerging adults as well. The data we have at this point in time do not allow for a full examination of the factors that might facilitate such a return. Given the close links between religion and family formation that we see in previous research, as well as in our data, we do expect that the experience of marriage and having children will likely serve as a motivator for young people to re-engage with religious faith.[14]

These motivating life events will come at later average ages than in the past, and based on current demographic trends, we expect that small but increasing numbers of today's emerging adults will not make these transitions at all, forgoing marriage or parenthood altogether. For the majority of emerging adults who will marry and have children, however, the theoretical desires to incorporate religion into their newly formed families will be balanced against the practical considerations that contribute to the likelihood of increased religious participation. We expect that the ability to translate motivation into action will be most likely among those emerging adults who have maintained at least some sort of ties to religion or communities of faith. Among the emerging adults in our study, the Marginal and even the Disaffiliated seem better positioned to make a return to religion than those who have embraced a Not Religious identity and who have few, if any, remaining ties to religion.

Another recurring theme throughout the NSYR project has been the importance of parents in shaping the religious outcomes of their children. Parents, as well as the overall home atmosphere related to religion, are important predictors of whether emerging adults remain religiously committed (i.e., on the "Stable High" trajectory), at least as they have moved into emerging adulthood. Emerging adults whose parents were religiously engaged during their adolescent years are less likely than their peers to exit from religion in the first place. But to the extent that they do experience religious decline, we expect that a future return to religion will be more likely among those emerging adults who have religiously engaged parents.

A religiously engaged family environment contributes to an enduring sense of religious identity among emerging adults that can persist even when they are not actively participating in religious practices. In addition, a religiously engaged family can facilitate continued ties to religious communities that make it more feasible for young people to re-engage with religion in the future. Understanding how emerging adults were socialized toward religion as adolescents is an important key to understanding where they may end up as adults—as either religious or not religious, or perhaps somewhere in between. We would argue that if emerging adults were to return to religion at some point in their lives, the group most likely to return would be those who were raised in homes that were actively engaged with religion.

Potential Futures: Religion for Individuals and Institutions

What might the findings we've presented in this book mean for the future of religion in America, both for emerging adults and for religious institutions? Although the dominant trend of decline in affiliation and participation does not bode well for traditional religious institutions, there are, as we have shown, still emerging adults who remain active in religious organizations. Yet these young people demonstrate an increasingly customized religious and spiritual outlook intended to fit their personal needs and desires. As leaders of religious institutions consider their future, they will have to decide whether and how they can adapt to meet the challenges presented by emerging adults who are less interested in the long-established expressions of many religious traditions.

We believe there are at least four potential strategies that religious institutions may pursue as they consider their futures and any role that emerging adults may have in them. First, religious institutions may stay the course and make no changes, expecting that emerging adults will remain engaged participants and perhaps those who have left might return some day. Second, religious institutions may change their traditions, doctrines, or practices to meet the needs and demands of emerging adults, and in the process change their core identity, becoming something other than what they have been historically. Third, they could maintain their allegiance to their core identities, but push those identity boundaries as they reimagine and redefine their message to show how it can have resonance in the lives of emerging adults.[15] Or, finally, new types of religious institutions may emerge that better serve the needs and desires of emerging adults. There are examples of religious movements on each of these paths with varying degrees of success, but it remains to be seen how successful they can be over the longer term.[16]

Regardless of the response of religious institutions – whether staying the course, wholesale change, reimagining themselves, or the development of entire new forms – they will have to contend with the religious sensibilities of emerging adults like those we have come to know in this book. These young people are most interested in customizing or curating their beliefs and practices to suit their own desires and preferences, while leaving behind those beliefs and practices that are irrelevant or that do not have resonance in their lives. Thus, whatever seems comfortable, plausible, and, perhaps most important, allows them to live their lives as they wish without much, if any, intrusion from religious institutions or authorities will increasingly govern emerging adult choices about religion and spirituality.

Recall that we heard from emerging adults who said that they were happy with their church or religious identity, but who didn't really believe everything that was taught. We also saw this in some individuals who had exited religious institutions yet were still hanging onto certain beliefs and practices that they had tailored to their own particular needs. Thus, for emerging adults, religion as an institution maintains little authority in their lives. Religion might be true, or it might offer something that is of use in an individual's life, but it isn't really something that is authoritative in the claims that it makes in a person's life or as a conspicuous source of moral guidance.

This has significant implications for religious beliefs, practices, and institutions. At the most basic level, if the trends of disaffiliation and lack of participation continue, religious institutions of all types will have a declining pool of potential members and a concomitant decline in resources. Thus, keeping current and future members in the fold is one of the most significant tasks for religious organizations such as churches and synagogues, but also for institutions like religious schools and other faith based institutions.

Further, it is clear from our findings that emerging adults have embraced a highly individualistic perspective that seems to color all parts of their lives, not least how they understand and participate in religion and religious institutions. It remains to be seen whether this is simply a stage that emerging adults are passing through or if this is a more enduring shift in the role of religion and spirituality in their lives. Will they ultimately return to some form of traditional religious involvement as they reach full-fledged adulthood, or will this qualitatively different way of thinking about religion, religious beliefs and practices, and religious institutions persist as they move through the life course?

Whatever the future holds, the present reality includes emerging adults whose viewpoints range from a general lack of interest in religion to a religiosity that is curated and customized from traditional religious beliefs and practices. The changes evinced by these young people will require religious institutions to take their perspectives into account as they think about how to respond to the ways that emerging adults are changing the religious landscape.

APPENDIX

Research Methodology

This appendix describes the methods used to collect the survey and interview data analyzed in this book.

SURVEY METHODOLOGY AND SAMPLE STATISTICS

For the Wave 4 National Study of Youth and Religion (NSYR) survey, every attempt was made to reinterview all Wave 1 youth respondents. At the time of the fourth survey, respondents were between the ages of 23 and 28. The survey was fielded between February 2013 and December 2013 and was administered through the Center for the Study of Religion and Society at the University of Notre Dame, using Qualtrics online survey software. The Wave 4 survey instrument replicated many of the questions asked in Waves 1, 2, and 3, with some changes made to questions to take into account the respondents' lives as they grew older, such as getting a full educational or relationship history; other questions were added to get greater specificity on old questions. Additional questions were added that were of interest to researchers involved with the project that had not been included in the survey previously.

The Notre Dame Center for the Study of Religion and Society conducted a pretest to ensure that the survey instrument was working properly and that the survey length was appropriate. Fifty respondents were recruited with the assistance of Survey Sampling International (SSI), a research firm that specializes in digital research. The survey link was sent to SSI, and they distributed the link by email to respondents in February 2013. Responses from the 50 respondents were not included in the Wave 4 dataset.

Between Waves 3 and 4, NSYR project staff maintained all in-between survey tracking efforts. This included maintaining contact each year through US Postal Service–mailed birthday cards and then recording change of address information for returned cards. All program mailings included a link to the respondent website that allowed respondents to submit changes to contact information and other questions or comments. Approximately six months before the survey was fielded, all Wave 1 respondents for whom we had a mailing address were sent a postcard and a $2 bill asking them to contact us with their current contact information and informing them that the Wave 4 survey would soon be fielded.

Of the total 3,328 original respondents, the 2,144 complete responses in Wave 4 represented a 65 percent retention rate from Wave 1, which was fielded in 2002. Of the 2,144 who participated in the Wave 4 survey, 81 percent had participated in all three previous waves, while another 14 percent had participated in two of the three previous waves. In the first three waves, 100 percent of surveys were conducted by telephone. In Wave 4, only 15 percent of surveys were conducted on the telephone; the other 85 percent were completed online. All but two phone surveys and all of the online surveys were fielded in English.

On key demographic variables, the Wave 4 respondents were very similar to the Wave 1 respondents. Table A.1 shows a column for the sample distribution from each wave of the survey. The demographic characteristics were collected at Wave 1. In the Wave 4 survey, there were only minor fluctuations in the region, age, and income demographics of respondents who remained in the survey compared with the original Wave 1 sample. The percentages of female respondents increased slightly with each wave of the study, suggesting that retention was marginally higher for females than males. Similarly, white respondents made up 72 percent of the Wave 4 sample compared with 65 percent of the Wave 1 sample and 69 percent of the sample from Waves 2 and 3. The percentages of black and Hispanic respondents declined by 4 and 1 percent, respectively. The other noticeable change is in the percentage of the sample whose parents were married at the time of the Wave 1 survey. Those respondents made up 57 percent of the sample in the Wave 4 survey compared with just 51 percent at Wave 1. These are not large differences, such that the final sample still is demographically very similar to the original sample. The changes that are present, however, reflect the fact that retention was slightly lower among people of color and respondents from nonintact families.

METHODOLOGICAL DESIGN AND PROCEDURES FOR THE NSYR
WAVE 4 PERSONAL INTERVIEWS

The fourth wave of in-person interviews for the NSYR involved in-depth personal interviews with 303 of the Wave 4 survey respondents, resulting in 292 useable interview transcripts. The purpose of the interviews was to provide extended follow-up discussion about the religious, spiritual, family, and social lives of emerging adults. The questionnaire included much of what was used in Waves 1, 2, and 3, with the addition of several new topics that were relevant to their lives as 23- to 28-year-olds. The length of the interviews ranged from slightly less than one hour to approximately

Table A.1 Comparison of Waves 1, 2, 3, and 4 Respondents on Key Demographic Characteristics*

Wave 1	W1 Respondents	W2 Respondents	W3 Respondents	W4 Respondents
Census Region				
Northeast	15	15	15	15
Midwest	23	24	25	26
South	42	41	41	38
West	20	20	19	21
Gender				
Male	51	50	49	47
Female	49	50	51	53
Age				
13	19	19	19	18
14	20	20	20	20
15	21	22	22	22
16	20	20	20	21
17	20	19	19	19
Race/Ethnicity				
White	65	69	69	72
Black	17	16	16	12
Hispanic	12	10	10	9
Asian/Pacific Islander/American Indian/mixed/other	5	5	5	5
Missing	1	1	1	1
Family Structure†				
Lives with two biological/ adoptive parents	51	56	55	57
Parent Income				
Less than $10K	3	3	3	2
$10K–20K	7	6	6	6
$20K–30K	12	11	11	10
$30K–40K	13	12	12	11
$40K–50K	13	14	14	14
$50K–60K	11	11	11	12
$60K–70K	7	8	8	8
$70K–80K	6	7	7	8

(continued)

Table A.1 Continued

Wave 1	W1 Respondents	W2 Respondents	W3 Respondents	W4 Respondents
$80K–90K	5	6	6	5
$90K–100K	4	4	4	5
More than $100K	11	12	13	14
Missing	6	6	6	6
N‡	3,259	2,530	2,458	2,071

*Numbers represent unweighted percentages. Percentages may not add up to 100 because of rounding.

†Family structure contains some missing data.

‡N does not include the Jewish oversample cases ($N = 80$ for Wave 1; $N = 74$ for Wave 2; $N = 78$ for Wave 3; $N = 73$ for Wave 4).

Source: National Study of Youth and Religion surveys 2003, 2005, 2008, 2013.

three hours, with most lasting about two hours. Respondents were offered a cash incentive ranging from $110 to $200 to participate in the study.

The in-person interviews were conducted between May 6, 2013 and December 19, 2013, with 92 percent of the interviews conducted between May and August 2013. To be interviewed, respondents were required to have completed the survey, and all interviews were completed between three and six months following respondents' completion of the survey. All respondents who were interviewed in Wave 1 were recontacted for Wave 4 interviews. Of the 303 individuals who were interviewed, 205 had been interviewed as teens in Wave 1, and 41 were added to the interview pool to refresh the sample and provide additional diversity.

Our sampling strategy for Wave 1 interviews represented a range of demographic and religious characteristics and took into account region, residential location (urban/suburban/rural), age, sex, household income, religion, and school type. The new in-person interview respondents were chosen by combinations of geographic region, religious type, race/ethnicity, and sex to balance out the original sample. The researchers clustered the respondents with whom they were still in contact into geographic areas for ease of travel in interviewing. Table A.2 provides demographic information about the 292 interview respondents.

Fourteen interviewers conducted interviews with respondents living in 44 states, Washington DC, and several other countries. While the majority of the interviews were conducted in person and near where the respondent lived, some of the interviews took place by phone or Skype because of costs and other logistics related to traveling to where the respondents were located. Each interviewer conducted between nine and 47 interviews. Eight of the interviewers had conducted personal interviews for the NSYR in either Wave 1, 2, or 3 (or all waves), and respondents were matched with their previous interviewers as much as possible. Before the fielding of the in-person interviews, all new interviewers participated in a day-long training meeting held by the NSYR project manager and the principle investigator. The training covered the logistics of the interview process, procedural requirements, Institutional Review Board (i.e., Human Subjects) concerns, protection of human participants, safety and liability concerns, and keys to NSYR interview success. In addition to that training, all interviewers were required to obtain Human Participants Training Certification.

The 14 project interviewers were assigned to sets of specific geographic locations around the United States. Each interviewer was provided with groups of contact sheets for respondents in their assigned geographic areas. The contact sheets included respondent name, respondent nickname (if known), parent name, address, phone number, respondent birth date, respondent gender, respondent race, household income, religious affiliation, and religious denomination or tradition. The contact sheet also included space to note any changes to the contact information provided (e.g., new phone number, additional email address) and provided a call record. Interviewers recorded each household contact, noting the date, time, person with whom they spoke, and content of each contact. In addition to the original sample, as the project progressed through the interviews, the priorities shifted somewhat according to what types of respondent interviews were still needed (e.g., location, religion, gender). In this way, the researchers attempted to match the demographics of the original Wave 1 in-person interview sample as much as possible.

In addition to the demographic information on the contact sheet, before their interviews, NSYR interviewers were asked to review the transcripts of the previous in-person interviews. If an interviewer had not conducted the previous personal interviews with his or her respondents, the transcripts provided background information about that respondent to help facilitate a smooth interview. Using a standard call script provided by the NSYR, interviewers made contact with potential interviewee households. Interviewers identified themselves as researchers with the "National Youth Study." The full name of the project was not used in order to avoid introducing any response bias by identifying religion as a key focus of the study. It was often helpful for interviewers to explain their connection with the project, for example, graduate student, coinvestigator, and so on. However, since much of the interview was about religion and the researchers did not want to bias the respondents' answers, interviewers were instructed to avoid divulging revealing information about their own personal beliefs and commitments (of which there was considerable diversity on the interviewing team).

Interviewers were required to obtain initial verbal consent from the respondent during the phone call to conduct the interview. If respondents seemed hesitant about participating, an additional script provided more information about the project and offered the phone number of the principle investigator, whom they could call with questions or concerns. In addition, interviewers offered to mail written information

Appendix

Table A.2 Wave 4 Personal Interview Demographics[*]

	N		N
Gender		**Region**	
Female	150	Midwest	67
Male	142	Northeast	51
		South	101
Age		West	73
23	33		
24	58	**Religious Tradition**	
25	60	Conservative Protestant	46
26	57	Mainline Protestant	15
27	60	Black Protestant	17
28	24	Catholic	32
		Jewish	20
		Latter-day Saints	15
Race		Not Religious	111
White	200	Indeterminate Christian	24
Black	35	Indeterminate Other	3
Hispanic	30		
Asian	8		
Native American	6		
Other	13		

[*]$N = 292$.
Source: National Study of Youth and Religion.

about the project to hesitant respondents and then call back in a few days. When a respondent seemed reluctant to participate or was hesitant about the time commitment, an additional incentive was offered. However, in cases in which respondents refused to participate even after being offered additional information, the interviewers made no further attempts to convert those who refused. On receiving verbal consent from the respondents and scheduling an interview time and location, interviewers mailed packets of information to households. The packet contained a cover letter from the principal investigator, multiple copies of respondent written consent forms, and an appointment letter, including a portrait photo of the interviewer. Interviewees were required to bring the written signed consent with them to their interviews. Interviewers also called the respondents at least one week before the interview and again the day before the interview to confirm that the respondents were planning to participate.

Interviews were conducted in public settings that still provided confidentiality for the respondent. The ideal location for these interviews was in study rooms at local libraries. However, when these were not available, interviews were also conducted in restaurants, coffee shops, mall food courts, and outdoor settings. Interviewers were given guidelines for how to present themselves during the interviews as well as appropriate attire to be worn in order to ensure consistency in the presentation of interviewers across the interviews. Specifically, interviewers did not attempt to "relate" to respondents by dressing down or dressing in a more "trendy" fashion. Interviewers presented themselves as professional researchers with a sincere interest in young people's lives. At the close of the interview, respondents were given the cash incentive for their participation and in appreciation of their time and effort.

Notes

INTRODUCTION

1. Richard Flory. Throughout the book we use "we," "us," and "our" when referencing interviews with emerging adults unless otherwise noted. We use pseudonyms for all of our interview participants.
2. See, for example, Pew Research Center, "Religion among the Millennials"; and Lipka, "Millennials Increasingly Are Driving Growth of 'Nones.'"
3. See, for example, Gill, "Millennials and Religion"; and Taylor, "Crossing Borders."
4. On the former, see, for example, Thurston and ter Kuile, "How We Gather." On "spiritual but not religious," see Linda Mercadante, *Belief without Borders*; and Kaya Oakes, *The Nones Are Alright*.
5. Clydesdale and Garces-Foley, *The Twentysomething Soul*. For a similarly positive view of "millennial" evangelical Christians, see Bevins, *Ever Ancient, Ever New*. For a positive view of religious decline among evangelical young people, see Stanton, *Myth of the Dying Church*.
6. Clydesdale and Garces-Foley, *The Twentysomething Soul*, pp. 11–13.
7. Pew Research Center, "Religion among the Millennials."
8. Smith and Cooperman, "The Factors Driving the Growth of Religious 'Nones.'"
9. See Appendix for details on each wave of data collection.
10. Smith and Denton, *Soul Searching*.
11. Pearce and Denton, *A Faith of Their Own*.
12. Smith and Snell, *Souls in Transition*.
13. Arnett, *Emerging Adulthood*.
14. Arnett, *Emerging Adulthood*.
15. Flory and Miller, *Finding Faith*. See also Costanza, "Can We Please Stop Talking about Generations as if They Are a Thing?"
16. Cf., Arnett and Jensen, "A Congregation of One."

17. Throughout the book, we use the masculine pronoun for God for convenience of writing, but it is important to keep in mind the multiple ways that emerging adults expressed how they conceptualized God, whether as female, male, plural, or not embodied.

CHAPTER 1

1. Melinda Denton.
2. Smith and Snell, *Souls in Transition*.

CHAPTER 2

1. For a review of this literature, see Arnett, *Emerging Adulthood*. For a classic study of the transition of youth to adulthood in the United States, see Modell, *Into One's Own*.
2. Arnett, *Emerging Adulthood*, chapter 13.
3. Fry, "For First Time in Modern Era, Living with Parents Edges Out Other Living Arrangements for 18- to 34-Year-Olds"; Chris Kirkham, "Percentage of Young Americans Living with Parents Rises to 75-Year High."
4. Smith and Snell, *Souls in Transition*.
5. The higher reported rates of giving and volunteering among our respondents may be explained by "social desirability bias," in which respondents overestimate their volunteering or financial donations.
6. US Department of Labor, Bureau of Labor Statistics, "Volunteering in the United States, 2015."
7. On financial giving, Smith and Davidson, *The Paradox of Generosity*.
8. It is important to note that the NSYR Wave 4 data was collected before the 2016 elections, and with the results from that election, the responses from our respondents in regard to their political perspectives could potentially be different— either more liberal or more conservative. However, based on what else we know about emerging adults through our work, we do not believe that the results would be significantly different than how they responded to our survey and interview questions. In fact, regardless where they placed themselves on the political spectrum, they likely would have responded much the same way even after the 2016 election; that politicians are mainly out for themselves and have little regard for creating actual positive social change.
9. See Smith and Denton, *Soul Searching*, chapter 4, "God, Religion, Whatever: On Moralistic Therapeutic Deism."
10. Haidt, "The Emotional Dog and Its Rational Tail"; also Haidt, *The Righteous Mind*.
11. On the role of inarticulate or "tacit" knowledge in cultural life and how it motivates action, see Mukerjee, "The Cultural Power of Tacit Knowledge."

CHAPTER 3

1. See, for example, Pew Research Center, "Nones on the Rise"; Lipka, "Millennials Increasingly Are Driving Growth of 'Nones' "; Pew Research Center, "Religion among the Millennials."

2. TRADREL is the variable categorizing respondents into major religious types. It is the combination of RELIG1 and RELATT, but it always prioritizes attendance. So, in essence, this variable starts as an exact replication of RELATT, but then uses RELIG1 to classify all those who could not be classified based on attendance (i.e., nonattenders and indeterminate). TRADREL is similar to the RELTRAD variable from Wave 1, with slight differences. First, TRADREL always prioritizes named attendance. Next, it splits the "no affiliation" group into two separate categories: not religious (respondents who do not attend and do not self-identify with a religion) and indeterminate (respondents who participate in or identify with a group that cannot be categorized, e.g., "just Christian"). Additionally, we were able to use prprot1 to help categorize indeterminate individuals who answered this question. The variables used to determine TRADREL included: ATTREG, CHURTYPE, BAPTIST, METHST, PRSBIAN, LUTHAN, REFMED, CONGAL, CHCHST, RELIG0, RELIG0A, RELIG0B, ATHEIST1, HALF1, OTHREL1, PRPORT, and TEENRACE.

3. Steensland et al., "The Measure of American Religion."

4. Blumberg, "American Religion"; Lipka, "Religious 'Nones' Are Not Only Growing."

5. Just more than half of the Indeterminate "just Christian" respondents do not regularly attend religious services, while the other half reported that they do attend services at a religious congregation.

6. Black Protestant loss may be due in part to sample attrition over the 10 years of the project.

7. Religious switching percentages for the entire sample (Waves 1–4): same religious affiliation = 48 percent; switch from one religious affiliation to another = 11 percent; switch from specific religious affiliation to Indeterminate affiliation = 12 percent; switch from religious affiliation to Not Religious = 26 percent; switch from Not Religious to Indeterminate affiliation = 1 percent; switch from Not Religious to religious affiliation = 2 percent.

8. Smith and Denton, *Soul Searching*.

9. Smith and Denton, *Soul Searching*; Pearce and Denton, *A Faith of Their Own*; Smith and Snell, *Souls in Transition*.

10. See note 2 in this chapter for a description of how the religious tradition variable was constructed.

11. We chose to exclude Wave 2 data from this analysis because we are particularly interested in understanding the changes across the 10 years of the study. Wave 2, while interesting in its own right, was collected two years after Wave 1 and thus

does not provide a large number of years to add significant information to this analysis.

12. Specifically those who were identified with that tradition at Wave 1. Not all would have necessarily been raised in that particular tradition, but this is the case for most.

13. Religious service attendance is subject to known social desirability bias that leads to overreporting of attendance frequency, and these percentages should be read within that context (see Hadaway and Marler, "How Many Americans Attend Worship Each Week?"; and Presser and Chaves, "Is Religious Service Attendance Declining?"). Assuming that the overreporting bias persists over time, we can learn much from the relative differences in attendance reports across the time frame of the study.

14. For the Wave 4 survey, the majority of respondents were given the option to complete their survey online instead of over the telephone. In the original telephone survey (Waves 1–3), the *none of these views* option was not read to respondents but was available if they volunteered this answer. In Wave 4, this option was visible in the online version of the survey and, for consistency across formats, was also read to respondents who completed the survey by phone. The presentation of this option likely explains much of the increase in this response category.

15. Pearce and Denton, *A Faith of Their Own.*

16. Smith and Denton, *Soul Searching*; Smith, Longest, Hill, and Christoffersen, "*Young Catholic America.*"

17. Pearce and Denton, *A Faith of Their Own.*

18. For example, Kaya Oakes, *The Nones Are Alright*; Linda Mercadante, *Belief without Borders*; Elizabeth Drescher, *Choosing Our Religion.*

19. See Flory and Miller, *Finding Faith*; for a personal account from a former Conservative Protestant emerging adult that also includes the appeal of more open cultural and political perspective of Mainline Protestantism, see Evans, *Searching for Sunday.*

20. See Smith and Snell, *Souls in Transition*, for a discussion of declines among Mainline Protestants.

21. For the Wave 4 survey, the majority of respondents were given the option to complete their survey online instead of over the telephone. In the original telephone survey (Waves 1–3), the *I Don't Know* option was not read to respondents but was available if they volunteered this answer. In Wave 4, this option was visible in the online version of the survey. The presentation of this option likely explains some of the increase in this response category.

22. Smith and Snell, *Souls in Transition.*

CHAPTER 4

1. Pew Research Center, "'Nones' on the Rise."

2. See, for example, Lipka, "A Closer Look at America's Rapidly Growing Religious 'Nones' "; Drescher, *Choosing Our Religion*; Hout and Fischer, "Explaining Why More Americans Have No Religious Preference"; Oakes, *The Nones Are Alright*.

3. By "congregation" we include all meeting places for religious groups such as churches, temples, synagogues, mosques, and the like.

4. Previous books from the National Study of Youth and Religion (NSYR) have developed different typologies of youth and emerging adult religion that describe how the young people in this study expressed how they were thinking about religion at the time of each wave of data collection. These typologies ranged from four types (Smith and Denton, *Soul Searching*) to five types (Pearce and Denton, *A Faith of Their Own*), to six types (Smith and Snell, *Souls in Transition*), in which each described the different levels and types of religious commitment and belief that these young people were expressing at that point in their lives. Similarly, Arnett (*Emerging Adulthood*) used Wave 3 NSYR data to develop a four-part typology that ranged from most religious to least religious. We took these different typologies into account in developing our typology, while also allowing our categories to emerge from the qualitative and quantitative data. The result is a similar set of categories that allow for understanding where emerging adults are now in how they express their religious identity, commitments, and involvements.

5. There are a handful of respondents who do not claim any religious identity, yet do attend religious services with some regularity. In these cases, respondents are coded as Marginal or Committed based on patterns of religious service attendance.

6. Lim, McGregor, and Putnam, "Secular and Liminal"; Pew Research Center, " 'Nones' on the Rise"; Lipka, "A Closer Look at America's Rapidly Growing Religious 'Nones' "; Baker and Smith, "None Too Simple"; Baker and Smith, "The Nones."

7. See, for example, Edgell, Hartmann, and Gerteis, "Atheists as Other"; Cimino and Smith, *Atheist Awakening*, pp. 42–45.

8. Hout and Fischer, "Explaining Why More Americans Have No Religious Preference."

9. Pearce and Denton, *A Faith of Their Own*.

10. Dean, *Almost Christian*, p. 28.

11. Lim, McGregor, and Putnam, "Secular and Liminal"; Mercadante, *Belief without Borders*; Oakes, *The Nones Are Alright*; Drescher, *Choosing Our Religion*.

12. Tong and Yang, "Internal Diversity among 'Spiritual but Not Religious' Adolescents in the United States."

13. Burton, "Spiritual but Not Religious"; Oppenheimer, "Examining the Growth of the 'Spiritual but Not Religious' "; Barrie-Anthony, "Spiritual but Not Religious."

CHAPTER 5

1. Growth mixture modeling (GMM) is a variant of latent growth curve analysis. Instead of making the assumption that individual trajectories are deviations

from one grand trajectory, GMM assumes that multiple normative trajectories better characterize the data (or, alternatively, that we are sampling from distinct subpopulations that have qualitatively distinct growth patterns). These different classes of trajectories are a latent function of the data, so no a priori assumptions concerning how individuals change religiously are necessary.

2. There are two common ways to present GMM results graphically: one relies on the statistical estimates based on the coefficients, and the other on the actual means for each group. We choose to present the actual group means because they are a more natural comparison to the overall means presented in Figure 5.3. The estimated growth curves are very similar to the group means.

3. Because this is a combination of three measures, each measured from zero to four, we considered a shift in three to be roughly equivalent to moving a single category in each of the three measures (even though we realize this isn't the only way to see a change of three in our composite measure). In our judgment, this is a fairly small shift in religious faith. The standard deviation for this composite measure varies by survey wave, but it is always greater than three (it varies from 3.2 to 3.9). So, even judging by the distribution of scores, these individual shifts are fairly small.

4. Although these figures do not include individual tests for whether one growth curve group is significantly different from every other group in that figure, this can be approximated by visually estimating whether the error bars of one group overlap the point estimate of another group. It's important to note that error bars from two groups that "cross" one another do not necessarily mean these groups are not statistically different. Rather, it is the error bar from one group compared with the specific percentage estimate of the other group that matters.

5. Socioeconomic status (SES) is measured by the income and educational attainment of parent(s). High SES is defined as having at least one parent who graduated with a bachelor's degree or higher and a household income of $80,000 or more in 2002–3.

6. Wuthnow, "Religious Involvement and Status-Bridging Social Capital"; Verba, Schlozman, and Brady, *Voice and Equality*; Cnaan and DiIulio, *The Invisible Caring Hand*; Wuthnow, *All in Sync*.

7. Norris and Inglehart, *Sacred and Secular*; Smith, *Religion*.

8. To investigate this, we ran logistic regression models predicting being in the Stable High category versus the Shallow Decline or Steep Decline categories. The odds ratio of Conservative Protestant to Mainline Protestant was 2.02 without any controls and 1.55 after controlling for religious talk in the household. The odds ratio of Conservative Protestant to Catholic was 2.13 without any controls and 1.67 after controlling for religious talk in the household. The equivalent odds ratios for Black Protestant to Mainline Protestant was 3.41 without controls and 2.43 with the additional measure of religious talk. Black Protestant to Catholic was 3.59 without controls and 2.61 with the religious talk variable. In

all cases, a substantial portion of the differences between religious traditions can be accounted for by the measure of the frequency of religious talk.

9. The index contains measures of how often the father and mother praise and encourage, hug, tell the teen they love them, talk about personal subjects, and "hang out" with the teen. It also includes measures of how well the teen and parent get along, how close the teen feels to his or her mother and father (or similar figures), and how close the parent feels to his or her teen. Last, it includes measures of whether the parent has taken the teen to a museum, a play, or a library; worked on a project together; or played a game or sport together in the past six months. Thank you to Kyle Longest for providing the coding for this index.

10. This index contains measures of how often the teen reported that his or her parent figure knows what music, television, and movies are watched, whom he or she spends time with, and what he or she is actually doing when not at home. It also includes the parents' report of how often they monitor the teen's television and movie watching, along with the teen's Internet use. Again, thanks to Kyle Longest for providing the coding for this index.

11. Wilcox and Robinson, *Onward Christian Soldiers?*

CHAPTER 6

1. Wilcox, Chaves, and Franz, "Focused on the Family?"; Denton and Uecker, "What God Has Joined Together."
2. US Census Bureau, "Median Age at First Marriage."
3. Cherlin, *The Marriage-Go-Round.*
4. Collapsed data from the 2012 and 2014 General Social Survey indicates that 30 percent of young people ages 25 to 28 are currently married, while 65 percent have never married. GSS 2012–14 calculated using "GSS 1972–2016 Cumulative Datafile."
5. Matthews and Hamilton, "Mean Age of Mothers Is on the Rise."
6. Uecker, "Religion and Early Marriage in the United States"; Xu, Hudspeth, and Bartkowski, "The Timing of First Marriage?"; Rendon, Xu, Denton, and Bartkowski, "Religion and Marriage Timing"; Amato et al., "Precursors of Young Women's Family Formation Pathways."
7. Manning, Brown, and Payne, "Two Decades of Stability and Change in Age at First Union."
8. Carlson, McLanahan, and England, "Union Formation in Fragile Families"; Cunningham, Beutel, Barber, and Thornton, "Reciprocal Relationships between Attitudes about Gender and Social Contexts during Young Adulthood."
9. In a multivariate model that controls for demographic factors, the Committed respondents reported an ideal age of marriage that is lower than each of the other groups by a statistically significant margin. Multivariate models are available from the author.

10. Willoughby and James, *The Marriage Paradox*; Gibson-Davis, Edin, and McLanahan, "High Hopes but Even Higher Expectations"; Addo, "Debt, Cohabitation, and Marriage in Young Adulthood."

11. Cherlin, *The Marriage-Go-Round.*

12. In multivariate regression models, differences in reports of disappointment about never getting married are statistically significant for Disaffiliated, Marginal, and Committed compared with Not Religious.

13. Regnerus, *Forbidden Fruit*; Rostosky, Wilcox, Wright, and Randall, "The Impact of Religiosity on Adolescent Sexual Behavior"; Kirby, "Reflections on Two Decades of Research."

14. Buhi and Goodson, "Predictors of Adolescent Sexual Behavior and Intention."

15. Uecker, "Religion and Early Marriage in the United States."

16. In a multivariate logistic regression model, those who are not willing to cohabit in the future are 1.85 times as likely to be married at Wave 4 than those who are willing to cohabit (odds ratio = 1.85, $p < 0.000$).

17. In a multivariate logistic regression model, those who have never cohabited are 2.55 times as likely to be married at Wave 4 than those who have cohabited at some point (odds ratio = 2.55, $p < 0.000$).

18. Manning, Brown, and Payne, "Two Decades of Stability and Change in Age at First Union Formation."

19. Amato et al., "Precursors of Young Women's Family Formation Pathways."

20. The majority (72 percent) of the cohabiting and single with children respondents have never been married. The remaining 28 percent reported being previously married or currently in a civil union partnership.

21. Multivariate models reveal statistically significant differences in the family status of respondents in the very/extremely important category as teenagers compared with those in the not important category.

22. Of those Conservative Protestants who are currently unmarried without children, 3 percent have been previously married or are in a civil union, leaving just 41 percent who have not experienced any family transition.

23. In multivariate analyses, however, there is not a statistically significant difference between the family statuses of Mainline Protestant and Jewish respondents when compared with Conservative Protestants.

24. The statistics for the Black Protestants are more likely a reflection of racial patterns in marriage and childbearing than something distinct about the religious ideology of Black Protestants. In multivariate analyses that control for race, there are no statistically significant differences between Black Protestants and other religious groups.

25. In multivariate analysis, both Catholic and Not Religious respondents are significantly less likely to be married than their Conservative Protestant peers.

26. Pew Research Center, Religious Landscape Study: Marital Status.

27. Multivariate analysis reveals statistically significant differences in family status between Marginal and Not Religious and between Committed and Not Religious. There are no statistically significant family status differences between the Disaffiliated and Not Religious respondents.

28. Uecker, "Religion and Early Marriage in the United States"; Xu, Hudspeth, and Bartkowski, "The Timing of First Marriage"; Rendon, Xu, Denton, and Bartkowski, "Religion and Marriage Timing"; Amato et al., "Precursors of Young Women's Family Formation Pathways."

29. Uecker, Maryl, and Stroppe, "Family Formation and Returning to Institutional Religion in Young Adulthood"; Schleifer and Chaves, "Family Formation and Religious Service Attendance."

30. In a multivariate model, respondents who are cohabiting or single without children reported significantly less importance of faith compared with the married with children group.

31. Multinomial logistic regression was used to predict the odds of becoming more or less religious compared with staying the same religiously. Using married with children as the family status reference category, all of the other groups have significantly lower odds of saying that they became more religious over time, with those cohabiting without children having the lowest odds of becoming more religious. The odds ratios for reporting becoming less religious over time (as opposed to staying the same) were significant for the cohabiting without children group and the single without children group when each was compared with the married with children group. In other words, individuals who have not yet transitioned into a family-of-formation status were the most likely to report becoming less religious during the years of emerging adulthood. See also Denton and Uecker, "What God Has Joined Together."

32. Uecker, Maryl, and Stroope, "Family Formation and Returning to Institutional Religion in Young Adulthood"; Schleifer and Chaves, "Family Formation and Religious Service Attendance."

33. Smock, "Cohabitation in the United States."

34. Denton and Uecker, "What God Has Joined Together."

35. Ashley and Carla were both interviewed by Melinda Denton.

CONCLUSION

1. Mercadante, *Belief without Borders*; Oakes, *The Nones Are Alright*; Clydesdale and Garces-Foley, *The Twentysomething Soul*; Thurston and ter Kuile, "How We Gather."

2. Smith and Denton, *Soul Searching*.

3. See the Pew Research Center report, "U.S. Religious Knowledge Survey"; see also Prothero, *Religious Literacy*.

4. See Smith, *Religion*, pp. 198–199 on "The Default Religious Laxity Tendency."

5. Mukerjee, "The Cultural Power of Tacit Knowledge"; Haidt, "The Emotional Dog and Its Rational Tail." See also Vaisey and Lizardo, "Cultural Worldviews."

6. See Arnett, "A Congregation of One." See also Bellah et al., *Habits of the Heart* on "Sheilaism." What we are describing among emerging adults is different from what Bellah and colleagues described as "Sheilaism," in that Sheila was actively pursuing her own religion, while emerging adults are on average not engaged in such a pursuit and are not interested in creating their own religion so much as simply accepting, rejecting, or ignoring those elements of religion that may or may not suit their particular interests.

7. We do not have a survey question for belief in karma, so we don't know how many emerging adults in our study would say that they believe in karma. However, in our in-person interviews, karma and associated similar concepts were common across the majority of emerging adults in the study.

8. Smith and Denton, *Soul Searching*.

9. Roof, *A Generation of Seekers*; Bengtson, Putney, and Harris, *Families and Faith*.

10. Jones, Cox, Cooper, and Lienesch, *Exodus*.

11. Pearce and Denton, *A Faith of Their Own*.

12. Klinenberg, *Going Solo*; Arroyo, Payne, Brown, and Manning, "Median Age at First Marriage."

13. Arnett, *Emerging Adulthood*.

14. Schleifer and Chaves, "Family Formation and Religious Service Attendance"; Uecker, Maryl, and Stroope, "Family Formation and Returning to Institutional Religion in Young Adulthood."

15. For examples of "reimagining religion," see USC Center for Religion and Civic Culture, *Reimagining Religion Conference*.

16. Christerson and Flory, *The Rise of Network Christianity*.

Bibliography

Addo, Fenaba. 2014. "Debt, Cohabitation, and Marriage in Young Adulthood." *Demography* 51 (5): 1677–1701.

Amato, Paul, Nancy Landale, Tara Havasevich-Brooks, Alan Booth, David Eggebeen, Robert Schoen, and Susan McHale. 2008. "Precursors of Young Women's Family Formation Pathways." *Journal of Marriage and Family* 70 (5): 1271–86.

Arnett, Jeffrey Jensen. 2015. *Emerging Adulthood: The Winding Road from the Late Teens through the Twenties*, 2nd ed. New York: Oxford University Press.

Arnett, Jeffrey Jensen, and Lene Arnett Jensen. 2002. "A Congregation of One: Individualized Religious Beliefs among Emerging Adults." *Journal of Adolescent Research* 17 (5): 451–67.

Arroyo, Julia, Krista K. Payne, Susan L. Brown, and Wendy D. Manning. 2019. "Median Age at First Marriage, 2017." National Center for Family and Marriage Research. https://www.bgsu.edu/content/dam/BGSU/college-of-arts-and-sciences/NCFMR/documents/FP/FP-13-06.pdf

Baker, Joseph O., and Buster Smith. 2009a. "None Too Simple: Examining Issues of Religious Nonbelief and Nonbelonging in the United States." *Journal for the Scientific Study of Religion* 48 (4): 719–33.

Baker, Joseph O., and Buster G. Smith. 2009b. "The Nones: Social Characteristics of the Religiously Unaffiliated." *Social Forces* 87 (3): 1251–63.

Barrie-Anthony, Steven. 2014. "'Spiritual but Not Religious': A Rising, Misunderstood Voting Bloc." *The Atlantic*, January 14, 2014. https://www.theatlantic.com/politics/archive/2014/01/spiritual-but-not-religious-a-rising-misunderstood-voting-bloc/283000/.

Bellah, Robert N., Richard Madsen, William M. Sullivan, Ann Swidler, and Steven M. Tipton. 1985. *Habits of the Heart: Individualism and Commitment in American Life*. Berkeley: University of California Press.

Bengtson, Vern L., Norella M. Putney, and Susan Harris. 2013. *Families and Faith: How Religion Is Passed Down across Generations*. New York: Oxford University Press.

Bevins, Winfield. 2019. *Ever Ancient, Ever New: The Allure of Liturgy for a New Generation*. Grand Rapids, MI: Zondervan.

Blumberg, Antonia. 2016. "American Religion Has Never Looked Quite Like It Does Today." *Huffington Post*, April 15, 2016, sec. Religion. https://www.huffingtonpost.com/entry/american-religion-trends_us_570c21cee4b0836057a235ad.

Buhi, Eric R., and Patricia Goodson. 2007. "Predictors of Adolescent Sexual Behavior and Intention: A Theory-Guided Systematic Review." *Journal of Adolescent Health* 40 (1): 4–21.

Burton, Tara I. 2017. "'Spiritual but Not Religious': Inside America's Rapidly Growing Faith Group." *Vox*, November 10, 2017. https://www.vox.com/identities/2017/11/10/16630178/study-spiritual-but-not-religious.

Carlson, Marcia, Sara McLanahan, and Paula England. 2004. "Union Formation in Fragile Families." *Demography* 41 (2): 237–61.

Cherlin, Andrew J. 2010. *The Marriage-Go-Round: The State of Marriage and the Family in America Today*. Vintage. New York: Vintage Books.

Christerson, Brad, and Richard Flory. 2017. *The Rise of Network Christianity: How Independent Leaders Are Changing the Religious Landscape*. Global Pentecost Charismatic Christianity. New York: Oxford University Press.

Cimino, Richard, and Christopher Smith. 2014. *Atheist Awakening: Secular Activism and Community in America*. New York: Oxford University Press.

Clydesdale, Tim, and Kathleen Garces-Foley. 2019. *The Twentysomething Soul: Understanding the Religious and Secular Lives of American Young Adults*. New York: Oxford University Press.

Cnaan, Ram, and John DiIulio. 2002. *The Invisible Caring Hand: American Congregations and the Provision of Welfare*. New York: New York University Press.

Costanza, David. 2018. "Can We Please Stop Talking about Generations as If They Are a Thing?" *Slate*, April 13, 2018. https://slate.com/technology/2018/04/the-evidence-behind-generations-is-lacking.html.

Cunningham, Mick, Ann M. Beutel, Jennifer S. Barber, and Arland Thornton. 2005. "Reciprocal Relationships between Attitudes about Gender and Social Contexts during Young Adulthood." *Social Science Research* 34 (4): 862–92.

Dean, Kenda Creasy. 2010. *Almost Christian: What the Faith of Our Teenagers Is Telling the American Church*. New York: Oxford University Press.

Denton, Melinda Lundquist, and Jeremy E. Uecker. 2018. "What God Has Joined Together: Family Formation and Religion among Young Adults." *Review of Religious Research* 60 (1): 1–22.

Drescher, Elizabeth. 2016. *Choosing Our Religion: The Spiritual Lives of America's Nones*. New York: Oxford University Press.

Edgell, Penny, Douglas Hartmann, Evan Stewart, and Joseph Gerteis. 2016. "Atheists and Other Cultural Outsiders: Moral Boundaries and the Non-Religious in the United States." *Social Forces* 95 (2): 607.

Evans, Rachel Held. n.d. *Searching for Sunday: Leaving, Loving and Finding the Church.* Nashville, TN: Nelson Books.

Flory, Richard, and Donald E. Miller. 2008. *Finding Faith: The Spiritual Quest of the Post-Boomer Generation.* New Brunswick, NJ: Rutgers University Press.

Fry, Richard. 2016. "For First Time in Modern Era, Living with Parents Edges Out Other Living Arrangements for 18- to 34-Year-Olds." Washington, DC: Pew Research Center. https://www.pewsocialtrends.org/2016/05/24/for-first-time-in-modern-era-living-with-parents-edges-out-other-living-arrangements-for-18-to-34-year-olds/.

Gibson-Davis, Christina M., Kathryn Edin, and Sara McLanahan. 2005. "High Hopes but Even Higher Expectations: The Retreat from Marriage among Low-Income Couples." *Journal of Marriage and Family* 67 (5): 1301–12.

Gill, Andy. 2018. "Millennials and Religion." *Faith, Justice, & Culture* (blog). February 5, 2018. https://www.patheos.com/blogs/andygill/millennials-and-religion/.

"GSS 1972-2016 Cumulative Datafile." n.d. SDA: Survey Documentation and Analysis. http://sda.berkeley.edu/sdaweb/analysis/?dataset=gss16.

Hadaway, C. Kirk, and Penny Long Marler. 2005. "How Many Americans Attend Worship Each Week? An Alternative Approach to Measurement." *Journal for the Scientific Study of Religion* 44 (3): 307–22.

Haidt, Jonathan. 2001. "The Emotional Dog and Its Rational Tail: A Social Intuitionist Approach to Moral Judgment." *Psychological Review* 108 (4): 814–34.

Haidt, Jonathan. 2013. *The Righteous Mind: Why Good People Are Divided by Politics and Religion.* New York: Vintage.

Hout, Michael, and Claude S. Fischer. 2014. "Explaining Why More Americans Have No Religious Preference: Political Backlash and Generational Succession, 1987-2012." *Sociological Science* 1 (24): 423–47.

Jones, Robert P., Daniel Cox, Betty Cooper, and Rachel Lienesch. 2016. "Exodus: Why Americans Are Leaving Religion—and Why They're Unlikely to Come Back." Washington, DC: Public Religion Research Institute. https://www.prri.org/wp-content/uploads/2016/09/PRRI-RNS-Unaffiliated-Report.pdf.

Kirby, Douglas. 1999. "Reflections on Two Decades of Research on Teen Sexual Behavior and Pregnancy." *Journal of School Health* 69 (3): 89–94.

Kirkham, Chris. 2016. "Percentage of Young Americans Living with Parents Rises to 75-Year High." *Wall Street Journal*, December 21, 2016, sec. U.S. https://www.wsj.com/articles/percentage-of-young-americans-living-with-parents-rises-to-75-year-high-1482316203.

Klinenberg, Eric. 2012. *Going Solo: The Extraordinary Rise and Surprising Appeal of Living Alone.* New York: Penguin Books.

Lim, Chaeyoon, Carol Ann Macgregor, and Robert D. Putnam. 2010. "Secular and Liminal: Discovering Heterogeneity among Religious Nones." *Journal for the Scientific Study of Religion* 49 (4): 596–618.

Lipka, Michael. 2015a. "Millennials Increasingly Are Driving Growth of 'Nones.'" Fact Tank. Washington, DC: Pew Research Center. https://www.pewresearch.org/fact-tank/2015/05/12/millennials-increasingly-are-driving-growth-of-nones/.

Lipka, Michael. 2015b. "A Closer Look at America's Rapidly Growing Religious 'Nones.'" Fact Tank. Washington, DC: Pew Research Center. https://www.pewresearch.org/fact-tank/2015/05/13/a-closer-look-at-americas-rapidly-growing-religious-nones/.

Lipka, Michael. 2015c. "Religious 'Nones' Are Not Only Growing, They're Becoming More Secular." Fact Tank. Washington, DC: Pew Research Center. https://www.pewresearch.org/fact-tank/2015/11/11/religious-nones-are-not-only-growing-theyre-becoming-more-secular/.

Manning, Wendy D., Susan L. Brown, and Krista K. Payne. 2014. "Two Decades of Stability and Change in Age at First Union Formation." *Journal of Marriage and Family* 76 (2): 247–60.

Matthews, T. J., and Brady E. Hamilton. 2016. "Mean Age of Mothers Is on the Rise: United States, 2000-2014." 232. National Center for Health Statistics. https://www.cdc.gov/nchs/products/databriefs/db232.htm.

"Median Age at First Marriage, American Community Survey." 2012. U.S. Census Bureau. 2012. https://factfinder.census.gov/faces/tableservices/jsf/pages/productview.xhtml?pid=ACS_12_1YR_B12007&prodType=table.

Mercadante, Linda A. 2014. *Belief without Borders: Inside the Minds of the Spiritual but Not Religious.* New York: Oxford University Press.

Modell, John. 1989. *Into One's Own: From Youth to Adulthood in the United States, 1920-1975.* Berkeley: University of California Press.

Mukerjee, Chandra. 2014. "The Cultural Power of Tacit Knowledge: Inarticulacy and Bourdieu's Habitus." *American Journal of Cultural Sociology* 2 (3): 348–75.

"'Nones' on the Rise: New Report Finds One-in-Five Adults Have No Religious Affiliation." 2012. Washington, DC: Pew Research Center. https://www.pewforum.org/2012/10/09/nones-on-the-rise-new-report-finds-one-in-five-adults-have-no-religious-affiliation/.

Norris, Pippa, and Ronald Inglehart. 2011. *Sacred and Secular Religion and Politics Worldwide,* 2nd ed. Cambridge Studies in Social Theory, Religion and Politics. New York: Cambridge University Press.

Oakes, Kaya. 2015. *The Nones Are Alright: A New Generation of Believers, Seekers, and Those in Between.* Maryknoll, NY: Orbis Books.

Oppenheimer, Mark. 2014. "Examining the Growth of the 'Spiritual but Not Religious.'" *The New York Times,* July 18, 2014. https://www.nytimes.com/2014/07/19/us/examining-the-growth-of-the-spiritual-but-not-religious.html.

Pearce, Lisa D., and Melinda Lundquist Denton. 2011. *A Faith of Their Own: Stability and Change in the Religiosity of America's Adolescents.* New York: Oxford University Press.

Presser, Stanley, and Mark Chaves. 2007. "Is Religious Service Attendance Declining?" *Journal for the Scientific Study of Religion* 46 (3): 417–23.

Prothero, Stephen. 2008. *Religious Literacy: What Every American Needs to Know—and Doesn't.* New York: HarperOne.

Regnerus, Mark D. 2009. *Forbidden Fruit: Sex and Religion in the Lives of American Teenagers.* New York: Oxford University Press.

"Reimagining Religion Conference Program and Livestream." 2017. USC Center for Religion and Civic Culture. February 9, 2017. https://crcc.usc.edu/feb-9-reimagining-religion-conference/.

"Religion among the Millennials." 2010. Washington, DC: Pew Research Center. https://www.pewforum.org/2010/02/17/religion-among-the-millennials/.

"Religious Landscape Study: Marital Status." n.d. Pew Research Center. Accessed May 30, 2018. https://www.pewforum.org/religious-landscape-study/marital-status/.

Rendon, Joshua J., Xiaohe Xu, Melinda Lundquist Denton, and John P. Bartkowski. 2014. "Religion and Marriage Timing: A Replication and Extension." *Religions* 5 (3): 834–51.

Roof, Wade Clark. 1993. *A Generation of Seekers: The Spiritual Journeys of the Baby Boom Generation.* San Francisco, CA: Harper.

Rostosky, Sharon Scales, Brian L Wilcox, Margaret Laurie Comer Wright, and Brandy A Randall. 2004. "The Impact of Religiosity on Adolescent Sexual Behavior: A Review of the Evidence." *Journal of Adolescent Research* 19 (6): 677–97.

Schleifer, Cyrus, and Mark Chaves. 2017. "Family Formation and Religious Service Attendance: Untangling Marital and Parental Effects." Edited by Michael Hout. *Sociological Methods & Research* 46 (1): 125–52.

Smith, Christian. 2017. *Religion: What It Is, How It Works, and Why It Matters.* Princeton, NJ: Princeton University Press.

Smith, Christian, and Hiliary Davidson. 2014. *The Paradox of Generosity: Giving We Receive, Grasping We Lose.* New York: Oxford University Press.

Smith, Christian, and Melinda Lundquist Denton. 2005. *Soul Searching: The Religious and Spiritual Lives of American Teenagers.* New York: Oxford University Press.

Smith, Christian, Kyle Longest, Jonathan Hill, and Kari Christoffersen. 2014. *Young Catholic America: Emerging Adults In, Out of, and Gone from the Church.* New York: Oxford University Press.

Smith, Christian, and Patricia Snell. 2009. *Souls in Transition: The Religious Lives of Emerging Adults in America.* New York: Oxford University Press.

Smith, Gregory A., and Alan Cooperman. 2016. "The Factors Driving the Growth of Religious 'Nones' in the U.S." Fact Tank. Washington, DC: Pew Research Center. https://www.pewresearch.org/fact-tank/2016/09/14/the-factors-driving-the-growth-of-religious-nones-in-the-u-s/.

Smock, Pamela J. 2000. "Cohabitation in the United States: An Appraisal of Research Themes, Findings, and Implications." *Annual Review of Sociology* 26: 1.

Steensland, Brian, Lynn D. Robinson, W. Bradford Wilcox, Jerry Z. Park, Mark D. Regnerus, and Robert D. Woodberry. 2000. "The Measure of American Religion: Toward Improving the State of the Art." *Social Forces* 79 (1): 291–318.

Taylor, Katherine. 2018. "Crossing Borders: For LDS Families, Millennials Leaving Religion Causes Faith Divide." Utah Public Radio. https://www.upr.org/post/crossing-borders-lds-families-millennials-leaving-religion-causes-faith-divide.

Thurston, Angie, and Casper ter Kuile. 2017. "How We Gather." How We Gather. https://www.howwegather.org/s/How_We_Gather_Digital_41117.pdf.

Tong, Yunping, and Fenggang Yang. 2018. "Internal Diversity among 'Spiritual but Not Religious' Adolescents in the United States: A Person-Centered Examination Using Latent Class Analysis." *Review of Religious Research* 60 (4): 435–53.

Uecker, Jeremy E. 2014. "Religion and Early Marriage in the United States: Evidence from the Add Health Study." *Journal for the Scientific Study of Religion* 53 (2): 392–415.

Uecker, Jeremy E., Damon Mayrl, and Samuel Stroope. 2016. "Family Formation and Returning to Institutional Religion in Young Adulthood." *Journal for the Scientific Study of Religion* 55 (2): 384–406.

"U.S. Religious Knowledge Survey." 2010. Washington, DC: Pew Research Center. https://www.pewforum.org/2010/09/28/u-s-religious-knowledge-survey/.

Vaisey, Stephen, and Omar Lizardo. 2010. "Can Cultural Worldviews Influence Network Composition?" *Social Forces* 88 (4): 1595–1618.

Verba, Sidney, Kay Leman Schlozman, and Hentry E. Brady. 1995. *Voice and Equality: Civic Voluntarism in American Politics.* Cambridge, MA: Harvard University Press.

"Volunteering in the United States, 2015." 2016. United States Department of Labor, Bureau of Labor Statistics. February 25, 2016. https://www.bls.gov/news.release/volun.nro.htm.

Wilcox, Clyde, and Carin Robinson. 2010. *Onward Christian Soldiers?: The Religious Right in American Politics,* 4th ed. New York: Routledge.

Wilcox, W. Bradford, Mark Chaves, and David Franz. 2004. "Focused on the Family? Religious Traditions, Family Discourse, and Pastoral Practice." *Journal for the Scientific Study of Religion* 43 (4): 491–504.

Willoughby, Brian J., and Spencer L. James. 2017. *The Marriage Paradox: Why Emerging Adults Love Marriage yet Push It Aside.* Emerging Adulthood Series. New York: Oxford University Press.

Wuthnow, Robert. 2002. "Religious Involvement and Status-Bridging Social Capital." *Journal for the Scientific Study of Religion* 41 (4): 669–84.

Wuthnow, Robert. 2003. *All in Sync: How Music and Art Are Revitalizing American Religion.* Berkeley: University of California Press.

Xu, Xiaohe, Clark D. Hudspeth, and John P. Bartkowski. 2005. "The Timing of First Marriage: Are There Religious Variations?" *Journal of Family Issues* 26 (5): 584–618.

Index

For the benefit of digital users, indexed terms that span two pages (e.g., 52–53) may, on occasion, appear on only one of those pages.

Tables, figures, and boxes are indicated by an italic *t*, *f*, and *b* following the page number.